The
Woodworker's
Guide
to
HAND
TOOLS

The Woodworker's Guide to HAND TOOLS

PETER KORN

Illustrations by Kathy Bray

The Taunton Press

Taunton
BOOKS & VIDEOS
for fellow enthusiasts

Printed in the United States of America
10 9 8 7 6 5 4 3 2 1

The Taunton Press, Inc., 63 South Main Street, PO Box 5506,
Newtown, CT 06470-5506
e-mail: tp@taunton.com

Library of Congress Cataloging-in-Publication Data

Korn, Peter, 1951-
        The woodworker's guide to hand tools / Peter Korn.
            p.   cm.
        ISBN 1-56158-216-6
        1. Woodworking tools.   I. Title.
TT186.K67   1997   97-30981
684'.082 — DC21   CIP

To my mother and father, Peggy Liss and Stephen Korn, with love and respect

Acknowledgments

In writing this book, I have made every attempt to confirm and correct my own understanding of woodworking tools with the most reliable authorities available. I am grateful to the many friends, colleagues, and strangers who took the time to share their knowledge with me.

In particular, I would like to thank John McAlevey and Stephen Proctor for their criticisms and suggestions as they reviewed the manuscript-in-progress. Brian Boggs, John Burt, Bob Flexner, John Fox, Darryl Keil, Silas Kopf, James Krenov, Tom Law, Harv Mastalir, Alan Peters, Monroe Robinson, and Mario Rodriguez were particularly helpful with specific areas of expertise. Many other woodworkers, more than I can name here, have been kind enough to discuss their preferences and prejudices regarding hand tools, and I thank them all.

In addition, I appreciate the patience with which many people in industry and commerce responded to what must have seemed an inundation of technical questions. It is impossible to list everyone I spoke with, but I would especially like to thank the following:

John Bryan, Norton Company

Larry Cavalier, 3M

Pat Cooper, Anchor Tape

Bill DeBruhl, Cooper Tools/Nicholson Operations

Bob Dunstan, Whitechapel Ltd.

Eric Feldborg, Norton Company

Brian Gandy, Crown Tools

Drew Geldart, Neill Tools

Ken Hreha, Stanley Tools

John Hyde, Norton Company

Ken Jackman, DMT

Doug Johnson, Spyderco

Ralph Johnson, EZE-LAP Diamond Products

Terry Kane, GMT Rhodes American

Bob Kaune

Larry Kee, Cooper Tool/Plumb Hammer

Kayoko Kuroiwa, Misugi Design

Patrick Leach, Independence Saw Company

Leonard Lee, Lee Valley Tools Ltd.

Jimmy Lewter, Cooper Tools/Lufkin

Tom Lie-Nielsen, Lie-Nielsen Toolworks

Jean Longford, Stanley Tools, U.K.

Jim Martin, Stanley Tools

Barney Newberry, Cooper Tools

Chuck Olson, Olson Saw Company

Philip Proctor, Robert Sorby

Dick Ranney, Coors Ceramic Company

Alan Reid, Clico Tooling Ltd.

Alan Steyler, Alpha Fabrication

Carl Stoutenberg, Stanley Tools

Derek Taylor, Garlick Saw Company

Frank Tielli, Sanvik Saws & Tools

Craig Waldon, DML Industrial Products, Forest City Tool Division

Michael Watkins, Adjustable Clamp Company

Mark Weigel, Sanvik Saws & Tools

Special thanks are due to Ian Turner at Garrett Wade and to Doug White at Woodcraft for sharing their wide-ranging knowledge of tools and suppliers. Also to Kathy Bray for her lovely, clear illustrations. And, finally, I would like to thank Peter Chapman, my editor at The Taunton Press, with whom it is a pleasure to work.

Contents

Introduction

A common assumption of our age is that machines make things better than people can. For this reason, and because it is so much easier to push a switch than to nurture hand-eye coordination, most of us begin our woodworking journeys reliant on power tools. Then, along the way, as our sensitivity to wood and under-standing of craftsmanship grow, we may begin to appreciate the practical benefits and subtle pleasures of traditional hand skills.

There is a romance to hand tools that should not over-shadow their utility. They are far more than charming accents with which to decorate country cottages or ornament workshops. No contemporary woodshop is complete without functioning hand tools. No craftsman achieves excellence without first mastering their use.

Although hand tools are essential to the highest level of craftsmanship, there is a lack of information available to the woodworker who desires to attain proficiency with them. A new thickness planer comes with a detailed manual explaining setup, use, and maintenance and an exploded diagram to facilitate repair. A new handplane often comes only with wrapping tissue. Yet, of the two, the handplane requires more skill, knowledge, and time to set up and use successfully. Think of this book as the missing manual for your woodworking hand tools.

In these pages you'll find a comprehensive representation of the specialized hand tools commonly employed by the contemporary wood furniture maker. You'll learn what each tool is used for, what to look for when buying one, how to tune it up for maximum performance, and, where appropriate, how to use it efficiently. Of necessity, more demanding tools such as bench planes merit longer treatments, while there is no need to belabor the obvious by explaining how to swing a hammer.

This book is intended as an ongoing source of information as you work. For ease of reference, I have set it up much like the Yellow Pages of a telephone book. Tools are listed alphabetically within functional groupings (abrading, cutting, sawing...), which are likewise arranged alphabetically. Two categories that you will not find in these pages are woodturning tools and carving tools—they are such extensive specialties as to require books of their own.

A word of advice: You don't need to rush out and buy all the tools you see within these pages in order to be a good woodworker. I have found it best to wait until I have a specific need and understand how a new tool will fulfill it. Even in our school shop at the Center for Furniture Craftsmanship, which I believe to be well equipped by any standard, you won't find every tool that is presented here.

What is the place of hand tools in the workshop? In part, the answer is a matter of temperament. Each craftsman finds a personal balance between machine and hand work. There is no "right" way to work. The 20-plus years that I have been making furniture have been, and continue to be, a learning process. As my experience increases, so does my respect for the practical advantages and aesthetic pleasures that hand tools provide.

Simply, you can do more things with wood using hand tools than you can using machinery. Hand tools enable the woodworker to create the widest possible range of designs. Of course, machines are reliable and fast, and great for straightforward tasks such as milling wood four-square or cutting simple mortises. And with enough capital expenditure, jigging, and fussing, they will also perform exceedingly complex tasks dependably. But for the one-of-a-kind or limited-production furniture maker who wants to incorporate compound-angle joinery in a chair, marquetry or carved detail in a casepiece, or a unique molded edge on a tabletop, a mastery of hand tools will get the job done quicker, better, and less expensively.

Wood is a sensuous, seductive material unlike any other. Every tree, every board, is individuated by characteristics of color, density, grain pattern, and workability. Hand tools enable the craftsman to meet wood on intimate terms, sensitive to every nuance, and endow him with finer control of the medium. There are extraordinary pieces of furniture in which the life of the tree and the subtle presence of the maker's hand live on together, such as the work of James Krenov. This is a level of excellence well beyond the capability of machine work.

At the heart of the idea of "craftsmanship" is the notion of skill—of hand-eye coordination won through years of practice. Certainly, the part of furniture making that I love best is being at the bench working with hand tools, whether cutting joinery or using a handplane. The joy of surfacing a lovely piece of ash with a well-tuned jack plane is exceptional—the feel, sound, smell, and sight of the blade throwing off translucent shavings and leaving behind a surface of smoothness and clarity.

More than anything else, I go into my workshop for the experience of being there, for the joy of making. The furniture I create is the measure of that process, and hand tools are essential to it in every way. Whether you look to hand tools as a source of pleasure, quality, or efficiency, I'm sure you will find this book of assistance.

ABRADING

For most woodworkers, there is far less romance to rubbing wood with abrasive materials than there is to sawing or cutting it with edge tools. Yet all three methods of shaping wood are equally essential. Abrasives, primarily in the form of files, rasps, and sandpaper, are excellent for forming wood to flat and curvilinear shapes and for smoothing its surface.

The distinction between "abrading" and "cutting" blurs when we consider the action by which rasps and files remove wood. At least one author on the subject compares the teeth of a rasp to tiny chisel points and calls the rasp a cutting tool. From the point of view of the wood, however, metallic rasp teeth work in quite similar ways to the sharp mineral particles that coat sandpaper. In fact, sandpaper, files, and rasps are often used for identical tasks, such as shaping and fairing curved surfaces and cleaning up end grain. For these reasons, I've included them in the same chapter, along with steel wool and nonwoven nylon abrasive pads, which are abrasives used primarily in finishing.

Most sanding in contemporary workshops is done with stationary and portable electric sanders, which vary quite a bit in their precision and aggressiveness. Belt sanders are capable of committing mayhem on wood with just a split second's inattention. Random-orbit disc sanders are more docile and leave a decent surface behind. But no matter how reliable a machine sander is, there always comes a point when the human hand takes over if control and surface quality are paramount. Hand sanding is still indispensable to the highest level of workmanship.

Files and sandpaper are important to a woodshop's metalworking needs, too. Scraper preparation, saw sharpening, and plane tuning are but three examples. I must admit that, like many woodworkers, I have spent my life in relative ignorance of metalworking tools. For example, only when spurred by writing this book have I clarified for myself the difference between second-cut and double-cut files. I say this not to praise ignorance, but to point out that it is possible to make wonderful furniture without knowing every last bit of tool arcana. You don't have to know the specific hardnesses of silicon carbide and aluminum oxide to be able to sand.

What follows is a compendium of those abrasive tools most commonly employed in the woodshop.

FILES

Files are steel bars on which patterns of sharp ridges have been formed by repeated blows with a hardened chisel. They are specified according to pattern configuration, length, cross-sectional and longitudinal shapes, and coarseness.

Files (and rasps) fall into two broad categories: American pattern and Swiss pattern. American pattern includes virtually all the files and rasps that are used for woodworking and woodshop metalwork. Swiss pattern files have more teeth per inch and are manufactured to tighter tolerances for precision filing by jewelers, modelmakers, and die makers.

Within American pattern files there are two predominant ridge patterns: single-cut and double-cut, double-cut being the more aggressive of the two. Curved-tooth files are also available but more difficult to find. Within each pattern, there are four grades of ascending smoothness: coarse, bastard, second-cut, and smooth.

File lengths generally graduate in 2-in. increments. For example, a mill file (see p. 7) can be 4 in., 6 in., 8 in., 10 in., 12 in., 14 in., or 16 in. long. Longer files have larger cross sections and more widely spaced teeth, which makes them cut more aggressively. Specified file lengths do not include the tang.

AMERICAN PATTERN FILES

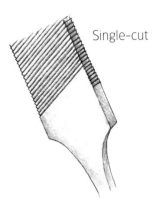

Single-cut

Double-cut

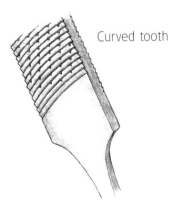

Curved tooth

Woodworking files are generally flat, half-round (flat on one side, curved across the other), or round in section. Metalworking files come in a greater variety of shapes, including the triangular taper saw files listed on pp. 7-8.

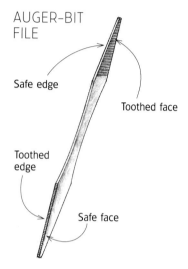

AUGER-BIT FILE

Safe edge

Toothed face

Toothed edge

Safe face

Auger-bit files

Few woodworkers use auger bits anymore. They originated for use with a brace and have been pushed aside by bits better suited to the electric drill. As the name implies, the auger-bit file was originally intended for sharpening auger bits (see pp. 19-21), but it also works well with contemporary high-carbon-steel drill bits such as brad points (though not with high-speed-steel or carbide bits, which are harder). The auger-bit file has two heads connected by a thin handle. One head has single-cut teeth on its faces and safe, uncut edges. The other head is the opposite, with safe faces and toothed edges. This configuration allows you to file one facet of a bit without affecting adjacent surfaces.

Cabinet and wood files

The two varieties of files made specifically for use on wood are cabinet files and wood files. Compared to metalworking files, these files have fewer teeth per inch, with cutting faces that slope back at a greater angle. The backs of their teeth have a slight convex curve for a greater clearance angle. The tip of the tooth (the scallop) is wider to form a broader cutting surface. The net effect of these alterations is that a woodworking file has less aggressive teeth but unloads waste more efficiently.

Cabinet and wood files are half-round in section, gradually tapered in width, and double-cut. Wood files are coarser than cabinet files and shaped just like half-round metalworking files. Cabinet files have a larger cross-sectional radius and are thinner. Cabinet files are sold in 8-in. and 10-in. lengths, wood files in 10-in. lengths.

The round files that are sold as woodworking tools are actually standard metalworking files.

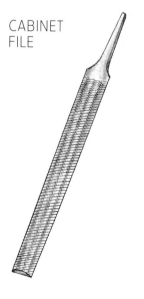

CABINET FILE

Metalworking files

The four metalworking files that the woodworker is most likely to encounter are the mill, flat, half-round, and round. All are manufactured in bastard, second-cut, and smooth versions, with lengths ranging from 4 in. to 16 in.

METALWORKING
FILES

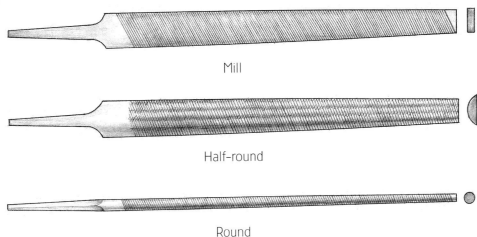

Mill

Half-round

Round

Mill files are single-cut, flat with square edges, and taper slightly in width. They are best for fine finish work on metal. The 8-in. mill bastard seems to be the file most readily available at local hardware stores, so it is the one most generally used for metalwork around the shop, including preparation of scraper edges.

Flat files are similar in shape to mill files but have double-cut faces, which make them better for rapid removal of metal where a fine finish isn't necessary. They are much more likely to be found in a metalworking shop than in a woodshop.

Half-round files are double-cut on the flat side. The rounded sides vary. Bastard-cut half-round files and second-cut files over 6 in. long are double-cut on the rounded side, whereas smooth files are single-cut.

Round files taper toward the point and are made in single- and double-cut versions.

Taper saw files

Taper saw files are single-cut, tapered, triangular-sectioned files made for sharpening handsaws. They are specified by cross-sectional size and length, not by coarseness. Sizes are regular, slim, extra slim, and double extra slim. Lengths range from 4 in. to 10 in. and generally graduate by the inch, although there is also a 4½-in. size.

The recommended file sizes for sharpening crosscut saws according to the number of teeth per inch (tpi) are shown in the chart on p. 8. Ideally, the width of each face of the file will be a little more than double

TAPER SAW
FILE

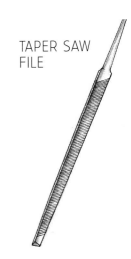

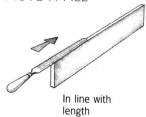

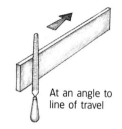

In line with
length

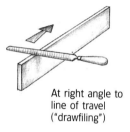

At an angle to
line of travel

At right angle to
line of travel
("drawfiling")

the length of the saw's teeth. This allows use of all three file corners in the gullets without overlapping wear on the faces. (For more on saw sharpening, see pp. 158-162.)

How to use files

Almost all files have teeth that cut only on the forward stroke; even so, there are many ways to handle a file. As shown in the drawing at left, you can push it in line with its length, keep it at an angle to its direction of travel, or hold it at right angles to the line of travel. This last technique is called "drawfiling" and, done with a light touch, yields the smoothest cut.

In most cases, you should lift the file clear of the work on the return stroke or bring it back with no downward pressure beyond its own weight to prevent unnecessary dulling and clogging. For drawfiling, however, at least one manufacturer recommends working the file in both directions: the forward stroke to cut and the return stroke to burnish.

The woodshop uses of files are too numerous to catalog. Some of the more frequent applications are leveling proud joints and pins (see the bottom drawing on the facing page), shaping edges, cleaning up end grain, fairing curves, preparing scraper edges, and sharpening handsaws. If you don't know the "proper" way to use a file for a given task, let trial and error be your guide. It's not difficult.

Recommended Taper-Saw-File Sizes for Sharpening Crosscut Saws

Teeth per inch (tpi) of saw	File size
5, 5.5	7-in. regular
6	7-in. or 8-in. slim
7	6-in. or 7-in. slim
8	6-in. slim, 7-in. extra slim, or 8-in. double extra slim
9	6-in. extra slim or 7-in. double extra slim
10	5-in. or 6-in. extra slim
11	5-in. extra slim or 6-in. double extra slim
12	5-in. extra slim
13, 14	5-in. double extra slim
15, 16	4-in. double extra slim

File handles

Although files are generally sold with bare tangs, the addition of handles greatly improves the comfort and dexterity with which they can be used. Handles sold commercially are generally made of turned wood, with a metal ferrule to prevent splitting. Some ferrules are like caps, and the tang is inserted through a threaded hole in the metal with a screwing motion. Others are like rings, so that the tang is driven directly into the wood of the handle.

You can also make handles from dowels or pieces of scrap wood by drilling out one end and rounding over any hard edges for a comfortable grip. These shopmade handles can be bound against splitting with ferrules made from cut-off sections of metal pipe.

WOODEN FILE
HANDLE

Metal ferrule

Maintaining files

Files are simple tools, but they need maintenance to ensure continued good performance. Working soft materials, such as wood and aluminum, files easily clog and lose efficiency. To combat this, clean them often with a file card. The steel wire used in a file card is too soft (about Rc32 on the Rockwell C hardness scale) to damage file teeth. The type of card I prefer has stiff nylon bristles on one side and fine wire bristles on the other (see the top drawing on p. 10). The other type has only the wire bristles.

LEVELING PROUD PINS

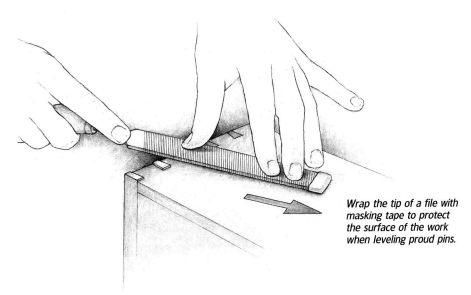

Wrap the tip of a file with masking tape to protect the surface of the work when leveling proud pins.

FILE CARD

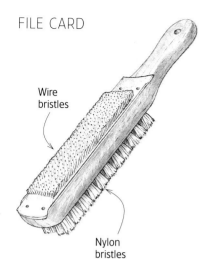

Wire
bristles

Nylon
bristles

To clean a file I begin with the nylon bristles, working along the grooves between the teeth. If more aggressive action is called for, I switch to the wire side. For single-cut files with seriously embedded material, another method is to take a piece of brass of any thickness and push it along the diagonal of the teeth. The teeth score the soft brass into a matching pattern that thoroughly scours the grooves.

There is a commercial process for restoring worn files that employs an acid bath to etch the teeth. Such services can be hard to find, however, and they are not necessarily worth the time and expense, since files are fairly inexpensive to begin with. You can also give new life to old files by regrinding them into knives and other sorts of tools. Just be sure not to overheat the steel as you grind, since that would rob it of hardness.

Store files so they won't dull themselves against each other or through contact with other metal surfaces.

Buying files

Nicholson, the largest domestic manufacturer, makes over 2,000 files (and rasps), but only a small selection are available to woodworkers through normal distribution channels. Woodworking specialty stores and mail-order catalogs often offer a better selection than the local hardware store, but even this is quite limited. The best selection can be found through industrial-supply distributors and mail-order catalogs.

NONWOVEN
NYLON
ABRASIVE PAD

NONWOVEN NYLON ABRASIVES

Nonwoven nylon abrasives are better known by trade names such as "Scotch-Brite" and "Bear-Tex." They are pads of nylon fiber to which abrasive grains have been bonded. As the abrasive wears off in use, the pads lose effectiveness much as sandpaper does. In the woodshop, nonwoven nylon abrasives perform many of the same tasks as steel wool: The finer grades rub out finishes, and the coarser grades remove paint and scrub surfaces clean.

Nonwoven nylon abrasives are manufactured in many forms, including belts, discs, and wheels, for industrial use on metal and other materials. For small-shop woodworking they are usually sold in the form of flat 6-in. by 9-in. pads with silicon carbide or aluminum oxide as the abrasive.

There is no standard grading system for nonwoven abrasives such as there is for sandpaper. Usually you can at least learn the steel-wool equivalency from the vendor or the manufacturer's literature. Nonwoven abrasives have a real advantage over steel wool, which tends to contaminate the pores of raw wood with broken-off steel fibers.

Buying abrasive pads

Nonwoven nylon abrasive pads are available through woodworking specialty stores and catalogs. They may also be found in paint stores, in metalshop supply houses and, sometimes, in hardware stores.

RASPS

RASPS

Manufacturers consider the rasp to be a subspecies of file. Similar in appearance, rasps have individual raised teeth instead of patterned ridges. Rasps remove wood more quickly than files and leave a coarser surface.

The three types of rasp used in furniture making, in descending order of aggressiveness, are wood, cabinet, and patternmaker's rasps. Technically, rasps are categorized as coarse, bastard, second-cut, and smooth, but, in fact, only a few grades are actually made. Another closely related tool that is often included as a rasp is the surform. Surforms have only one grade of coarseness. The specialized rasps employed by carvers and sculptors (some of which are called "rifflers") are not within the purview of this book. A good selection of rasps is available from most woodworking specialty stores and mail-order catalogs.

Cabinet rasps

Cabinet rasps are half-round, either second-cut or smooth, and come in 8-in., 10-in., and 12-in. lengths. They are similar to half-round wood rasps, but with finer teeth and a larger radius to the curved side. Although cabinet rasps are less aggressive than wood rasps, they still leave a fairly rough texture behind.

Patternmaker's rasps

Patternmaker's rasps have small teeth individually raised in random patterns. No two rasps are identical. They are offered in second-cut and smooth versions, half-round only, and in 10-in. lengths. They cut quickly, without the tendency to ride in their own tracks that other rasps have. Patternmaker's rasps leave a relatively smooth finish, given the rapidity with which they work. They are the woodworker's first choice among rasps.

Cabinet
rasp

Pattern-
maker's
rasp

SURFORM

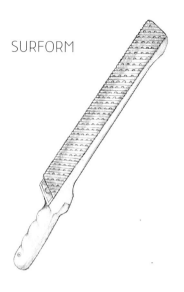

Surforms

Surforms were developed around 1950 in Sheffield, England, and are used much like rasps. Their cutting surface is a thin plate of ridged and perforated steel fitted to a handle (see the drawing at left). Each perforation forms a sharp, forward-facing lip, which cuts more like a plane blade than a rasp's tooth. Shavings exit upward through the hole, as they might through the throat of a plane. Surforms are available in flat, half-round, and round (cylindrical) forms. The soles of the flat and half-round versions are replaceable and can be reversed to cut on the pull stroke where desired.

Surforms do not perform anywhere near the level of handplanes in terms of quality of surface, accuracy, and speed on flat work and harder woods. However, they are good tools for shaping and fairing curves, as well as for rough sculpting. The tool marks left by a surform are easier to remove than those of a rasp. The narrow teeth of rasps leave small canyons among broad plateaus, while the wider teeth of a surform leave broad valleys separated by narrow ridges. For the same reason, rasps are less likely to tear out difficult grain.

Wood rasps

Wood rasps are the most aggressive rasps. The regular pattern of their teeth tends to leave a pattern on wood much like a cheese grater on cheddar. They are manufactured with flat, half-round, and round sections. Flat wood rasps come bastard-cut in 10-in. lengths. Half-round wood rasps are available in bastard-cut or smooth in 6-in., 8-in., 10-in., 12-in., and 14-in. lengths. Round wood rasps are bastard-cut in 8-in. and 10-in. lengths.

4-in-hand

The 4-in-hand was originally a shoemaker's tool. It is half-round in section, with each side being half rasp and half file. Like most two-for-one tools, it doesn't perform either of its tasks as well as two, separate stand-alone files would—it lacks a handle and has a short stroke.

Although I haven't used one in decades, the 4-in-hand was one of the first tools I came across in the winter I began to make furniture. I spent many absorbed hours filing and rasping red oak in an unheated barn, wearing heavy gloves to protect my hands from the cold and from whichever end of the 4-in-hand I was grasping.

4-IN-HAND

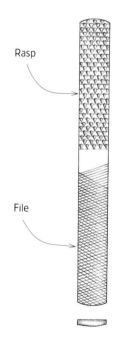

Rasp

File

How to use rasps

Rasp teeth are designed to cut on the forward stroke and should be lifted on the return to avoid excessive wear. For maximum control, grasp the handle in one hand and, when possible, the tip of the rasp in the other. The rasp can be pointed straight ahead or at an angle to its line of travel, but you cannot drawfile with a rasp (see p. 8).

A rasp with a handle is more comfortable to use and easier to control. Rasp handles are the same as file handles (see p. 9).

Maintaining rasps

Rasp maintenance is like file maintenance. Rasps should not jostle against each other or any metal surfaces. If necessary, they can be cleared of waste buildup with a file card.

SANDING MATERIALS

Sanding seems to be everyone's least favorite part of woodworking. It is dusty, noisy (if you use a power sander), and tedious where there are intersecting parts to work around. Woodworkers will go to great lengths to avoid sanding: I have known them to texture entire pieces of furniture with gouges or to char them with torches.

If you are looking for a clear, smooth surface, a handplaned finish is the best alternative to sanding, but doing it well requires a great deal of skill, a design limited to essentially flat surfaces, and properly selected wood. Scraping, too, can leave an acceptable final surface, but only on the hardest of woods, such as ebony and hard maple. For those of us looking for a flawless surface on our work, some amount of sanding is inevitable most of the time.

The theory of sanding is that you begin with a grit coarse enough to remove whatever defects there are on the surface of the wood. Subsequently, you sand with finer and finer papers, each meant to obliterate the tracks of its predecessor. Most woodworkers I know sand up to 220 grit prior to applying a finish. During the finishing process they may sand with finer grits, often up to 600, and even to 1000 grit and above for rubbing out lacquers and varnishes.

On my first pieces of furniture I began sanding at 80 grit and worked through each successive grit—100, 120, 150, 180—up to 220. Eventually I learned to prepare wood with a scraper first, which allowed me to begin sanding at 120 grit; I also learned that I could skip directly from 120 to 220 grit and still get satisfactory results. Since then, as my understanding of planes and scrapers has improved, I have jumped the initial grit to 150 or 180. Starting with finer paper yields a clear surface with less sanding, because there is no need to remove deep scratches left by coarser papers.

How do you know when to sand with a machine and when to sand by hand? There is no precise answer since the applications of the two overlap considerably. Hand sanding avoids the cross-grain scratches and swirls commonly left by orbital sanders, especially in the coarser grits. On the other hand, machine sanders are well suited to large, flat surfaces, where they save time and sweat. We each develop our own preferences as to where machine sanding leaves off and hand sanding begins. A common practice is to machine-sand at coarser grits and conclude by hand sanding with 220 grit. My own approach is to sand fine furniture entirely by hand, but to use an orbital or random-orbit disc sander on cabinetry.

SANDING BLOCKS

Cork

Rubber

Urethane foam

Sanding blocks

It is often advantageous to back up sandpaper with another material. A sanding block provides more even pressure than the hand does and leaves a more uniform surface. It also reduces muscle fatigue and skin abrasion.

Sanding blocks should have some yield to their surfaces. The grit on sandpaper is imperfectly graded, with the result that a hard backing forces the largest particles to the fore. This reduces the overall efficiency of the paper and leaves a scratchier surface. Cork, rubber, urethane foam, and felt backing allow more particles of grit to come into play.

Sanding blocks can be bought commercially or improvised in the shop. Store-bought blocks hold one-sixth or one-quarter of a standard 9-in. by 11-in. sheet of sandpaper. They come in all sorts of designs. Some have clips to hold the paper in place; others take self-adhesive sandpaper. My own preference, however, is for a plain cork block. You can also create special sanding blocks for unusual applications. A simple example is wrapping sandpaper around a dowel in order to sand a cove.

Sandpaper

There are three elements to sandpaper: abrasive particles, a flexible backing sheet, and an adhesive binder. Between them, they determine the working properties of the product. The right sandpaper is the one that will do the job at hand well, with the least expense.

Sandpaper meant for high-speed machine use must meet demanding requirements: The adhesive must survive friction heat, the backing of belts must be flexible and resist fatigue, and the abrasive must stay effective through strenuous use. The demands on sandpaper meant for hand sanding and random-orbital machine sanding are less severe.

Abrasive particles

The abrasives most commonly employed for slow-speed sanding are aluminum oxide, silicon carbide, and garnet.

Aluminum oxide is the most frequently used abrasive for hand and machine sanding. Its particles are tougher than those of silicon carbide and garnet, meaning that it doesn't break apart or wear down as easily. Toughness makes aluminum oxide preferable for coarse and medium sanding where material removal, speed, and sandpaper longevity are the most important factors. However, grit for grit, aluminum oxide leaves a scratchier surface than the other two abrasives, making it less desirable when surface smoothness becomes the predominant consideration, as it normally does in the finer grits. There is no defined transition point at which "fine" sanding begins. For some woodworkers it may be 150 grit, for others it starts above 220.

Silicon carbide is the hardest of the three primary abrasives and sharper than aluminum oxide, though not as tough. As it breaks down, silicon carbide exposes fresh, sharp edges. The result is a relatively evenly abraded surface, which is why silicon carbide is preferred as grit fineness increases and surface finish becomes paramount. Silicon carbide is the abrasive on wet/dry sandpaper, which is used primarily in the finishing process.

Garnet, which is orange-red in color, is made by crushing semiprecious stone. Like silicon carbide, it is sharper than aluminum oxide, but it lacks toughness and breaks down more quickly than either of its competitors. Once widely employed, particularly for finish sanding, garnet's position has steadily eroded in the face of the superior performance and low cost of man-made abrasives. Nevertheless, there are still craftsmen who swear by garnet paper, since it arguably leaves the most scratch-free surface of all three abrasives and is particularly effective on end grain.

Zirconia alumina and ceramic aluminum oxide are two newer abrasives that stay sharp from 5 to 10 times longer than normal aluminum oxide. Being more expensive, they are mostly of interest to production shops for rapid stock removal via machine and may not prove economically attractive to the small shop.

Sandpaper is available in open-coat and closed-coat forms. Open-coat sandpaper has abrasive covering 50% to 60% of the coated side, closed-coat is completely covered. With more space between particles, open-coat paper resists clogging better, making it the first choice for woodworking. Open-coat abrasives are sometimes treated with a lubricant (zinc stearate) to further prevent "loading." Closed-coat paper provides a more uniform finish and wears longer but is more applicable to metalwork.

Domestic manufacturers grade abrasive particles for size according to American National Standards Institute (ANSI) specifications. The requirements are typically that 60% to 70% of the particles on a sheet of sandpaper must be on grade, while up to 30% may be over grade (coarser) and up to 10% can be under grade (finer).

Backing sheets

Sandpaper used for wood is generally backed with paper or cloth; paper is less expensive and more common for slow-speed sanding. Mylar and other specialty backings offer higher performance but are more costly. Sheet sandpaper in grits above 150 usually has an A-weight paper backing, which is the lightest, most flexible paper available. Below 150 grit, the backing is C-weight, which is stronger, less flexible, and better suited for use with small portable sanders. The superior flexibility and tear resistance of cloth-backed sandpaper don't make much difference for hand sanding, but they are real advantages for sanding belts and other heavy-duty applications. Both paper and cloth are available with pressure-sensitive adhesive or hook-and-loop backings for adhesion to the surfaces of portable machines and sanding blocks.

Adhesive binders

The adhesive that binds an abrasive material to a backing can be animal-glue-based, resin-based, or a combination of the two. Animal glue is softer and produces a more even, less scratchy finish but also loses its grip more quickly and is adversely affected by heat. Resin has more heat resistance, wears longer, and is resistant to liquids. Aluminum-oxide and garnet papers meant for hand and light machine use are usually made with animal glue. Silicon-carbide papers are generally bonded with resin.

Storing and cutting sandpaper

After sandpaper has been removed from the package it should be stored flat, ideally with a board on top to keep the edges from curling. A good method for tearing sheets into smaller sizes is to use a hacksaw blade. Mount the blade parallel to a flat surface, with a washer under each end as a spacer so the sandpaper can slide underneath. Lift and tear the paper much as you do aluminum foil against the serrated lid of its packaging.

Buying sandpaper

Standard 9-in. by 11-in. sheets of sandpaper are often sold by the sheet or the sleeve, although some vendors repackage paper into 5-sheet packs, and so forth. The quantity in a sleeve may vary from 50 to 200 sheets, depending on the size, weight, and cost of the sandpaper.

SANDPAPER
STORAGE BOX

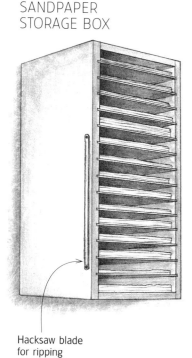

Hacksaw blade
for ripping
sheets to size

Potential sources of supply include hardware stores, paint stores, woodworking stores and catalogs, specialty sandpaper mail-order companies, industrial-supply houses, and stores that cater to metal-working trades. If you find a wide divergence in the price of sandpaper, keep in mind that you generally get what you pay for. There can be real differences in the quality of sandpaper from one manufacturer to another.

STEEL WOOL

STEEL-WOOL PAD

Steel wool was first developed commercially about 1900. It consists of continuous steel shavings that are wound together on reels. Depending on the precise manufacturing process, the shavings are crescent-shaped or triangular in section so that they have sharp edges. Steel wool sold in bulk comes in long skeins; sold retail it is cut and folded into pads. While steel wool has remained virtually unchanged for most of the century, currently some new products are being introduced to the finishing market. These are sheets of steel wool with pressure-sensitive-adhesive or hook-and-loop backing.

Steel wool has eight grades of coarseness, which are determined by fiber width. The finest is 0000 (four-aught), in which the mean fiber width is between six and ten ten-thousandths of an inch (0.0006 in. to 0.0010 in.) The coarsest is "4," in which mean fiber width is in the range of one hundred ten-thousandths of an inch (0.0100 in.).

The primary use of steel wool by woodworkers is for smoothing and polishing finishes to impart a uniform degree of abrasion—that is, an even sheen. Unlike sandpaper, though, steel wool is not a flattening agent. Whereas sandpaper knocks off high spots such as drips to create a level surface, steel wool adapts to irregular contours. Only the two finest grades, 000 and 0000, are commonly employed in finishing. They will also impart a dull patina to polished brass hardware when desired. Coarser grades of steel wool are often used for rust and paint removal.

Never rub raw wood with steel wool. If steel particles lodge in the pores of the wood and moisture is introduced, the steel will begin to rust. The resultant iron oxide reacts with tannic acid in the wood to turn the wood black or gray. Believe me, I learned this the hard way and barely saved two lovely English brown oak display cases by extensive application of bleach.

Steel-wool pads are easy to find at your local paint or hardware store. Skeins are available from finishing-supply stores.

BORING

Fifty years ago the hand drill and brace were indispensable parts of any woodshop. Today they have become the exception, replaced by electric drills that are less strenuous to use and equally fast and accurate, if not more so.

In the contemporary workshop, the practicality of hand-powered drills is limited to making holes where electric drills cannot easily reach. A good example would be holes that tuck in close to an interior corner where the larger chuck of an electric drill can't get as close as a hand drill. There is also an aesthetic argument in favor of hand-powered drills, particularly for those craftsmen who prefer their workshop unplugged and for those who specialize in traditional hand tools.

As demand has decreased, the commercially available selection of hand-powered boring tools has shrunk considerably. In many instances, the best designs have been discontinued. Yet excellent tools may still be found in the antique, collectibles, and second-hand markets. This chapter presents hand-powered drills and bits that are still manufactured commercially, are available through regular distribution channels, and have some relevance to the contemporary woodshop.

BITS

Woodworking drill bits are interchangeable between hand-powered and electric drills (excluding variations in shank design). After all, the function of a drill is simply to grasp and spin a cylindrical shaft of steel. The electric drill's ability to achieve higher speeds is rarely an advantage in woodworking, where it is often critical to avoid overheating the bit. When a standard carbon-steel drill bit gets hot enough to turn blue or black, it loses its temper and won't retain a sharp edge. As the bit dulls, it generates even more heat. By the time the wood starts to smoke, the bit is history. The proper way to drill is to get the bit in and out quickly, but at a reasonably slow speed to minimize friction. This is particularly true for Forstner and multispur bits, which have continuous rims.

Over the historically short span of my woodworking career, various styles of drill bits have come and gone in popularity. Manufacturers are still trying to build a better mousetrap—experimenting to find a bit that works better and costs less. What follows is a list of the prevalent woodworking drill bits available for use in hand drills, braces, and portable electric drills.

Auger bits

For a century prior to the reign of the electric drill, auger bits were the dominant, all-purpose drill bit used in the woodworking trades. Handled correctly, they deliver as clean, precise, and straight a hole as one could want.

AUGER BITS

Head   Twist   Shank   Tang

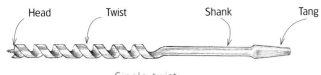

Single twist

Double twist

Solid center

ANATOMY OF AN AUGER-BIT HEAD

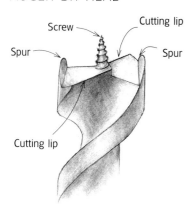

Screw

Cutting lip

Spur

Spur

Cutting lip

There are three different types of auger bit, each distinguished by the form of its helical shaft (see the drawing on p. 19). The single-twist auger, first patented in 1809 by Ezra L'Hommedieu, was made by wrapping a thin bar of steel around a cylinder to give a consistent spiral. The double-twist auger, patented in 1855 by Russell Jennings, was made by twisting a straight steel bar along its length to form a spiral. The solid-center auger bit, patented by Charles Irwin in 1884, has a drop-forged continuous core, around which winds a single spiral, and either one or two cutting lips and spurs. Drop-forging is a forming process in which hot steel is hammered into molds.

All three types of auger bit work in the same fashion. The screw point contacts the wood first; its job is to center the hole and then pull the auger through at a steady pace. Next, the spur(s) outline the hole and sever the wood fibers (when boring across the grain) to prevent tearing on the perimeter. Then the cutting lip(s) begin to lift wood out in what would be a continuous peel, except that it chips as the short grain splits across. Finally, the helical shaft feeds the shavings up and out of the hole to prevent clogging.

Of the three types of auger bit, the Jennings-style double-twist makes the cleanest, most accurate holes. On the other hand, single-twist and single-spiral solid-center bits cut faster and remove chips more efficiently.

Auger bits are made with three different screw pitches: fast, medium, and fine. A fast pitch pulls the bit through the quickest and is best suited for smaller-diameter bits and softer woods, where there is less resistance. Fine is the opposite, best for larger-diameter bits and harder woods where the auger is going to have slower going. In general, medium is the best all-purpose pitch. Also, fast and medium threads are better for end-grain boring, where a finer thread increases the likelihood that the short-grained wood between the threads will break out and clog the screw.

Traditionally, auger bits were made with square, tapered tangs for use with a brace. Today you will also find auger bits with round or hexagonal straight shanks designed to fit electric drills.

How to use an auger bit

It takes a little practice to use an auger bit well, but it does bore with remarkable efficiency, assuming the bit is sharp and well maintained. The trick is to provide enough pressure to keep the rate of penetration consistent with the feed of the screw point. Otherwise the screw threads can clog and obstruct the bit's progress. A small bit drilling soft wood pulls itself along with no backup pressure at all, but more force is required with larger bits and harder woods.

Buying auger bits

Auger bits are usually sold in diameters from ¼ in. to 1 in. The size is marked on the shaft as a single number indicating the number of sixteenths, so that, for example, the number 12 signifies a ¾-in.-diameter bit. Most auger bits, except those manufactured specifically for doweling, are actually ground about ¹⁄₆₄ in. oversize to allow free passage of bolts and other fasteners.

Auger bits are available at hardware stores and wood specialty stores and through woodworking mail-order catalogs. Used auger bits are widely available on the second-hand tool market. When looking over used bits, make sure all the parts are in good condition, check the twist for straightness by rolling the bit on a flat surface, and expect to do some sharpening when you get home.

Maintaining auger bits

Sharpening an auger bit involves restoring the spurs and cutting edges with an auger-bit file (see p. 6), removing only as much steel as necessary to eliminate nicks and wear. File the spurs from the inside only. Filing them on the outside will change the hole's diameter and destroy the clearance for the twist. File the cutting edges from the tang end, taking the same amount of metal off both lips to maintain cutting balance. For a keen edge, the spurs and cutting edges may be honed subsequently with a slipstone, again from the inside and top, respectively.

Store auger bits in such a way as to prevent them from rubbing against one another and other metallic objects. They should also be wiped with an oily rag occasionally to prevent rust.

Brad-point bits

Most of the time, the brad point is the first choice for accurate drilling in wood with a drill press or handheld electric drill. The projecting point makes it easy to locate the hole, the spurs outline the hole cleanly (especially if the bit enters the wood slowly at first), and the spiral flutes clear out waste efficiently. Brad-point bits are available in sizes from ⅛ in. to 1 in. in diameter and in metric sizes as well.

There are three types of steel out of which brad points are made. The least expensive bits are of carbon steel with a Rockwell hardness of Rc48 to Rc50. They are good for nonproduction boring into all woods and perfectly satisfactory for small-shop furniture making.

Brad-point bits made of high-speed steel have a Rockwell hardness of Rc60 to Rc62, stay sharp twice as long as carbon-steel bits, and are good for continuous cutting of softwoods in production, as well as for all small-shop needs.

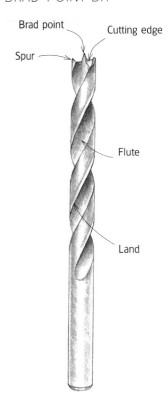

BRAD-POINT BIT

Brad point

Cutting edge

Spur

Flute

Land

BRAD-POINT
DESIGNS

Projecting
spurs

Acme grind

Carbide-tipped brad-point bits are the hardest of all, though not as sharp as the others when new. You won't find them in many small shops, but they are preferred for production boring in all hardwoods and softwoods, and especially for abrasive materials such as medium-density fiberboard (MDF).

There are two different styles of brad-point bit: those with projecting spurs and those with an "acme" grind (see the drawing at left). Projecting spurs are preferable for cross-grain boring because they sever wood fibers ahead of the cutting edge to make a particularly clean hole. Acme-style bits are better for end-grain boring, where spurs have nothing to sever and serve only to increase resistance. However, the distinction is minor enough that either style of bit may be used for both cross-grain and end-grain boring in the small shop.

FORSTNER BIT

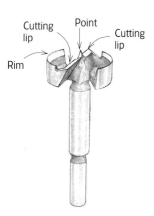

Cutting lip
Point
Cutting lip
Rim

Forstner bits

The Forstner is a specialty bit, not meant for everyday use because it is slow-cutting and tends to overheat. The Forstner bit is guided by its rim rather than its center. The rim and cutting lip lie in virtually the same plane, which creates a flat-bottomed hole with a particularly clean entry. Because the point sticks out a minimal distance, the Forstner bit is desirable for drilling holes where the point of a brad-point bit or auger bit might punch through to the other side.

Its unusual geometry makes the Forstner bit preferable to brad-point and screw-point bits for the following tasks: drilling a partial circle at the edge of a piece of wood without the bit walking; drilling angled holes cleanly; drilling end grain; drilling a larger hole over an existing hole; and drilling through knots. Forstner bits are available in diameters from ¼ in. to more than 2 in.

MULTISPUR BIT

Multispur bits

The multispur bit is a variation on the Forstner bit with teeth milled around the perimeter. It is somewhat more aggressive and less prone to overheating. Multispur bits don't cut quite as cleanly as Forstner bits, but they still do a quality job and share the ability to drill partial and angled holes. These bits are a good choice for large-diameter holes (from ¾ in. up) and come in sizes as large as 4 in. in diameter.

Spade bits

The spade bit is the most prevalent of the woodboring bits sold in hardware stores. It is quick-cutting and inexpensive, making it a good rough-carpentry tool. Spade bits aren't accurate enough for furniture making, however, because they tend to make somewhat ovoid holes of irregular diameter. They come in diameters from ¼ in. to 1½ in.

One instance in which spade bits outshine other woodboring bits is in drilling fibrous green wood, such as fresh-cut ash. Where a brad-point or multispur bit clogs up with spongy fiber, a spade bit eats its way through.

Sharpening spade bits

To sharpen a dull spade bit, file the lips with an auger-bit file at their original angle until you see fresh metal all along the cutting edge. Both lips should contact the wood simultaneously.

SPADE BIT

Spoon bits

Spoon bits were in common use in the 18th and early 19th centuries, particularly among chairmakers. They are half-cylindrical in section with either parallel or tapered sides (for making straight-sided and tapered holes). They will also ream a taper into a straight hole. Spoon bits are driven with a brace and will cut when spun in either direction.

The unique aspect of spoon bits is that you can change direction as you drill. This makes them desirable for Windsor-chair construction, where spindle holes are often drilled freehand at compound angles. To drill an angled hole, the bit is first started straight on to make a dish, and then angled as it bites. Any other bit would fail to make a clean hole when used in this fashion.

Today, spoon bits are rarely employed outside the Windsor-chairmaking community. Without brad points or screws, they cannot be accurately started the way all other bits can.

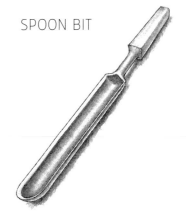

SPOON BIT

Buying spoon bits

One manufacturer in Britain still makes spoon bits. They are available through wood specialty stores and mail-order catalogs. Diameters range from ⅜ in. to ¾ in. by sixteenths.

Sharpening spoon bits

Sharpen spoon bits by honing the inside of the cutting edge with a slipstone or fine file. Never hone the outside of the cutting edge, because this would destroy its clearance.

TWIST DRILL

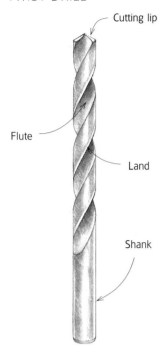

Cutting lip

Flute

Land

Shank

TWIST-DRILL GEOMETRY

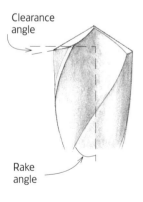

Clearance angle

Rake angle

Twist drills

The twist drill is the universal drill-bit design, able to make holes in wood, metal, stone, concrete, plastic, and just about anything else. For metal machinists, it is the primary drill bit. For woodworkers, it is often second or third choice.

The parts of a twist drill are as follows: The body is the main section in which the flutes are milled. The shank is the unfluted end of the bit that mounts in a chuck. The web is the core of metal that runs the length of the bit between the flutes. The lips are the cutting edges at the end of the drill. The land is a narrow, flat band that runs along the rim of each flute. The body of the drill adjacent to the land retreats to a smaller diameter.

The common twist drills you are likely to purchase are made to metalworking specifications. The included angle formed by the cutting edges of a standard twist drill is 118°, the rake angle of the flutes is 30°, and the clearance angle of the lip is 12°.

A better, but less commonly available style of twist drill has a split point (see the top drawing on the facing page). The geometry of a split-point drill differs in that the cutting lips are offset and the point angle is 135°. Its primary advantage is that it won't wander when you start a hole the way a standard twist drill normally does.

Twist drills of standard length are called "jobber's" drills. They are made to four different systems of diameter specification: fractions of an inch graduated by sixty-fourths from 1/64 in. to 1/2 in. (and sometimes beyond); metric sizes; letter sizes; and numerical wire gauge sizes. Most commonly, woodworkers use bits graduated by the inch system.

From a woodworker's point of view, there are several problems with a twist drill. The broad angle at the point makes it difficult to position the bit accurately. The lack of spurs makes for ragged-edged cross-grain holes that tend to be slightly oval-shaped. And the spiral flutes milled in the body have limited chip-clearing capacity. For the most part, twist drills are good for making small holes, such as pilot holes for screws, where the close graduation between sizes offers a welcome versatility. Also, they are necessary for the metalworking needs that crop up now and then in the woodshop.

Sharpening twist drills

The performance of a twist drill is critically affected by the precision and symmetry of the cutting lips. It's not a good idea to regrind the lips freehand, although I have seen practiced machinists do so. Many woodworkers I know simply throw a dull twist drill out and buy a replacement, particularly in the inexpensive smaller sizes. Larger drills may be sent out for professional sharpening. There are sharpening jigs on the market for small-shop use, but most woodworkers can't be bothered with them: Twist drills stay sharp so long on wood that the jig may not be worth the investment.

In my own shop, I sometimes refashion dull twist drills into brad-point bits, working freehand against the corner of a grinding wheel (see the drawing below). They don't come out as perfect as a properly manufactured brad point, but they work a whole lot better than they did dull.

To regrind a twist drill into a brad point, first establish the grinding angle with a real brad-point bit. This involves setting the grinder's tool rest and finding the oblique angle at which the bit must be held on it so the cutting lip meets the corner of the wheel flat on. Having established the approximate angle, grind one lip of the twist drill at a time. To start,

TWIST-DRILL
POINTS

Standard

Split point

MAKING A TWIST DRILL
INTO A BRAD-POINT BIT

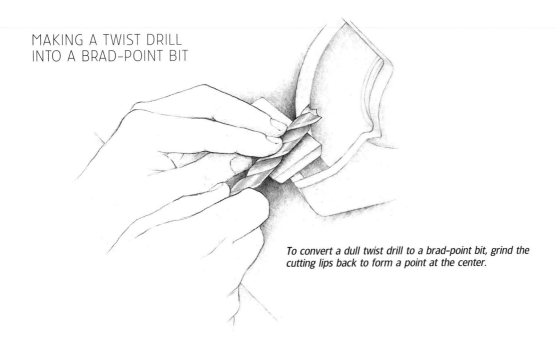

To convert a dull twist drill to a brad-point bit, grind the cutting lips back to form a point at the center.

place the mid-point of the lip (halfway between point and land) against the corner of the wheel. As the wheel begins to bite, spin the bit through about one-third of an arc, back and forth, watching to make sure you don't remove so much material as to lose the center of the bit, which is gradually forming into a brad point. Then do the same thing to the other lip. When the reground bit passes visual inspection for symmetry, place it in a drill press and lower it onto a piece of wood (with the motor off) to be sure the two spurs make contact simultaneously. If not, grind the protruding one to match.

COUNTERSINKS

The function of a countersink is to clear a conical depression at the entrance to a screw hole so the head of the screw can be set flush with or below the surface. Ideally, the lip angle of the countersink is matched to the taper of the screw head, but, depending on the screw's country of origin, this may not be the case. The standard angle of screw heads made in the United States is 82°, whereas in the United Kingdom it is 90°; with screws now being made all over the world, the heads can fall anywhere within this approximate range. The best bet is to use an 82° countersink so that all screw heads will pull tight around their rims, whatever their actual angle.

COUNTERSINKS

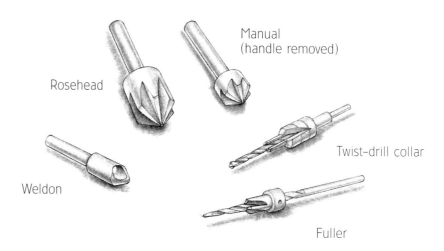

Rosehead

Manual
(handle removed)

Weldon

Twist-drill collar

Fuller

There are several designs for countersinks on the market. Most are made to work with a drill, but some come with attached handles for manual rotation. The best traditional design is the rosehead, which consists of a multitude of serrations radiating like spokes down a cone-shaped head. Modern descendants tend to have four or five spokes with deeper grooves in between. Other designs include Fuller countersinks, which mount on tapered drill bits that approximate the tapers of the various-size wood screws; Weldon countersinks; and collars made for twist drills. The collars are the least desirable; they dull quickly, burn the wood, and break easily.

Countersinks come in a range of diameters, each meant to span several different hole sizes depending on how deeply they enter the wood.

TRADITIONAL
ROSEHEAD
COUNTERSINK

Sharpening countersinks

Like all drill bits, countersinks do their best work when sharp, particularly in softer woods that are prone to crush and tear. Most woodworkers send their countersinks out to a professional sharpener or, in the case of the cheaper collars, throw them away and buy new ones.

To sharpen a rosehead yourself, you would run an oilstone or fine diamond file along each outer facet, maintaining the bevel angle and avoiding damage to the edges of adjacent teeth. To sharpen a modern five-spoke rosehead you would do the same, but you could also hone the inside faces of the cutters with slipstones since they have a more accessible geometry.

DRILLS

There are three basic types of hand-powered drills: the brace, the hand drill, and the push drill. Braces are traditionally used with auger-type bits for making holes from $\frac{1}{4}$ in. up to $1\frac{1}{2}$ in. in diameter, whereas hand drills are used with twist drills to make holes from $\frac{1}{4}$ in. down to $\frac{1}{16}$ in. in diameter. The push drill is less widely used in furniture making. Its specialized bits are called straight-flute drill points and are sized from $\frac{11}{64}$ in. down to $\frac{1}{16}$ in.

Braces

While the brace has been around since the 15th century, the contemporary version was first patented during the American Civil War, with some improvement to the chuck taking place over the next 50 years. The fully developed brace is distinguished by a ratchet mechanism and

BRACE

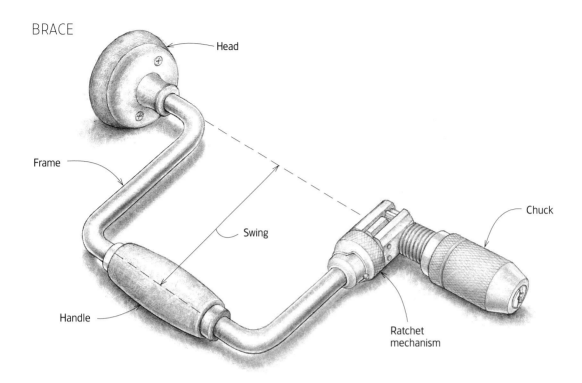

Head

Frame

Swing

Chuck

Handle

Ratchet
mechanism

a universal chuck. The ratchet has three positions so that the chuck may be engaged only on the clockwise swing of the handle, only on the counterclockwise swing, or both ways. The universal chuck will take straight-shanked bits up to ½ in. in diameter and any size of square-tapered tang—a feature that was particularly useful early on, when competing manufacturers were making nonstandardized auger bits.

Braces are specified for size according to their "swing" or "sweep." The swing is the distance from the central axis to the handle; the sweep is the diameter of the circle described by the handle and is double the swing. The size range of manufactured braces has narrowed considerably over the past half century. Those still made today have sweeps ranging from 6 in. to 12 in.

For an excellent, in-depth treatment of braces and other hand-boring equipment, get your hands on a copy of *Restoring, Tuning, & Using Classic Woodworking Tools* by Michael Dunbar (Sterling Publishing, 1989).

Buying braces

Better-quality braces are distinguished by the following traits: First, the underside of the head attaches to the shaft with a steel-housed ball bearing for ease of turning and long wear. Second, the ratchet mechanism is all-steel and enclosed. Third, the universal chuck has a square recess to firmly support taper shanks and will take round-shanked bits up to ½ in. in diameter.

As demand for braces decreases, manufacturers are continually pruning their lines. There is no guarantee that top-quality braces will be made at all in the future. For this reason, you may want to shop on the used-tool market to compare price and quality.

Maintaining braces

From time to time, place a drop of oil in the lubrication hole under a brace's head and on the ratchet mechanism (which may or may not have a lubrication hole).

Hand drills

The hand drill bears the nickname "eggbeater" because of the way it works. A hand crank turns a gear-and-pinion mechanism, which in turn spins a chuck. Hand-drill chucks usually have a ¼-in.-diameter capacity.

The best hand drills are distinguished by a double-pinion gear, meaning that the main gear to which the handle connects engages two separate pinions on the shank, one above and one below. Where a single-pinion gear might theoretically deflect away from the frame, disengage, and skip under heavy pressure, a double-pinion gear has no problem. Cast-iron (gray-iron) gears wear better than zinc or aluminum, but all three are far better than plastic gears.

The gears on a hand drill can be enclosed or exposed. Enclosed gears are less likely to pinch the operator, but the exposed gears on older drills can be quite lovely.

Buying hand drills

Hand drills may be purchased at hardware stores and through woodworking specialty stores and catalogs. As with braces, there are wonderful older hand drills available on the used-tool market at reasonable prices.

HAND DRILL

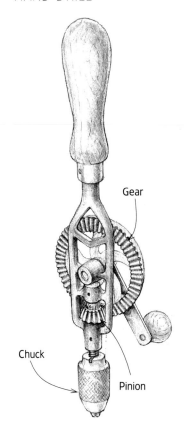

Gear

Chuck

Pinion

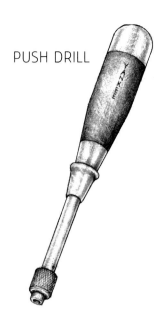

PUSH DRILL

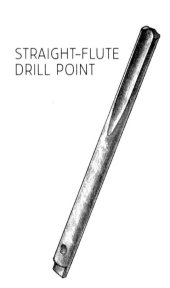

STRAIGHT-FLUTE
DRILL POINT

Push drills

The push drill is a boring version of the "Yankee" screwdriver. As you push the handle down and let it spring back you rotate a spiral-grooved shaft, which in turn spins the chuck back and forth. The chuck has a simple quick-release mechanism actuated by a retractable collar.

Specific bits, called straight-flute drill points, are made for use with the push drill in sizes from $\frac{1}{16}$ in. to $\frac{11}{64}$ in. They have straight-sided bodies with V-grooves milled down opposite sides. The cutting lips angle away from the point much like those of a twist drill. The shank of a straight-flute drill point is double-notched to fit the chuck.

Push drills are as much carpentry tools as they are cabinetmaking tools. Their bits lack the points and spurs that would make them highly accurate but are small enough to achieve reasonable accuracy if hole locations are first marked with a broad-pointed awl or centerpunch. Push drills are often used to make starter holes for screws.

Buying push drills

When buying a push drill, look for one with bit storage in the handle—an extremely convenient feature. Older push drills had durable metal caps that screwed on and off for access to the storage compartment. New drills are made only with plastic caps, but the better ones have a threaded metal insert built into the underside of the cap.

Another feature to look for is a fully enclosed mechanism with the spiral shaft housed in a metal sleeve to protect it from damage and to protect the user from pinching.

New push drills are available at local hardware stores, but better quality can be found on the used-tool market. Replacement points can be ordered through your hardware store if they're not available off the shelf.

Maintaining push drills

Oil the spiral shaft from time to time. Push drills with enclosed shafts provide an oil hole for this purpose.

CLAMPING & HOLDING

Even Vishnu, the four-armed god, would need a clamp or vise from time to time were he to take up woodworking. For mere two-fisted mortals such as ourselves, clamping and holding devices are absolute necessities. This chapter covers clamps, vises, and workbenches—the tools with which we hold wood in place and exert pressure during assembly.

CLAMPS

There are many types of clamps, with new variations being introduced all the time thanks to the confluence of human ingenuity and the profit motive. Clamps vary in reach and length, in the amount of pressure they exert, in the ease with which they adjust and tighten, in the degree to which they flex under load, in their durability, and in how much they are likely to mar unprotected wood. With so many variables being applied to the myriad clamping needs that arise in the woodshop, it's no wonder that the popular adage is "you can never have enough clamps."

This chapter includes the range of manufactured clamps most commonly used in the woodshop. Not every permutation in clamp design is included or anticipated. These are the tried-and-true basics, from an understanding of which you can satisfy your clamping needs and evaluate new products as they enter the market.

In addition to manufactured clamps, the woodworker has recourse to many low-tech clamping techniques. Components can be squeezed together with a loop of rope twisted by a stick. Free-form laminations may be assembled with windings of sliced-up inner tube. Thin stock can be edge-glued with wedges between fixed rails on a tabletop. Vertical pressure can be applied with spring poles run to the ceiling. The possibilities are endless.

The pressure a clamp is capable of exerting is measured in pounds per square inch. Limiting factors are the strength of the clamp's frame, the power of the clamping mechanism, and the amount of torque applied by the handle. The best clamp is not always the most powerful—for some jobs gentle, light pressure is preferable.

The secret of good clamping is to put pressure straight through the joint, at right angles to the faces being assembled. One instance is gluing together a panel with ordinary bar clamps (as shown in the drawing below). In the correct setup, the work is positioned at a height where the bar clamps' screws are directly in line with the center of the boards. This keeps the force straight through the joints, holds the clamp jaws square to the work, and pulls the boards together with a minimum of deflection. If the screw is above center, it will tend to force the work into a concave cup. If the pressure is below center, the work will cup upward.

CLAMPING PRESSURE

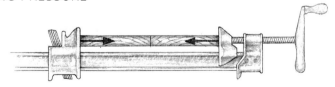

Ideal clamping pressure goes straight through the joints.

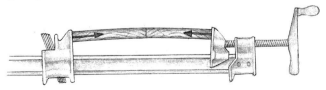

If the work is above the clamp screw, the jaw angles back and causes the assembly to cup.

The same principle of clamping through the joint applies to miters. Temporary glue blocks such as those shown in the top drawing at right allow clamping pressure to be exerted straight through the joint, ensuring maximum pressure and minimum slippage. The blocks can be glued to the work with a layer of brown paper in between to make their removal clean and easy.

Band clamps

The band clamp is a continuous loop of woven material closed by a tightening mechanism that reduces the web's circumference. Band clamps are particularly useful for assembling irregular forms such as staved barrels, columns, and hexagonal frames where straight clamps are at a disadvantage. Although they can exert significant pressure, band clamps are not very efficient at delivering that pressure where it is needed across the joints. Instead, they diffuse pressure around the entire circumference of the clamped object and direct it partially inward, toward the center of the loop.

Band clamps are distinguished by the width, length, and strength of the band material, by the power of the tightening mechanism, and by the ease with which they adjust for length, tighten, and release. Smaller band clamps typically have 1-in.-wide nylon or polyester webs 15 ft. to 25 ft. long, capable of exerting about 1,000 lb. of pressure. While that may sound like a lot of squeeze, it's spread over a large area. If you were to put a band clamp around a hexagonal frame, the amount of pressure on each of the six joints would be less than 167 lb.—considerably less than the pressure provided by an average-sized quick-action clamp. And the pressure would not be directed straight across the joint where it would do the most good.

Larger band clamps have 2-in.-wide, 25-ft.-long canvas or nylon straps capable of exerting over 3,000 lb. of pressure. A T-handled screw vise takes care of both tightening and releasing pressure. Strap length is adjusted by means of self-locking cams on either side of the vise head. Canvas band clamps are considerably more expensive than their little brethren, but they are proportionately more effective.

Bar and pipe clamps

Technically, the term "bar clamp" defines a wide range of clamp sizes and styles that share certain simple characteristics: a metal bar or pipe; a stationary head; a sliding tail stop; and a screw assembly that threads through the head or the tail. In practice, woodworkers apply the name "bar clamp" only to a subgroup comprising the heavy-barred, flat-jawed

CLAMPING A MITER JOINT

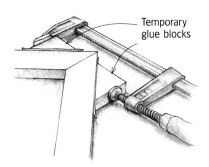

Temporary glue blocks

The best way to pull a miter joint together is to orient clamping pressure straight through the joint.

BAND CLAMPS

One-inch

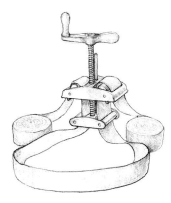

Two-inch

BAR CLAMPS

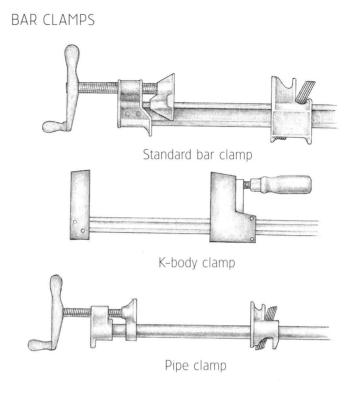

Standard bar clamp

K-body clamp

Pipe clamp

BAR-CLAMP
TAIL STOPS

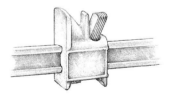

Clutch stop

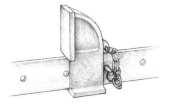

Pinned stop

clamps used for assembling wide panels and large carcases (they are called "sash cramps" in England). "Pipe clamps" serve the same purpose, but have round pipe in place of rectilinear steel bar. What I choose to call "quick-action clamps" (described under a separate heading) are technically bar clamps with lighter bars, swivel pads on their screws, and raised pads on their stationary heads.

In section, a bar clamp's bar may be I-shaped or simply rectangular. The thicker and wider the bar, the more resistance it has to deflection under load. The load limit for bar clamps ranges from 1,600 lb. to 7,000 lb. depending on the heaviness of construction. Length ranges from 2 ft. to 8 ft. Separate bar-clamp fittings are available for attachment to wood beams, but these tend to flex more than their metal counterparts.

Standard bar clamps come with several different styles of tail stop (see the drawing at left). The most popular has a quick-adjusting slip clutch made up of stacked steel plates. Another design that works well locks the tail stop in place with a steel pin inserted through one of a series of holes spaced along the bar. The quick-adjusting clutch is more convenient, but the pin style has the advantage that an extra-long clamp can be quickly made by removing the tail stops and bolting two clamps together end for end, as shown in the top drawing on the facing page.

Another style, called the K-body or parallel clamp, differs from the standard bar clamp. On the positive side, K-bodies have deeper throats and their jaws are engineered to stay square to the bar under load. This allows you to edge-glue without the fuss of lining up the vise screw with the center of the work. The K-body's deep-reach, plastic-covered steel jaws are also gentle on wood, so the hassle of slipping in protective pads as you clamp is usually eliminated.

On the negative side, the tail stops of K-body clamps can be more awkward to adjust for length and the vise screw is shorter, which can be inconvenient. For all that, K-body clamps are usually the first choice in our shop when a bar clamp is needed.

A pipe clamp consists of a threaded head and a quick-release sliding tail stop mounted on a length of pipe. Pipe-clamp fittings are made in two sizes, to fit ½-in. or ¾-in. I.D. black iron pipe. Generally, you purchase the head and tail fixtures separately from the pipe, which can be found at any plumbing-supply store and must be threaded at one end in order to mount the head. The load limit of pipe clamps is beyond the manufacturers' control since the limiting factor is the quality of the pipe, but it is definitely less than that of heavy-duty bar clamps.

Pipe clamps have two advantages over bar clamps, but these are more than outweighed by their major defect. On the upside, pipe clamps are far less expensive and infinitely more versatile in that one set of fixtures can be used with many lengths of pipe and two pipes can be coupled together if they are threaded at both ends. On the downside, pipe clamps flex so readily that they make it difficult to keep work flat and square. As they bow in tension, the jaws angle out and force the work to bow as well. The common solution when edge-gluing is to place clamps on alternate sides of the work, but this doesn't succeed nearly as well as using correctly positioned bar clamps.

C-clamps

C-clamps, known as "G-cramps" in England, have a C-shaped iron frame with a screw threaded through one end and an anvil formed on the other. The screw has a swivel pad where it meets the work and a handle on the outside. C-clamps are made in such a variety of weights and sizes as to be useful for everything from gluing tiny splinters back in place to laminating piano frames. C-clamps were once the dominant clamp design, but they have been largely superseded by the more convenient quick-action clamps.

The openings of C-clamps range from under 1 in. to over 18 in. in length, with throat depths from 1 in. to 8 in. C-clamps are made in light-duty, regular-duty, heavy-duty, and extra-heavy-duty versions. The load

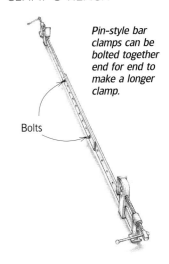

EXTENDING A CLAMP'S REACH

Pin-style bar clamps can be bolted together end for end to make a longer clamp.

Bolts

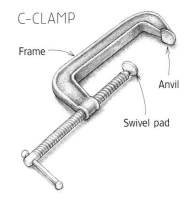

C-CLAMP

Frame

Anvil

Swivel pad

capacity of the lightest is around 250 lb.; that of the heaviest-duty is over 20,000 lb. (for metalwork only!).

Good-quality C-clamps have unitary frames formed from ductile iron, malleable iron, or drop-forged carbon steel. Poor-quality clamps have pressed- or stamped-steel frames that are made in cookie-cutter fashion. The handles of C-clamps are either fixed T-bars or sliding T-bars. The sliding ones are more versatile and often provide more torque, because they are longer and can be tightened next to obstructions. When buying new C-clamps, make sure the threaded rod aligns with the anvil.

CAM CLAMP

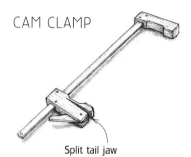

Split tail jaw

Cam clamps

Cam clamps are deep-throated clamps with two long jaws mounted on a steel bar. To tighten the clamp you rotate the cam against the split tail jaw, which forces the inner side of the jaw against the work. The jaws themselves may be wood or plastic; they are often lined with a soft material such as cork. The head is fixed, and the sliding tail holds its position as pressure is applied.

Cam clamps range in length from 8 in. to 31 in. and in throat depth from 4¼ in. to 8½ in. They are not notable for the amount of pressure they exert—approximately 300 lb.—yet this is sufficient for many holding and gluing tasks. It's great to have a couple of cam clamps around the shop because of their deep reach, light weight, and gentle, nonmarring jaws.

HANDSCREW

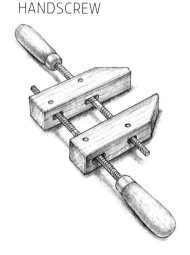

Handscrews

Handscrews look like objects from a 16th-century engraving. In fact, they have been around for centuries, but they are still quite relevant for the contemporary woodworker. Their wooden jaws are nonmarring, exert significant pressure over a relatively broad area, and angle to accommodate nonparallel shapes when necessary.

Early handscrews were made with threaded wood spindles. Modern handscrews adjust via threaded steel spindles and pivoting steel inserts mounted in the jaws. They are stronger and more durable, and their jaws adjust through a range of angles. The smallest handscrews have a throat depth of 2 in. and a 2-in. opening. The largest have a 12-in. throat depth and a 17-in. opening.

To set the opening quickly you grasp the two handles and rotate them in parallel circles, much like the movement of bicycle pedals. To adjust the relative angles of the jaws, you turn either handle separately. In most cases, the best assembly technique is to have the jaws flat against the work, applying broad, even pressure.

Because the jaws of handscrews are wood, they should be protected from glue. Otherwise you might glue the clamp to the work. A good preventive technique is to place wax paper between the glued surface and the clamp or to keep the jaws of the clamp waxed or finished.

Pinch dogs

Pinch dogs are shaped to pull edge joints together when driven into the ends of adjacent boards. Sometimes they are used alone and sometimes as positioning devices until other types of clamps can be brought into play.

PINCH DOG

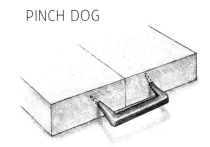

Quick-action clamps

Quick-action clamps are the most widely used, most versatile clamps in the contemporary workshop. They have a stationary head with a raised pad at its tip and a sliding head through which a screw assembly ending in a swivel pad is threaded. They are called "quick-action" and similar names because of the speed with which they adjust for length compared to C-clamps, which they have largely replaced.

There are two types of quick-action sliding heads: those that incorporate a slip clutch made of stacked steel plates and those that slide freely unless held in place by friction under load (see the drawing below). It's difficult to say which design is preferable—some woodworkers swear by one, some by the other.

The size range of quick-action clamps is extensive. Throat depth, also called "reach," varies from 2 in. to as much as 20 in., and open lengths from 4 in. to 60 in. Light-duty clamps have load limits of as little as 200 lb., while heavy-duty ones are capable of exerting at least 1,200 lb. of pressure. When you first begin putting a clamp collection together, it is probably wiser to begin with heavy-duty clamps because they are more versatile, even though they are also more expensive and cumbersome. As time goes on, you will want some lighter-duty clamps for convenience.

QUICK-ACTION CLAMP

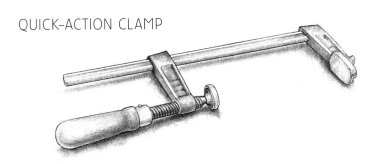

This recommendation does not apply to the smallest sizes of quick-action clamp, where the convenience of light weight may be more important than strength from the start.

When selecting quick-action clamps, there are a couple of things to look for besides weight and strength. The bar should in some way prevent the tail stop from sliding off. If it doesn't, you can always put a bolt or rivet through the end. You can also beat the bar on-end with a hammer to peen an edge. Some clamps feature fitted plastic or rubber jaw covers that protect the work—a convenience that saves the bother of placing pads between the clamp and the work. Fitted jaw covers are not an essential feature, since you can achieve the same effect by taping your own wooden, plastic, or rubber pads onto the jaws with double-sided tape, but they are handy to have. Finally, the screw assembly should align with the head so that clamp pressure is delivered straight through the joint.

An interesting variation on the quick-action clamp works by means of a squeeze grip. This allows you to hold the clamp in position and tighten it with one hand. Squeeze-grip clamps tend to be light-duty—pleasant to use, but not the sort of clamp you can rely on to pull a bent lamination together.

SPRING CLAMPS

Standard

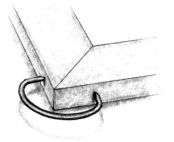

Arc type

Spring clamps

Standard spring clamps work like clothespins, except their springs are so strong you may need two hands to open them. They are great for all sorts of tasks such as placing stops on machine fences, holding components together while transferring marks from one to another, and clamping small parts and repairs where a moderate amount of localized pressure is sufficient.

When acquiring spring clamps, be sure to get those with plastic sleeves on their pincers and handles. They protect the work and your hands and are definitely a desirable feature. The smallest spring clamps have 1-in. openings and a 1¼-in. reach. The big biters have 4-in. jaw openings and 4 in. of reach.

A second, rarely used type of spring clamp is a plain arc of spring steel wire. This clamp is powerful enough to be sold with a mechanical spreader and is intended primarily to hold mitered corners together. It comes in two styles: one with sharp ends, one with protective buttons. The sharp-pointed clamps have the more positive grip, but they also make holes in the wood, so their application is limited unless you go to the trouble of first gluing protective blocks to the work (with brown paper glued in between for easy removal).

Tape

No discussion of clamping and holding would be complete without mention of masking tape and double-sided tape (also commonly referred to as "double-coated tape" and "double-stick tape"). Conventional masking tape is great for holding small repairs and parts in place during glue-up, for taping up veneer, and for many other tasks. Its backing is crepe paper, saturated with rubber latex. Crepe paper has been creased to give it elasticity, which is why it is particularly good for clamping. The adhesive on masking tape is a combination of rubber and tackifying resin.

Masking tape is made in a range of qualities from "general purpose" through "painter's grade" up to "premium grade." What distinguishes better-quality tapes are heavier paper with greater tensile strength and a higher proportion of rubber in the adhesive, making it harder and more cohesive so that it leaves less residue behind.

Conventional masking tape should be removed from a surface within 24 hours; otherwise, the adhesive begins to degrade and bond to the work. A newer variety, popularly called "blue tape" after its usual color, uses an acrylic-based adhesive with a longer life. It has more resistance to ultraviolet exposure and sunlight and can stay in place for up to seven days. However, blue tape has less tack than conventional tape, which is a disadvantage for clamping purposes.

There are two types of double-sided tape that can be used in the woodshop, crepe backed and plastic backed (often sold as "carpet tape"). Crepe-backed tape is thinner with a stronger bond, which makes it preferable. Tensile strength is not important in most cases where double-sided tape is used, but thinness is an advantage because it allows the two surfaces being attached to be closer together. Double-sided tape is incredible for making jigs and fixtures and for temporarily holding work where a clamp would be in the way.

Masking tape is manufactured in widths from ¼ in. to 57 in. (the latter for industrial special orders). The common widths available at hardware stores are ¾ in., 1 in., 1½ in., and 2 in.

Buying clamps

Building up a clamp collection is a slow process, given the expense and the great variety of clamps you will find desirable over time. What are the essential first clamps to have? Every experienced woodworker would probably give a different answer, but you won't go wrong with at least four 48-in. bar clamps for carcase and panel assembly, four 12-in. and four 24-in. quick-action clamps, a pair of spring clamps, and a few small, lightweight C-clamps or quick-action clamps with openings about 2 in. deep by 3 in. or 4 in. long. Clamps are sold in hardware stores, but a better selection is available from woodworking stores and catalogs.

VISES

Vises in the woodshop are sometimes described according to their position and function, sometimes according to their design. "Tail vise" and "front vise" refer to a vise's location and function on a workbench. "Woodworking vise" and "metalworking vise," as used here, describe styles of vise design.

A tail vise (see the drawing on p. 48) does not necessarily have jaws to grasp wood, though it usually does. Its defining function is to move a bench dog in line with a series of dog holes mortised down the length of the benchtop. The tail vise enables work to be held horizontally on top of the bench between bench dogs, free of clamps that would obstruct access with handplanes and other tools. A front vise, by contrast, holds wood between vertical jaws (see the drawing on p. 46). It is usually located on the long, front edge of a workbench at the far end from the tail vise. The tops of its jaws are flush with the bench surface.

Tail and front vises are desirable complements in a workbench. They are constructed as integral parts of many European-style benches (see pp. 45-49). Woodworking vises, on the other hand, are stand-alone pieces of hardware that can be attached to a bench to serve as either tail or front vises. Metalworking and universal vises mount on top of a bench and hold work well above the surface. Patternmaker's vises are versatile holding devices in a class of their own.

MACHINIST'S BENCH VISE

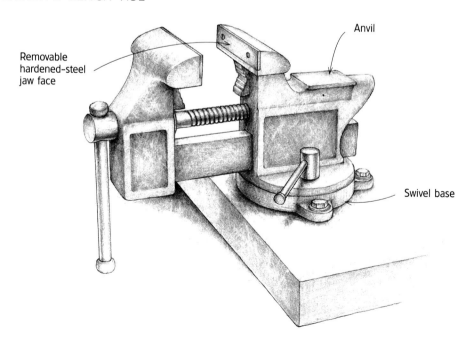

Removable hardened-steel jaw face

Anvil

Swivel base

Metalworking vises

Metalworking vises can be quite handy for holding wood as well as metal. They mount on a benchtop or tabletop, allowing the craftsman to work at a height that is often more comfortable than stooping over a front vise. Among the many tasks for which I prefer a higher vise are rounding spindles with a spokeshave and filing the edge of a scraper.

There are several styles of vises made for metalworking, such as the machinist's bench vise (see the drawing on the facing page), sheet-metal vise, and fitter's vise. They all share the same essential design, with some variation in the shape of the jaws. Metalworking vises have heavy cast-iron and steel construction and hardened-steel jaw faces. The jaws are relatively small and powerful compared to those of woodworking vises. Behind the fixed jaw there is often a flat, horizontal area on the body to serve as an anvil.

Metalworking vises come in a wide range of strength and quality levels, from light-duty economy to heavy-duty industrial. Acquiring a metalworking vise is one of the few times when a woodworker can feel comfortable not buying the top of the line. A light-duty vise is sufficient to the limited metalworking needs of woodworkers and powerful enough for any wood-holding required of it. Jaw openings on metalworking vises range from 3 in. to 12 in. Since the addition of wooden jaw protectors will diminish the opening size, 5 in. might be considered an acceptable minimum to start with. Jaw width ranges from 3 in. to 8 in.; 4 in. is a good minimum.

Vises that bolt down to a tabletop are better than those that clamp to a table edge, since sturdiness is preferable to portability in most shop situations. A swivel base is also desirable, because it is convenient to be able to approach the work from different angles.

Covering the jaws of a metalworking vise with wooden pads keeps them from crushing and indenting woodwork. Most metalworking vises have removable, hardened-steel jaw faces that you can replace with wider, thicker hardwood jaws. Dense hardwood plywood such as Baltic birch makes the best jaw covers, since it is so resistant to splitting. If a vise doesn't have removable jaw faces, you can simply attach wooden jaw covers with double-sided tape. (Make sure the taped-on pads don't overhang at the edges or they will quickly lever off.)

The most convenient place to mount a metalworking vise is on an auxiliary work surface close to the workbench. There, it is always within reach, but it doesn't disturb the plane of the benchtop, where it can get in the way, especially when working on large pieces. A standard alternative is to mount your metalworking vise on a T-shaped wood platform (as shown in the drawing above). The platform can then be gripped in a front vise as needed and be stored elsewhere the rest of the time.

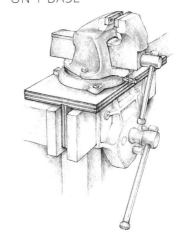

METALWORKING VISE MOUNTED ON T-BASE

PATTERNMAKER'S
VISE

Patternmaker's vises

The patternmaker's vise is an advanced form of woodworking vise with the ability to rotate, swing up from vertical to horizontal, and take tapered work between the jaws. In other words, it will hold work of varied shape in any position you can think of. This is more vise than most woodworkers need, which is fortunate given the fact that it is many times more expensive than a good woodworking vise.

Patternmaker's vises were widely used prior to World War II, when most steel and iron work was cast and the patterns for the molds required careful, often intricate modeling. At present, they are difficult to come by. Lee Valley Tools in Canada sells a version called the Tucker vise, which additionally features a quick-release mechanism for rapid adjustment and an automatic opening mechanism operated by a foot pedal.

Patternmaker's vises are not meant for heavy pounding, particularly when extended away from the bench. But if you have a particular need for controlled carving and shaping, you might find one worth the cost.

UNIVERSAL
VISE

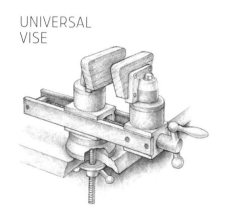

Universal vises

The universal vise bolts down through a single hole in a benchtop and can easily be turned through 360° by loosening the large wing nut beneath the bench. Its other special feature is that the outer jaw rotates, enabling it to grasp tapered and somewhat irregular forms. The universal vise is useful for holding work above the bench, much as a metalworking vise is, but it has the advantage of greater mobility and ease of removal.

However, the name "universal" must have been given by an advertising agency, not a craftsman. It would be more appropriately bestowed on the patternmaker's vise described above. A major limitation of the universal vise is that it cannot grip work that passes through it vertically. The rotating jaw angles away unless work passes across the center of the jaws. Another shortcoming is that only light to moderate pressure is possible due to the stress that results from the jaws' being so far above the screw. In both regards a metalworking vise is superior.

If I had to make a choice, I would take a metalworking vise over a universal vise. A metalworking vise handles wood reasonably well, but a universal vise lacks the strength and the hardened steel jaws to deal with metal.

Woodworking vises

Woodworking vises characteristically have broad, deep metal jaws to which protective wood faces may be attached. Better-quality vises have the movable outer jaw slightly canted in at the top. As the vise is tightened the jaw straightens and presses more uniformly than it would otherwise. Many woodworking vises house an adjustable bench dog in the movable jaw, which allows them to double as tail vises when mounted at the end of a workbench. Another extremely desirable option found on top-quality woodworking vises is a quick-release mechanism for rapid jaw positioning. Typical vise construction is shown in the drawing of a Record vise below.

The woodworking vise is such an essential tool that there is no justification for skimping on quality. Avoid vises that clamp to the benchtop or screw only into the table edge. What you want is a sturdy vise that bolts securely to the underside of the bench and can hold work without vibration or deflection. Similarly, don't skimp on size. The smallest vise I would recommend would have a jaw width of about 7 in., an effective depth of about 2½ in., and an open capacity of about 8 in. (before wood pads are attached). The largest vises available have jaw widths over 10 in., 4-in. depths, and open capacities of as much as 15 in. While it would be nice to have such a large vise, it's not necessary. Jaw width in a smaller vise can be increased an inch or two by putting on wider wooden jaw pads. Pads protect work from the metal jaws, but they also diminish vise capacity. For longevity, pads should be hardwood or a good-quality hardwood plywood.

There is one minor deficiency in the design of woodworking vises. When long work is clamped vertically, it must pass to the side of the center screw and guide rods. As a result, clamping pressure is offset and

WOODWORKING VISE

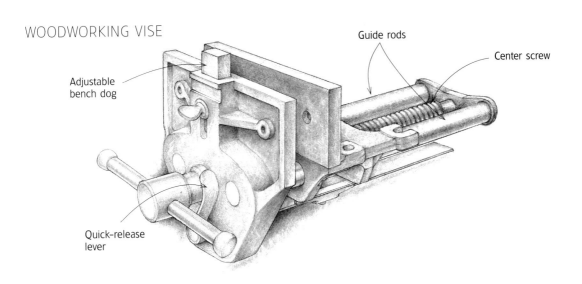

Adjustable bench dog

Guide rods

Center screw

Quick-release lever

USING A SPACER BLOCK

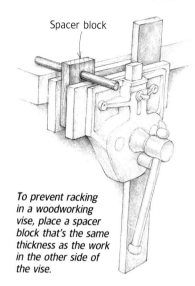

Spacer block

To prevent racking in a woodworking vise, place a spacer block that's the same thickness as the work in the other side of the vise.

the vise jaws want to rack. The farther away from the center the work is clamped, the more stress there is. This is not incapacitating, and scarcely noticeable on a well-built vise, but it does place some limit on the amount of pressure that can be brought to bear. If the angling of the jaw were to become a problem, perhaps on a cheaper vise, you could remedy it by placing a spacer block of the same thickness as the work in the other side of the vise (see the drawing at left). A dowel through the block keeps it from falling every time you open the vise.

A woodworking vise can be mounted in two positions on a workbench: either butted up against the side or let in flush (see the drawing below). The first position creates a space between the work and the bench. In the second, the bench side and the inner jaw pad form a continuous surface, which is advantageous when it comes to holding long boards on edge, since the free end can be easily clamped against the bench.

Vises usually come with clear mounting instructions, so there is no need to repeat them here. If you would like to read an extensive treatment of the woodworking vise, including tips for mounting and use, see *The Workbench Book* by Scott Landis (The Taunton Press, 1987).

Buying vises

Satisfactory metalworking vises are easy to find at hardware and automotive-supply stores. For the widest possible selection, however, consult an industrial-supply catalog. Woodworking vises are best purchased through woodworking specialty retail outlets and catalogs. Universal vises are sold through a few woodworking catalogs and retail outlets.

TWO WAYS TO MOUNT A
WOODWORKING VISE

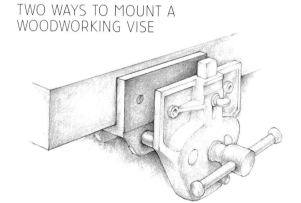

Vise proud of bench

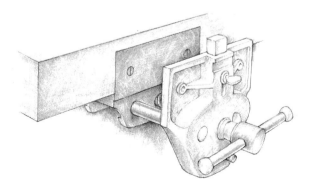

Vise inset into bench side

Maintaining vises

Keep the moving parts of your vise free of sawdust and grit accumulation. Lubricate them occasionally with oil or other metal-to-metal lubricants.

When replacing the steel jaw faces of a metalworking vise with thicker wooden pads, you'll need to replace the original machine screws with longer ones from your local hardware or automotive-supply store.

WORKBENCHES

The workbench is the heart of the workshop. As you build a piece of furniture, components circulate through the shop and return to the bench again and again—for handplaning, joining, shaping, scraping, sanding, assembling, and finishing. My own bench doubles as my lunch table, and I've even cleared it for a catnap from time to time.

A good workbench is sturdy, stable, heavy, and flat, with tail and front vises to hold work securely. A good workbench can also be an aesthetic inspiration—an embodiment of the connection between the useful and the beautiful.

The traditional European-style workbench is an unsurpassed woodworking tool, the product of centuries of evolution. It is long enough to hold boards up to 6 ft. or 7 ft. in length, which is the top end of the scale furniture makers generally encounter. It is relatively narrow so

EUROPEAN-STYLE
WORKBENCH

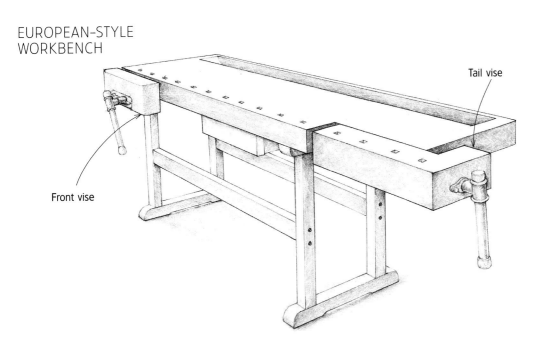

Tail vise

Front vise

FRONT VISES

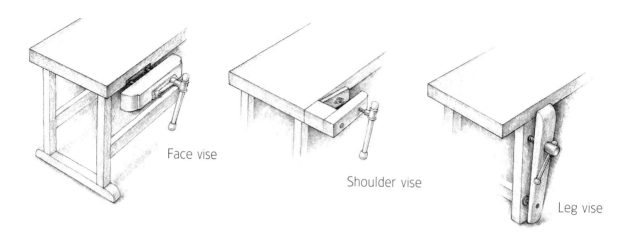

Face vise

Shoulder vise

Leg vise

you can reach work from both sides. It has a front vise for holding work vertically or on edge and a tail vise for holding work horizontally between bench dogs. A tool tray and drawers are optional.

Front vises

Historically, there are three different styles of front vise: face, shoulder, and leg (see the drawing above). On modern benches, the face vise predominates.

Face vises

Virtually all top-quality manufactured benches have a built-in face vise with a heavy wooden jaw. And most shopmade benches have them, too, often in the form of add-on woodworking vises. In fact, the traditional face vise is the progenitor of the woodworking vise. It has the same single screw flanked by one or two guide bars meant to keep the jaws parallel. A rarer version has double screws, one at each end of the vise. In general, the best qualities of a face vise are its broad clamping surface and the strength with which it can grasp boards held on a horizontal axis.

Predictably, the traditional single-screw face vise suffers the same design flaw mentioned in regard to the woodworking vise (see pp. 43-44). If a long piece of wood is to be held vertically, it must pass to the side of the screw. This makes the outer jaw want to cant inward as the vise tightens. The usual solution is to place a spacer of the same thickness as the work in the empty side of the vise. However, at least one contemporary workbench manufacturer solves the problem with a built-in adjustable stop: a wheel-shaped nut on a threaded rod anchored in the outer jaw and sliding freely through the inner jaw (see the drawing at right).

The double-screw face vise is more cumbersome to use than the single-screw vise, but it has the advantage that work can be placed upright between the screws and firmly clamped without racking the jaws. Double-screw face vises are found only on shopmade and antique workbenches, probably because they are too costly for manufacturers to install and less convenient to use.

Shoulder vises

The shoulder vise is of earlier origin than the face vise. Its screw threads through a built-out arm parallel to the front of the bench. A pivoting wooden jaw mounts on the screw to press work against the edge of the bench.

There are two main advantages to a shoulder vise. One is that the screw bears directly on vertical work, so there is no racking of the jaw. The other is that the outer jaw conforms to the angle of tapered work, as long as the taper is not too severe. The shoulder vise also has its drawbacks. First, building one involves considerably more labor than installing a face vise. Second, the large frame that juts out from the corner of the bench is physically awkward and makes the bench useless for left-handers. Third, it is impossible to extend a board beyond the end of the bench. Finally, tightening exerts leverage against the vise's outer arm, with potential structural damage. In the end, whether shoulder vises are better or worse than face vises comes down to a matter of personal preference often based on personal history. We like what we're used to.

Leg vises

The leg vise is the oldest front vise. It is traditionally a vertical board that screws against the bench leg. The jaw is at the top, the vise screw just below, and the fulcrum down at the bottom, where the board attaches either to the bench leg itself or to a beam extending outward from the leg.

The leg vise is strong but offers a relatively narrow clamping area. Keeping the jaws parallel up and down is difficult and requires that the fulcrum be attached to an adjustable beam that can be moved in and out as the thickness of the work dictates. Also, the leg vise is not well suited to holding work in a vertical orientation unless it is mounted out of plumb so that vertical work can be held in the center of the jaw and still clear the screw. The leg vise is found only on older or shopmade benches and is the least desirable type of front vise.

BUILT-IN FACE-VISE STOP

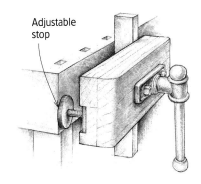

Adjustable stop

Some European workbenches have an adjustable stop to prevent the face vise from racking.

Tail vises

Tail vises, too, come in different guises. The standard on European-style benches is the traditional L-shape (see the drawing below). It is an excellent design that allows work to be held firmly between dogs or powerfully clamped between its front jaws. There is some argument among woodworkers as to whether or not it is appropriate to clamp with the rear jaw of an L-shaped tail vise, but certainly there should be no problem with only light pressure. Straight tail vises, made without the ell, also function well.

A second style of tail vise is called an end vise. Mechanically, it works like a traditional face vise mounted at the end of a bench with the jaw extending the full width. End vises usually have two dog holes corresponding with dog holes down both sides of the bench. They are good for holding wide work that spans both sets of dogs and irregularly shaped work for which the dogs can be staggered. However, when just one set of dogs is in use, which is most of the time, the end vise is at a disadvantage. The pressure of the screw doesn't line up behind the dogs, which causes the jaw to rack and limits the amount of pressure that can reasonably be exerted.

There is one end vise on the market that offers to solve the racking problem. It has twin screws connected by gears and a chain belt so that turning either screw automatically turns the other. As a result, the jaws should stay parallel at all times without any tendency to deflect.

The easiest way to create a tail vise on a shopmade bench is to install a woodworking vise with a dog (see p. 43). It works, but not nearly as well as the traditional L-shaped vise, which provides far better support under the work. The wider a woodworking vise opens, the more empty

TAIL VISES

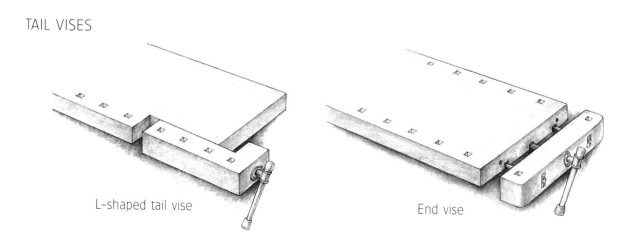

L-shaped tail vise

End vise

space there is under the work and the more spring and sag there is in the jaw. Also, the screw mechanisms of most woodworking vises extend under the first few dog holes in the bench, making the dogs difficult to insert. Some woodworking vises have off-center screws to address this problem.

Workbench size and location

In order to be effective, a workbench shouldn't slide or rack when you plane wood, nor should it have any yield when you chop mortises. It should be heavy and solid, ideally weighing at least 200 lb., preferably closer to 300 lb.

The precise width of the working surface is not critical, particularly if you have another table in the shop for assembly purposes. The bench surface should be narrow enough that work is accessible from both sides—anywhere from 18 in. to 24 in. The length should accommodate the longest board you are likely to handplane between dogs, typically 6 ft. or 7 ft.

Ideal bench height is a function of your own height and work methods. If you do a lot of handplaning, a lower height lets you get your weight over the plane, which is more efficient. If you do a lot of hand-cut joinery, detail work, or carving, a higher work surface makes it easier to see without constantly stooping over. Generally, you must compromise between the two. Commercially manufactured benches have heights in the range of 33 in. to 36 in. Shorter people usually find 33 in. or 34 in. satisfactory. In our school, tall students sometimes raise their benches on blocks to around 39 in.

The workbench should have excellent lighting, both natural and artificial if possible. The best working arrangement I have found is to place my bench in front of a second work surface, so I can easily turn from one to the other. The second surface gives me a convenient place to mount a metalworking vise and to put aside components and tools when I clear the deck of the workbench for action.

It is also desirable to have a wide, flat surface for assembly and work on projects too large for your bench. This could be the second work surface mentioned above, a large outfeed table on the table saw, or an entirely separate piece of shop furniture. Some woodworkers like their assembly table at a lower height, perhaps 26 in., to keep assembled work accessible. I am writing about the ideal, of course. If you are like most woodworkers, you barely have room for a piece of lumber in your shop, let alone a 7-ft. workbench and extra tables.

STEEL BENCH DOGS

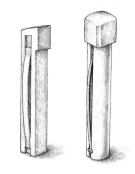

Fits square   Fits round
holes   holes

WOODEN BENCH DOG

Cork gasket
material

Wood
screws

Bench dogs

Bench dogs have flat faces for holding work in compression on a bench top. Their shanks are round or rectangular to match dog holes mortised through the bench. A spring on the shank provides enough friction to hold a dog at the desired height in the hole. When not in use, dogs push down below the surface of the bench.

Manufactured benches are equipped with steel dogs. They grip well and are indestructible but are heavy, resist adjustment, and can crush wood. In our school we replace them with cork-faced wooden dogs, which are lighter, easier to adjust, and much more considerate of the work they are holding. The master of our dog pack is California furniture maker Owen Edwards, who keeps us in good supply on his annual teaching visits. The bottom drawing at left shows Owen's design for wooden bench dogs.

It used to be that all commercially made benches had rectangular dog holes. The broader back surface of a rectangular hole holds up well, whereas a round hole might tend to compress and permit the dog to lean back under pressure, which in turn would change the angle of the dog face and diminish its holding power. Now, at least one top-quality maker has begun to offer a bench with round holes, probably as a matter of economy. The jury will be out on their longevity until some years have passed, but for the moment they seem perfectly solid. In any case, don't replace a round metal dog with a wooden one. The round wood shank will compress too easily.

Building a workbench

There are good arguments for and against building your own workbench. On the upside are the potential for satisfaction and a sense of self-reliance. In addition, you can tailor the scale, function, and design of the bench to your specific needs, and you will probably lay out less cash. On the downside, building a fine workbench demands such a large investment of time and effort that the top-quality commercial European-style benches begin to look reasonably priced. You may prefer to put that time into building actual furniture.

Fortunately for do-it-yourselfers, a good selection of vise hardware is available through woodworking catalog companies. If you are going to build a workbench, I strongly recommend that you first peruse Scott Landis's *The Workbench Book* (The Taunton Press, 1987).

Buying a workbench

A good workbench is a major purchase. It's big, heavy, and expensive, but it will provide you with a lifetime of pleasure. The only situation in which I would suggest compromise on bench size and weight would be where your shop is so compact that a full-size bench would just be in the way.

The three designs of European-style bench most commonly available are the standard bench with a face vise, L-shaped tail vise, and full-length tool tray; a wider version of the standard bench, minus the tool tray; and a wider version of the standard bench, with an end vise in place of the tail vise and double rows of dog holes (see the drawing below).

Unless you do a lot of work with large panels, one of the first two benches would be a better choice because of the superior performance of the L-vise over the end vise. Deciding between them is a matter of personal preference. Some woodworkers like a larger work surface, others want a place to keep tools out of the way.

Top-quality workbenches are available only through woodworking specialty stores and mail-order catalogs.

THREE DESIGNS FOR EUROPEAN-STYLE WORKBENCHES

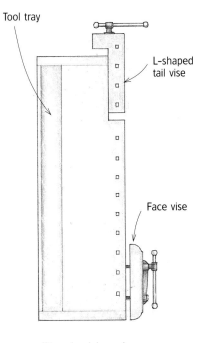

Tool tray

L-shaped tail vise

Face vise

Standard bench

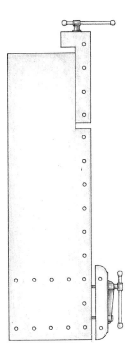

Standard bench without tool tray

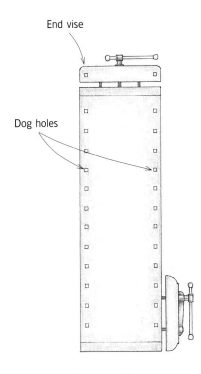

End vise

Dog holes

Bench with end vise and double dog holes

CUTTING

Tools assume an extraordinary familiarity when you work with them day in and day out. They enter the boundary of the self, as if it were natural to have detachable body parts to lay aside on the workbench and reconnect at will. They extend our sense of belonging in the world as they increase our ability to act upon it. Over time, tools assume recognizable histories and personalities; I would know my 1-in. chisel among a hundred just as I would know my left-hand ring finger by the scar a jagged tin can put there in 1962 at Flying Moose Lodge.

The tools that woodworkers invariably seem to have the most connection with (and most joy of) are cutting tools: those that have steel blades sharp enough to sever wood fibers cleanly. The cutting tools presented in this chapter—chisels, drawknives, inshaves, and scorps—have naked blades controlled entirely by hand. Planes, which are covered in a later chapter, are cutting tools in which the action of the blade is largely controlled by a sole. Scrapers are a third category of cutting tools. Their blades have the distinction of limiting their own penetration, and I have also accorded them a chapter of their own.

Contemporary woodworkers have access to cutting tools descended from two distinct cultural lineages: Western and Japanese. The differences are not only matters of posture and technique, such as planing on the push stroke versus the pull stroke, but also of balancing process against result. Japanese chisels and planes require more sensitivity and attention from the craftsman to the processes of tuning up, sharpening, and use in order to perform their best, but their best is truly excellent. For the craftsman using Japanese cutting tools, the process of working with the tools themselves assumes the first importance, whereas the Western craftsman generally subordinates his relationship to his tools to his interest in completing the project at hand. This is not to say that the "Japanese" craftsman is less dedicated to quality and efficiency, simply that he feels these attributes flow inseparably from the tools that create them.

The cutting tools presented in this chapter (and in the planing chapter) are those made for and used by contemporary furniture makers. The list is not static. Established manufacturers drop more specialized tools from their lines as they concentrate on volume sales. Enterprising smaller companies jump in to fill the niches. Since tools from the European/American tradition dominate the craft in countries where this book is likely to be published, they receive the greater attention.

Cutting wood with a dull chisel or plane is as hopeless as hacking at tomatoes with a butter knife. New cutting tools almost always need considerable attention before they work properly. In use, they require frequent sharpening. The appendix on pp. 185-195 offers detailed explanation of tools and processes for sharpening chisels and planes. Information pertinent only to specific tools is included with the descriptions of those tools in the relevant chapter.

CHISELS

The chisels that furniture makers and joiners have historically used at the workbench divide into three main families: paring chisels, mortise chisels, and firmer chisels. Paring chisels are long and thin, meant only for fine work under hand power. Mortise chisels have thick, sturdy blades designed specifically for chopping with a mallet. Firmer chisels bridge the two: They are thin enough for controlled hand paring and thick enough to be struck with a mallet.

Paring and firmer chisels further subdivide into those with square-edged blades and those with bevel-edged blades. Short firmer chisels are called butt chisels. In addition to all these varieties, there are a couple of specialty chisels that are of interest to furniture makers. They are corner chisels and crank-neck chisels.

CHISEL ANATOMY

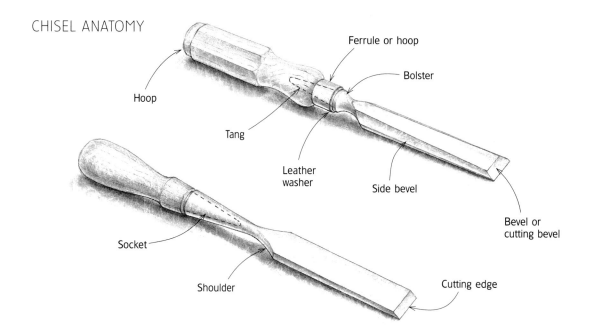

Hoop

Ferrule or hoop

Bolster

Tang

Leather washer

Side bevel

Bevel or cutting bevel

Socket

Shoulder

Cutting edge

Chisel manufacture

What makes one chisel superior to another are differences in steel quality, manufacturing procedure, and design. Steel must contain a certain amount of carbon in order to become hard enough to take and hold a cutting edge. Low-carbon steel is eternally soft and malleable. In addition to carbon, tool-quality steel may contain traces of various alloys, such as chromium and vanadium, which affect its characteristic qualities of hardness, toughness (ability to withstand fracture), edge retention, and sharpenability. In making a chisel, a manufacturer trades off these qualities against each other, always weighing cost.

The primary characteristic of high-carbon steel is that its crystalline structure alters to become extremely hard and brittle when raised to high temperature and quickly cooled. The same steel, cooled slowly (annealed), becomes relatively soft and malleable. Harder steel takes a sharper edge but is also more likely to fracture along the thin cutting edge. Much of the manufacturing process involves sequential hardening and softening.

Chisel handles

Wooden handles are traditional on chisels and can attach to the blade in two ways. Either they fit into a tapered socket, or they mount on a tang (see the drawing on the facing page). Socketed handles are superior for chisels that are struck heavily with a mallet, such as mortise chisels. The effect of impact is to tighten the connection between blade and handle, whereas impact on a tang might tend to split the handle. For this reason, tanged chisels designed for heavy work have metal hoops at the base of the handle.

Modern chisels have handles of wood or plastic, and it is not always easy to decide between them. Wood is handsome to the eye and pleasant to the hand, but plastic is more durable. My own choice is to get plastic handles on chisels that are going to feel a mallet often and wooden handles on chisels that will be used primarily for hand paring. If you prefer wooden handles for all uses, those with steel hoops around the top best withstand a mallet. On the other hand, hooped chisels are less comfortable to hold when hand paring, so there is a trade-off.

In a furniture workshop there would never be any reason to strike a chisel with a 16-oz. steel hammer, but a carpenter is much more likely to draw the claw hammer from his holster than to lug a mallet around a job site. A chisel that is to be struck with a heavy steel hammer should definitely have a plastic handle for longevity, preferably the type with an embedded steel cap. These are often found on the less expensive butt chisels sold at hardware stores.

Butt chisels

Butt chisels are firmer chisels with blades no more than 3 in. long. They can be either bevel-edged or square-edged and from ¼ in. to 2 in. wide. Few furniture makers use butt chisels, since their stubbiness is rarely an advantage. They are more practical for the carpenter who finds a short tool easier to carry around in his pouch.

Most of the butt chisels available today are of "handyman" quality, sold through hardware stores for use by carpenters and do-it-yourselfers working with softwoods such as pine and spruce. They are relatively low-priced, and the quality of their steel and forging is not up to furniture-making standards. The steel, while it is high carbon, is not tool steel and will not retain a sharp enough edge for work in hardwoods. Also, they are difficult to sharpen properly, because the backs are usually far from flat. Handyman-type butt chisels have plastic handles, often with a steel cap embedded in the top for striking with a hammer.

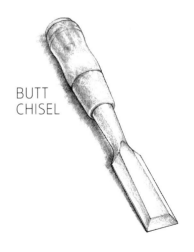

BUTT
CHISEL

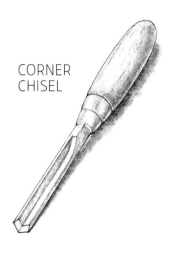

CORNER
CHISEL

Corner chisels

The corner chisel has two cutting edges that meet at 90°. Its primary use is to clean out the corners of mortises once the bulk of the waste has been drilled or machined out. Because it severs wood fibers in both faces of the mortise at once, a corner chisel is less likely to deflect or toe in as you chop down, which can be a particular problem for ordinary chisels in squirrelly or knotted wood.

Corner chisels are not widely used in furniture making. Ordinary firmer chisels are usually more than adequate for the task of squaring the ends of the relatively small mortises we make, and they are far easier to sharpen. However, corner chisels are commonly used by timber framers, who often encounter knots and contrary grain when chopping large mortises in framing stock. The timber framer's corner chisel is traditionally called a bruzz.

Because of its awkward interior corner, the cutting edges of a corner chisel must be maintained with files and flat slipstones instead of the more convenient grinding wheels and honing stones applied to ordinary chisels. To file close in to the corner without harming the adjacent bevel, grind the teeth off the edges of a mill file to make them safe. If the steel is too hard for a mill file, use a diamond file instead. The general principles are the same as those for sharpening normal chisels (see the appendix on pp. 185-195).

USING A CRANK-NECK
CHISEL

A crank-neck chisel can be used to clean out the bottom of a stopped dado.

Crank-neck chisels

These chisels are variously called "cranked-neck," "crank-shank," "dog-leg," and "trowel-shank." The handle is offset from the blade, which allows you to pare with the back of the blade flat on the work and the handle up out of the way. By their nature, offset chisels are meant for handwork, not to be struck with a mallet.

While many woodworkers live out entire careers without touching a crank-neck chisel, these tools are useful in certain situations. Examples would be paring plugs located in the center of a large panel or cleaning out the bottom of a stopped dado (see the drawing at left). However, in most cases, the work could be done as well or better with other tools, such as block planes and router planes.

Firmer chisels

Firmer chisels are the workhorses of the woodshop, the only set of chisels most woodworkers will ever need. They are thin enough for the fine work of hand paring and thick enough to clear out mortises with a mallet, obviating the need for paring and mortise chisels in most cases.

Bevel-edged firmer chisels are generally preferable to square-edged ones because they can maneuver into smaller spaces and acute corners, a ready advantage when trimming dovetails, among other things. They are also more commonly available. Bevel-edged firmer chisels have blades in the range of 3½ in. to 5 in. long and are made in widths from ⅛ in. to at least 1½ in. A minimal starting set might consist of ¼-in., ⅜-in., ½-in., ¾-in., and 1-in. chisels; ⅛-in., 5⁄16-in., and 1¼-in. sizes are welcome additions when you begin to do a lot of handwork. Chisels 1½ in. and larger are generally oversize to the scale of furniture making.

Firmer chisels come in a broad range of quality and price. The fanciest looking are not always the best. The key things to look for in a new chisel are a flat or mildly concave back, no pits or cracks in the blade, and straight alignment between the handle and the blade.

Why is a flat back so essential? It guides the chisel to make straight, flat cuts when paring and chopping (see the bottom drawing at right). If the chisel has a convex back, there is no reference for the cutting edge to work against, since only the cutting edge comes in contact with the wood as the tool tries to follow a straight course. A chisel with even the tiniest of back bevels along the cutting edge is even worse. As it cuts, the back of the blade rides up on the freshly exposed surface, continually pushing the chisel forward.

A mildly concave back is acceptable in a new chisel because it is so easily flattened with honing stones. A markedly convex back is virtually impossible to flatten. It rocks as you hone it. (The process of flattening is set forth in detail in the appendix on pp. 185-195.)

The extent of the side bevels affects a firmer chisel's performance. A relatively slight bevel leaves the chisel stronger and less flexible but also decreases its maneuverability into acute corners and small spaces. A heavily cut bevel is great for maneuverability but leaves a narrow surface at the top. Since this is the surface that rests on the tool guide of a grinding wheel, extreme narrowness can make grinding difficult, especially for beginners. On the other hand, legendary craftsman James Krenov purposely grinds such extensive bevels along the sides of his chisels that they meet to form spines at the ridge. There is no flat area whatsoever. He finds that this gives him maximum access into tight spots and reduces the tendency of the chisel to toe in when chopping. As with

FIRMER CHISELS

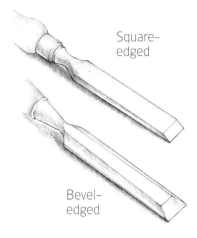

Square-edged

Bevel-edged

CHOPPING A SHOULDER

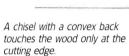

A flat back on a chisel guides it to make a straight cut.

A chisel with a convex back touches the wood only at the cutting edge.

A tiny back bevel on a chisel causes it to skid forward as it cuts.

FIRMER-CHISEL SIDE BEVELS

Heavily cut

Average

Slight

"Krenov"

many aspects of tool design, there are no right and wrong choices here, only a matter of establishing harmony between the way you work and the tools you use.

Cheap, handyman-quality firmer chisels usually offer inferior steel and/or overly thin blades. I have seen blades so thin that the heat of grinding caused them to warp.

Japanese chisels

Japanese chisels differ from Western chisels in shape and construction. The blades are shorter, the necks much longer, the backs of the blades are often hollowed, and, most significantly, the blades are bimetal. Where a Western chisel is forged from a single piece of high-carbon tool steel, a Japanese blade is composed of two layers of steel forge-welded together. The lower one that forms the cutting edge is high-carbon steel tempered to a Rockwell hardness of about Rc64. It is too brittle to stand on its own, so it is welded to an upper layer of mild (low-carbon) steel or wrought iron, which absorbs impact and resists fracture.

The high-carbon steel in a Japanese chisel may be "white" or "blue." The colors describe the paper in which the steel was wrapped, not the hue of the metal itself. The metallurgical difference is that blue steel contains additional alloys (chrome and tungsten) to give the cutting edge greater durability, but not to an extent most woodworkers could notice. What really distinguishes better-quality Japanese chisels are their forging and tempering by an individual craftsman sensitive to the nuances of steel. They push the balance between temper and brittleness to limits unobtainable in mass production. Compared to Western chisels, good Japanese chisels are harder, take a finer edge, and remain sharp longer.

The backs of many Japanese chisels are relieved with a hollow grind. This saves the craftsman time in keeping a flat back and reduces wear on sharpening stones. The handle of a Japanese chisel attaches with a combination tang/socket. Unlike Western chisels, the socket is a separate piece of metal, not an integral part of the blade. Chisels that are used with a hammer also have a steel hoop around the top of the handle.

Japanese chisels come in a great variety of shapes and sizes, as you might expect from a tradition where craftsmen are still so tuned into hand tools, much as they were in Europe a hundred years ago. They include chisels intended for mortising, chopping, and hand paring, as well as other, more specialized shapes. In general, the blades of Japanese chisels are much shorter than their Western counterparts. A Japanese "firmer chisel" has a blade of similar proportions to a Western butt chisel. This shortness can be disconcerting to the craftsman accustomed to working with Western-style chisels, and vice versa.

JAPANESE CHISELS

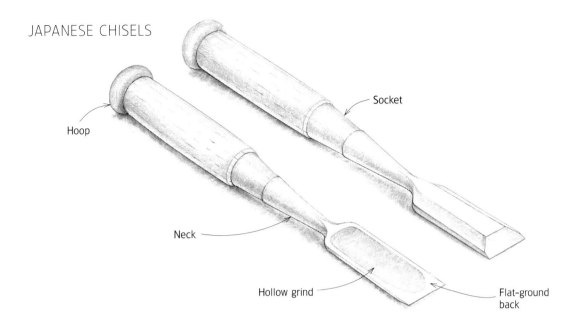

Hoop

Socket

Neck

Hollow grind

Flat-ground back

The best Japanese chisels are still forged by individual master craftsmen in small family-run workshops. Chisel making on this level is an art form, and the best chisels can cost hundreds of dollars apiece. These tools are for collectors and initiates. For the working craftsman or amateur, moderately priced Japanese chisels are as excellent tools as one could ever imagine needing.

Fitting the handle

When you acquire a new Japanese chisel, the steel hoop at the top of the handle is usually loose and needs to be fitted tight. The end of the wooden handle should stick out to serve as the striking surface. One way of accomplishing this is as follows:

1. Strip the finish off the handle with lacquer thinner.

2. Remove any burrs on the inside of the hoop with a small file.

3. Push the hoop down over the handle so it fits tightly (it is tapered on the inside).

4. Tap it down even farther with a hammer, carefully striking the edges. If the hoop won't go on far enough, remove it and try tapping the circumference of the handle with a hammer to compress the fibers. This works well on oak, which is what most Japanese chisel handles are made of. However, denser woods like ebony, which are more prone to splitting, should be gently pared instead.

5. Tap down the end grain of the handle with a hammer, working your way around the circumference, so that the wood mushrooms

over the hoop. This process requires patience, particularly since you want to avoid taking chips out of the dense end grain.

Another method of fitting the handle is to compress the circumference of the handle with a hammer (if it's a wood like oak and not brittle like ebony), situate the hoop, wet the handle to expand the compressed fibers, and, finally, hammer the end grain. No matter what method you use to fit the handle, the hoop is likely to come loose some winter when the wood is dry. When that happens, simply tap it back on and work the end grain over again with a hammer.

For in-depth information about Japanese chisels, see Toshio Odate's *Japanese Woodworking Tools: Their Tradition, Spirit, and Use* (The Taunton Press, 1984) and Henry Lanz's *Japanese Woodworking Tools: Selection, Care, and Use* (Sterling, 1985).

Mortise chisels

Mortise chisels have extremely thick, square-edged blades. They taper from about ¼ in. thick at the cutting end to ⁷⁄₁₆ in. at the shoulder. They are chopping machines, meant to efficiently knock out mortises under the impetus of a mallet. In an age when all work was handwork and cutting joinery was a specialized occupation, the mortise chisel was to the joiner what the horizontal slot mortiser is to the modern production shop.

What makes a mortise chisel so efficient is not just its sturdiness but also the extreme thickness of its edges. Used correctly, they guide the chisel fore and aft to leave a clean-walled mortise the precise width of the chisel. A good mortise chisel has tapered sides, so that seen in section a chisel measuring ¼ in. across the bottom might measure about 0.020 in. less across the top. This eases the action of the tool in the mortise.

MORTISE CHISEL

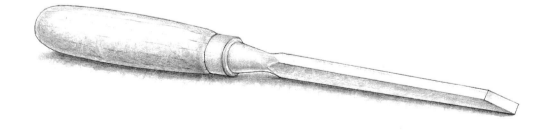

Mortise chisels are made in widths of ⅛ in., ¼ in., ⁵⁄₁₆ in., ⅜ in., and ½ in. and come with wooden or plastic handles. A wooden handle should be hooped at the top to prevent splitting. If it has a tang instead of a socket, the handle should also have a hoop around the base. A good-quality tanged mortise chisel may also have a leather washer between the wooden handle and the bolster to absorb impact.

Chopping a mortise

There is more than one way to chop a mortise with a mortise chisel. One method is as follows:

1. Mark out the cheeks with a mortise gauge set to the width of the chisel. Mark the ends of the mortise with a knife.

2. Stand in line with the length of the mortise, so you can clearly see that you are holding the chisel vertical in relation to the cheeks. If you are chopping a series of mortises along a board, approach them all from the same direction. That way, if you are prone to cut them somewhat off the vertical, they will at least be consistent.

3. Place the chisel about ⅛ in. from the end of the mortise in hardwood, farther away in softwood, with the bevel facing inward toward the center of the mortise. Strike the chisel firmly with a mallet, chopping straight down until you encounter moderate resistance. The unchopped portion at the end of the mortise will be a fulcrum against which you can pry out waste without damaging the real shoulder.

4. Turn the chisel around so the bevel faces back toward the first cut, and work your way along the mortise with a series of consecutive chops. (The cuts should be close enough together so the waste pops out easily. Hardwood and wild grain demand closer cuts than softwood and straight grain.) Stop chopping shy of the far end, again leaving some waste to pry against.

5. Turn the chisel around and work your way back across the mortise with another series of cuts, popping the waste out as you go along. Continue this process until you reach the desired depth.

6. Chop the ends square to the knife lines.

As you may imagine, it takes steady practice before one's hand and eye work together to chop consistently vertical, accurate mortises with a mortise chisel. An 18th- or 19th-century jointer performed the job day in and day out. But, being generalists, few contemporary craftsmen hand-cut enough mortises to master the process. When we aren't mortising with a plunge router or stationary mortiser, we are more likely to remove waste with a drill, and then pare the cheeks and ends square with firmer chisels.

CHOPPING A MORTISE
WITH A MORTISE CHISEL

Work along the mortise with a series of consecutive chops that are close enough together to let the waste pop out in between.

The one situation where mortise chisels are definitely a plus is in making deep mortises such as would be found in a large frame-and-panel door. In this case, machine bits may not be long enough to complete the job, and the extra length and strength of mortise chisels make them more efficient than firmer chisels.

Paring chisels

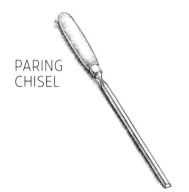

PARING
CHISEL

Paring chisels are built for finely controlled paring by hand, as when fitting dovetails or cleaning up tenon shoulders. The blades are long, thin, and too flexible to be driven with a mallet. While paring chisels were traditionally made in both square-edged and bevel-edged versions, only bevel-edged seem to be available today.

Few contemporary woodworkers work with paring chisels, most finding firmer chisels more than adequate to their needs. The largest market for paring chisels is among patternmakers.

Paring chisels come in widths from ¼ in. to 1½ in. Whereas the blade of a firmer chisel might be 3½ in. to 5 in. long, the blade of a paring chisel is 8 in. or longer.

Registered chisels

REGISTERED
CHISEL

These sturdy, square-edged chisels are thicker and heavier than firmer chisels, but thinner than mortising chisels. They were originally bargebuilders' tools. Some furniture makers use them to clean out mortises, particularly where most of the waste has already been removed by drilling or machining.

Registered chisels are made in widths from ¼ in. to 2 in. Like mortise chisels, they taper in thickness from shoulder to cutting edge.

How to use a chisel

A chisel may be used bevel up or bevel down, according to circumstances. The back of a chisel, placed against the work, guides it to leave a straight, flat surface (see the bottom drawing on p. 57). Working bevel down also has its advantages. One example is paring a groove up to a knife line. With the back down, the chisel would dig into the wood no matter how you held it. With the bevel down, you can closely control the cutting action by angling the handle, and you can lever against the bevel to pry out waste.

USING A CHISEL BEVEL DOWN

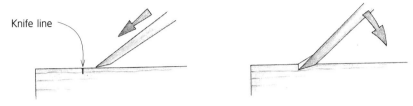

Knife line

When you pare up to a knife line with the chisel bevel down, you can lever against the bevel to lift the chip out smartly.

Chip lifted out

When chopping a shoulder, you get better results working in small increments and clearing waste away often. As the cutting edge of a chisel enters wood, it starts off by severing fibers cleanly. As it drives in further, the wedge-shaped bevel begins to pry heavily against the waste. If you apply too much force, the wood fibers tear out in advance of the cutting edge. This commonly occurs in chopping dovetail shoulders. Fortunately, the tearout is invisible once the joint is assembled. And because it's in end grain, it has no effect on the strength of the glue bond.

Buying chisels

The search for the perfect chisel is like the quest for the perfect chair. What pleases one person may not suit another. The factors that make a chisel superior are sometimes visible, such as the flatness of the back and the extent of the bevels, and sometimes tactile, such as handle shape, weight, and balance. There are also invisible factors, such as the quality of the steel, the way it has been forged and tempered, and the shape of the tang. The best indicator of invisible quality is the reputation of the manufacturer. Price is often (but not always) a guide. In any case, you don't need the world's best chisels to make beautiful furniture; a good set will do.

In reading about and buying chisels, you will find a certain amount of ambiguity in the nomenclature. For example, the term "bench chisel" is sometimes applied specifically to bevel-edged firmer chisels, sometimes as an inclusive term for all three families of chisel traditionally used by the craftsman at the bench: mortise, firmer, and paring. For this reason, you should ignore the name, look at the shape and construction of a tool to understand what you're getting, and decide if it is appropriate to your needs.

Whatever sort of chisel you buy, inspect it to make sure the handle is on straight, the back is flat or slightly concave (as explained in the section on firmer chisels), and the blade is free of cracks and other defects. A tiny dimple on the top near the bevel is not a defect. It reveals that the manufacturer has tested the chisel for hardness.

When assessing new chisels, beware of chrome-like polishes. A mirror polish is the result of extensive buffing, which also tends to round over the arrises where the back of the chisel meets the sides. This gives the tool a convex section across the back, so that extensive flattening is required.

The chisels sold through hardware stores are usually too poorly made to take and retain an edge for work in hardwoods. Better chisels are available through woodworking specialty retail outlets and catalogs.

DRAWKNIVES

The drawknife is a long, naked blade suspended between two handles, designed to work on the pull stroke. The blade ends in tangs that extend through the handles.

In skilled hands, a drawknife can do everything from rapid, rough shaping to controlled surfacing. It is even capable of leaving a glasslike finish on end grain. But few woodworkers bother to investigate its

DRAWKNIFE

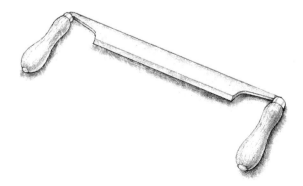

possibilities, and most contemporary furniture makers think of the drawknife as a relic. However, for those who work with green wood it is still one of the most essential tools in the shop, used to convert riven wood into chair spindles, legs, and slats, often with the work held in a shaving horse (see the drawing on p. 66). The drawknife is also useful for sculpting the perimeters of chair seats and other forms, as well as for chamfering corners.

Drawknives once took many forms to meet the specialized needs of coopers, turners, carpenters, wheelwrights, shipbuilders, and so forth. Even today, when only a few styles are made, blades may be straight or curved, lengths differ, and the positioning of the handles varies. Among experienced green woodworkers there is disagreement as to the best configuration and method of use. Some, for example, prefer to work with the bevel up, others with the bevel down. This is not too surprising. Woodworkers tend to disagree about the proper use and tuning of most hand tools.

The blade of a drawknife may be straight and flat, or modestly convex along the back and/or the cutting edge. A straight blade is more convenient to sharpen and is excellent for forming spindles. But a slight belly along the cutting edge confers certain advantages for shaving slats and other, wider surfaces. For quick, rough work, a curved blade takes a more aggressive bite with less resistance. For fine work, a curved blade takes shavings that thin out toward their edges to leave a cleaner transition. Also, a convex blade can approach a flat surface with greater maneuverability.

The back of a blade may be flat in section, slightly "dubbed" (back-honed) along the cutting edge, or mildly convex. All three conformations are recommended by various experts, so take your pick. A perfectly flat back is like that on a chisel, it directs the blade to make flat, straight cuts and allows consistency in sharpening. On the other hand, a chisel

BACK SHAPES FOR A DRAWKNIFE

Flat   Dubbed   Convex

generally begins paring from an edge, whereas a drawknife often must enter and exit the surface of the wood gracefully. A slightly curved or dubbed back gives the craftsman more steerage. It provides leverage for turning the blade within the cut, much like a carving tool.

As you might guess, the recommended bevel angle for the drawknife varies from source to source, ranging from 15° to 35°. This is as it should be. The correct bevel angle depends upon the hardness and quality of the blade, the inclusive angle formed by any dubbing, the technique of the craftsman, the material, and the type of work being done. Trial and error is the best way to find what works for you. If you are just starting out with a drawknife, you might as well stick with the original bevel angle until you get the feel of it.

FORMING A SPINDLE WITH A DRAWKNIFE

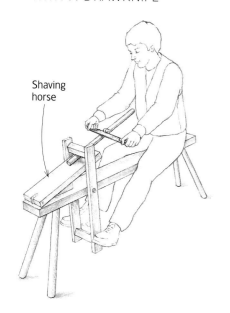

Shaving horse

How to use a drawknife

Whether the drawknife is used bevel up or bevel down depends on the way in which the back is ground and on the type of work being done. Often, either position will work. But to follow a tight radius the bevel should be down, and to achieve a modicum of straightness and rapid stock removal the bevel should be up.

Ideally, work is held in a shaving horse so its position can be changed quickly and often, as is necessary when shaving spindles and other cylindrical parts. A shaving horse places the work at a convenient height to the seated craftsman and puts his center of gravity in line with the stroke. Otherwise, he is best off standing at an upright, table-mounted vise.

Like other cutting tools, the drawknife meets the least resistance if the blade is used with a shearing cut, that is, with the cutting edge at an angle to its line of travel. Generally, the knife is pulled in long strokes, but to remove a lot of stock from an edge quickly it may also be pulled in a series of short, deep, consecutive cuts from which large chunks can be split out.

Sharpening a drawknife

Drawknives can be a challenge to sharpen. The handles limit access to a grinding wheel, and the blade is long and awkward.

The first step with a new knife is to prepare the back. If you want it perfectly flat, you might lap it on a flat, abrasive surface such as a piece of ⅜-in. plate glass about 5 in. wide and 12 in. long, covered with a strip of self-adhesive sandpaper. Mount the glass on a fully supportive, flat surface (such as a block of wood) high enough to keep the handles of the drawknife from hitting the tabletop. If the back of the blade requires extensive flattening, you might begin with 100- or 120-grit aluminum oxide and, when the back appears flat, switch to 220 grit. Clean the sandpaper often with an air hose or brush.

You can also flatten the back or put a slight convexity on it with sharpening stones. To do so, hold one handle of the drawknife in an upright bench vise and place the other on a block. With the blade elevated off the bench in this way it is easier to get at it with sharpening stones. Lap the back freehand, preferably with oilstones or diamond stones. Ceramic stones are too slow, and waterstones saddle and gouge so easily. (For more on sharpening stones, see the appendix on pp. 185-195.)

If the bevel needs reshaping, you can grind it on a stationary belt sander or the corner of a grinding wheel. The steel is probably too hard to file, but you could also shape it with a diamond stone. Once the bevel is at the desired angle and free of nicks, hold the drawknife in a vise and refine the edge with a honing stone to a very slight convexity. As with the back, this gives the knife more maneuverability than a hollow grind would.

After the back and bevel of a drawknife are prepared as above, sharpening is a matter of working both sides of the cutting edge with increasingly finer stones until no burr is left and the edge is razor sharp. Be careful how you handle a sharp drawknife: It's a lot of metal to sling around. Cover the blade with a grooved softwood block or similar protector when it's not in use.

Buying a drawknife

Drawknives available through woodworking catalogs and specialty stores range from small carver's knives with blades about 4 in. or 5 in. long up to full-size knives with blades 8 in. to 12 in. long. A greater variety are available on the used-tool market here in New England, and perhaps in other areas of the country as well.

Handles are subject to considerable stress and must be firmly anchored on their tangs so they won't pull off or spin. The extent to which the tangs penetrate through the handle is crucial, but, unfortunately, they are often hidden behind decorative steel buttons. Drawknife handles should be long and slightly pear-shaped to ensure a firm grip.

INSHAVE

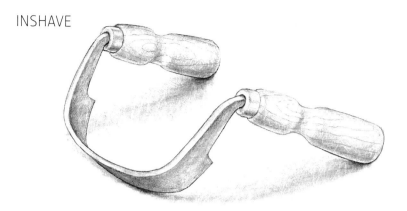

INSHAVES

The inshave is a specialized drawknife for hollowing and scooping and can be an aggressive wood remover. The bevel is on the convex side of the blade. The tool is used on the pull stroke, bevel down. Among furniture makers, it is most likely to be found in the shops of Windsor chair makers who still make solid-wood seats by hand.

Sharpening an inshave isn't much fun until you're good at it. The same considerations apply to the sectional shape of the blade as explained previously for drawknives. To give the back its initial "flattening" you might use a drill-mounted drum sander in long, sweeping strokes. Finer grits of abrasive can be applied by wrapping sandpaper around a curved piece of wood or by using conical sharpening stones. The bevel may be ground against a stationary belt sander. The final bevel should be slightly convex, as on a drawknife.

Once the back and bevel are properly ground, final honing may be done with slipstones on the inside and flat stones on the outside. An alternative honing technique used by carvers is to impregnate the surfaces of shaped wood blocks with abrasive buffing compounds such as chromium dioxide.

SCORPS

SCORP

The scorp is really a carving tool for hollowing bowls, spoons, and similar shapes. It could be described as a one-handed, miniature inshave and is an aggressive means of wood removal. Scorps are sharpened like inshaves.

DRAFTING

Drafting implements are not specialized to the woodworking trades, but they are indispensable to the furniture-making process. Their obvious use is in design, for drawing out small-scale and full-scale plans, but they are also useful for layout and tracing of templates, establishing curves, and other tasks that crop up in a day's work.

The drafting tools listed in this chapter are those most applicable in the woodshop, not the full arsenal of the professional draftsman and architect. The best selection of drafting materials can be found in stores and catalogs that specialize in artist's and architect's supplies.

COMPASSES

Compasses are typically used to draw arcs of circles. The most prominent style is the bow compass, which has two legs joined at the top by a spring and a threaded axle farther down for adjusting the span. One leg ends in a metal pin, the other in a holder that takes 2mm-diameter lead. Bow compasses are constructed on the same mechanical principal as spring-

BOW COMPASS

divided dividers (see p. 82) and calipers (see p. 80). Other styles of compass include the beam compass, which works on the same principal as trammel points (see p. 99), and friction dividers, which maintain their setting solely by the tightness of the connection at the top of the legs.

CURVES

A fair, irregular curve is often more pleasing to the eye than one that has a constant radius. Such curves may be sketched freehand, traced from French or ship curves, or generated by bending a flexible rod.

FLEXIBLE STEEL CURVE

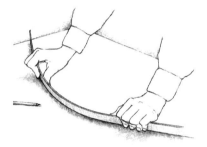

A steel rule can be flexed to make a fair curve.

Flexible curves

There are many types of rod that will yield a fair curve. In our shop we use steel straightedges, thin sticks of ash, and plastic splines. My own preference for making gradual curves is steel, which is rigid enough that a tracing pencil won't deflect it. Where steel is too stiff to negotiate a curve comfortably, I prefer plastic to wood. A wooden spline must have exceedingly regular grain to yield a consistent curve, whereas plastic and steel are homogeneous materials.

Highly flexible plastic splines $\frac{5}{16}$ in. thick and up to 5 ft. long are available through art and drafting suppliers. They can be held in curved positions with "ducks," which are actually whale-shaped weights with little hooks on their end that grip a groove in the spline (see the drawing below). However, flexing the spline by hand gives you subtler control, as long as there is someone else around to do the actual tracing.

A second type of flexible plastic curve is vinyl with a lead core. Because it doesn't have any spring, it is not a good tool for generating fair curves, but it will retain any shape to which it is bent and can copy an existing curve to a different location.

PLASTIC SPLINE AND DUCKS

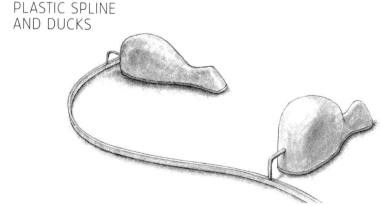

French curves

French curves are irregularly curved pieces of acrylic about ⅟16 in. thick. They come in dozens of shapes ranging from approximately 5 in. to 12 in. in length. Most have cutout interior shapes as well as complex exteriors.

French curves are used to create new lines or firm up portions of hand-drawn ones. Because of their limited size and pronounced curvature, they are more helpful at one-eighth or one-quarter scale, where a single curve can encompass an entire chair leg, than they are at full scale. But even there they may match up to smaller details.

French curves are available with square edges for pencil work and beveled edges for inking. (Ink tends to suck under a squared-off edge and blot.)

Ship curves

Like French curves, ship curves are usually made of ⅟16-in.-thick acrylic. They come in 56 standard configurations and a range of sizes from a few inches to 2 ft. The arcs of longer ship curves tend to be milder than those of French curves, and their transitions more gradual. There is no need to acquire the full set of ship curves, but I wouldn't want to do without some of the longer "sweeps" for full-scale drafting, particularly of chairs. The ones we use in our shop are numbers 36, 40, 43, 44, and 48 (as shown in the drawing below).

FRENCH CURVES

SHIP CURVES

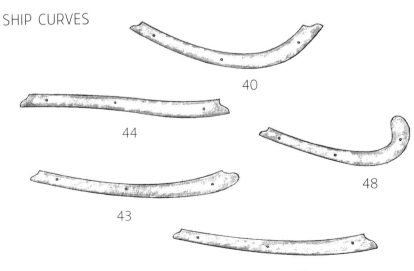

40

44

48

43

36

DRAFTING BRUSH

DRAFTING BRUSHES

Drafting brushes are excellent for dusting eraser and lead particles off of drafting paper. They are thin, resembling ½-in. sections resawn from normal bench brushes. Better drafting brushes have natural horsehair bristles that are close-packed and flexible. Handles are wood or plastic.

DRAFTING TAPE

DRAFTING TAPE

Drafting tape is relatively low-tack masking tape with a slow-curing tackifier, which makes it easier to remove without damaging paper. The tape commonly comes in rolls ½ in., ¾ in., and 1 in. wide or as round ⅞-in.-diameter dots. As with all masking tapes, drafting tape will eventually dry hard and become impossible to remove if left in place too long.

You can use regular masking tape or the blue painter's tape available in hardware stores as a substitute for drafting tape, but neither should be left in place for more than a couple of days. By comparison, drafting tape should have a life of at least a week.

ERASERS

ERASERS

There are quite a few erasers made for pencil. The most familiar is probably the "pink pearl" type at the end of a No. 2 school pencil. It is a good drafting eraser, but has some tendency to smear lead and rough up paper, especially as it stiffens with age.

"Plastic" or "vinyl" erasers work better and stay soft longer. An example is the Staedtler Mars 526 50. It is gentle enough not to damage paper, highly effective at removing lead, and virtually smear-free.

ERASER SHIELDS

An eraser shield is a thin, flexible piece of steel measuring about 2 in. by 3½ in. It protects lines adjacent to those you wish to remove. A variety of perforations enables precise erasure in areas where lines intersect or run close together. A series of small, round holes can be used to dot a line.

An eraser shield can be difficult to pick up from a flat surface, so it's a good idea to bend it enough to put a permanent curve along its length.

ERASER SHIELD

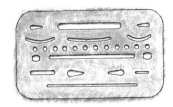

PAPER

In the offices of architects and engineers, paper has been largely displaced by "drafting film," a coated polyester material that is relatively indestructible and has superior reproduction quality for making blue-line and black-line prints. It also costs about twice as much. Furniture makers, being both thrifty and wedded to "natural" materials, are likely to continue drafting on paper for a long time to come.

For archival, finished full-scale drawings the best paper is 100% rag tracing vellum. It is available in 20-yd. or 50-yd. rolls, in widths from 24 in. to 42 in. It is strong, translucent enough to overlay and trace, has enough tooth to hold lead well, erases cleanly, stores with minimal deterioration, and is a good medium from which to make blue-line and black-line prints. Vellum is made in weights from 16 lb. to 22.5 lb., lighter paper being more transparent. I generally draft on 16-lb. or 17-lb. vellum, 42 in. wide. Anything narrower would be too small for full-scale work. Vellum is also made with an imprinted grid, like graph paper, but it's not appropriate for furniture drafting.

For design development, you can't beat a tissue paper with excellent transparency. Generations of drawings can build one atop the other, each tracing what needs to be saved from below. A common name for this paper is yellow trace (my design students at Drexel University called it "yellow trash"). It actually comes in canary yellow, pale yellow, and white. Yellow trace has the great virtue of being inexpensive, so you feel free to revise, experiment, and throw away drawings to your heart's content. It takes lead and erases well, although care must be taken not to rip it. Yellow trace comes in 20-yd. and 50-yd. rolls from 12 in. to 48 in. wide.

The least expensive source of paper I've found is the local newspaper's printing plant, from which I buy end rolls. They are approximately 3 ft. wide and wonderfully inexpensive. Newsprint doesn't take lead as crisply or erase as cleanly as vellum and tissue, but the price is right. I often use it as a first-draft base upon which to build. It also comes in handy for protecting benchtops when finishing, packaging items for shipping, and so forth.

PENCILS, LEADS, AND SHARPENERS

There are two types of pencil that are particularly good for drafting: mechanical pencils and leadholders. They leave fine, consistent lines that make a drawing clear and crisp.

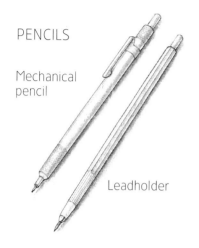

Leadholder

Mechanical pencils

Mechanical pencils take leads in thickness of 0.3mm, 0.5mm, 0.7mm, or 0.9mm. These leads are so thin that they never need sharpening. Any size works for drafting, so you can choose according to the "weight" of your hand (thinner leads break more easily) and the look you prefer. Mechanical pencils come with a variety of lead-advancing mechanisms, from the standard push button at the top to models that you shake.

Leadholders

Leadholders take thicker leads (2mm) than mechanical pencils. A push button at one end controls a set of expanding jaws at the other. Unlike mechanical pencils, leadholders must be sharpened. Nonetheless, I prefer them for drafting, drawing, and rendering because they are more versatile instruments. I find that with a leadholder I can put on the finest or bluntest of points, vary line weight, shade with control, and easily interchange leads of different hardnesses.

Because their leads take such fine points and are thick enough to extend a reasonable distance without breaking, leadholders make excellent marking tools for laying out joinery, tracing dovetails, marking from templates, and so on.

LEADS

Leads

Leads are rated for hardness on the following scale: 6H (hardest), 5H, 4H, 3H, 2H, H, F, HB, B, 2B, 3B, 4B, 5B, and 6B (softest). The hardest are as likely to crease paper as they are to leave a discernible amount of lead behind. The softest make dense, black lines. They also require constant sharpening and snap easily. The right hardness for drafting and marking seems to be about H or 2H.

Leadholders take the full range of leads, but mechanical pencils don't take anything softer than 2B. Colored leads are also available for both types of pencil.

Sharpeners

The tools with which leadholders are sharpened are usually called leadpointers. They come in stationary and hand-held models. I prefer the latter, since it so easily travels around the shop with me. Some leadpointers come with a large entry hole and a set of guide bushings to adapt to different diameters; but fixed-mouth pointers do a better job of sharpening, and most leadholders are standard size.

To use a leadpointer, extend the lead, insert it into the pointer, and use the holder as a crank to rotate the top of the pointer. As the lead travels round and round it abrades against a steel cutter on the inside.

SCALE RULES

Technically called "hand scales," these are flat or triangular rules for measuring out scale drawings. Three common versions are architect's, engineer's, and metric scales. Triangular architect's hand scales offer the greatest versatility for furniture designers who work in feet and inches. They are marked with ⅛-in., 3/16-in., ¼-in., ⅜-in., ½-in., and 1-in. scales.

When an architect draws with the ¼-in. scale, one-quarter of an inch on paper represents one foot in real life. But since furniture is considerably smaller than buildings, a woodworker uses the same quarter of an inch to represent a single inch. This is called a quarter-scale drawing.

To the left of the zero mark on each scale, a single unit of the scale is often subdivided in twelfths. These represent inches to the architect, not the sixteenths of an inch a furniture maker might prefer.

SHARPENING A LEAD

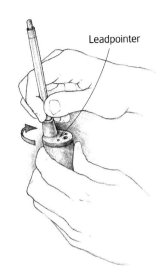

Leadpointer

TRIANGULAR ARCHITECT'S SCALE

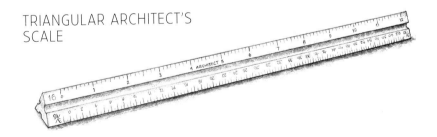

T-SQUARES

T-squares are used to lay out consistent vertical lines when making full-scale drawings. They also provide the physical standard against which drafting triangles register to make horizontal and angled lines. There are more sophisticated mechanisms for laying out vertical and horizontal lines, such as drafting machines and parallel rules, but the T-square is more than sufficient to the needs of most craftsmen.

T-squares are made in a range of qualities. Wood squares are at the bottom of the heap, steel at the top. Inexpensive, acrylic-edged, maple T-squares are satisfactory, although you should check the straightness of their edges from time to time. They can always be trued up with a handplane. It doesn't matter so much if the blade is square to the head. As long as a T-square works off a consistent face of the drawing board, vertical and horizontal lines will be square to each other, which is what matters.

For best results, press a hip against the head of a T-square as you draw. This keeps the square from drifting out of position.

T-SQUARE

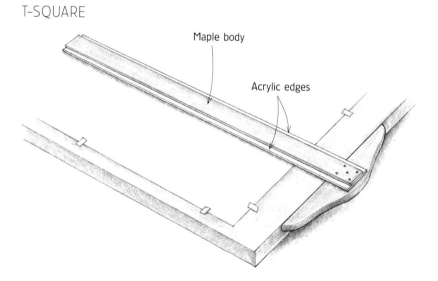

Maple body

Acrylic edges

TRIANGLES

Drafting triangles are usually made from transparent acrylic and are held against T-squares and parallel rules to draw lines at 90°, 45°, 30°, and 60° angles. They come in two shapes: 45°-45°-90° and 30°-60°-90°. Triangles are specified for size according to the length of the longer leg, which can be anywhere from 4 in. to 24 in. It's good to have at least one long triangle of each type (12 in. or 14 in.), plus a small 45° triangle for detail work. Triangles are also useful for setting up machinery and jigs.

Adjustable triangles can be set to any angle from 0° to 90° with a reasonably precise graduated protractor scale and a locking nut. Some adjustable triangles have their arrises beveled on top, but plain, square edges are better. A beveled edge tends to slide under a T-square.

Adjustable triangles are a necessity when your work departs from the rectilinear. They also come in handy for setting sawblades and fences to make angled cuts. Common sizes for adjustable triangles are 8 in., 10 in., and 12 in.

Triangles and adjustable triangles with beveled undersides are specifically for drawing with ink, which tends to blot under a square edge.

TRIANGLES

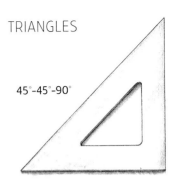

45°-45°-90°

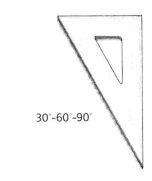

30°-60°-90°

ADJUSTABLE TRIANGLE

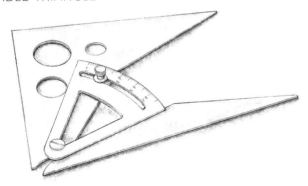

MARKING & MEASURING

The level of precision appropriate to furniture making is an odd amalgam—somewhere between that of the house carpenter satisfied with tolerances measured in sixteenths of an inch and the metal machinist measuring in thousandths. When we join together two pieces of wood there are times when even a couple of thousandths of an inch appears as an unsightly gap. Yet when it comes to dimensioning stock to thickness and width, wood makes a mockery of the craftsman who measures in thousandths. Being an inherently unstable biological material, wood constantly changes dimension in response to humidity.

The tools we use for accurate marking and measuring reflect this dichotomy of precision. For measuring, we generally work with tapes and rules marked in sixteenths. You can find rules scaled in finer increments, but they are too small to see and manipulate easily, at least for those of us over 40 years of age. However, there is an imaginary calibration called a "hair" that gives the craftsman working with sixteenths a level of accuracy closer to a sixty-fourth. If I measure the thickness of a board, I can easily tell the difference between ¾ in., ¾ in. plus a hair, midway between ¾ in. and ¹³⁄₁₆ in., ¹³⁄₁₆ in. minus a hair, and a full ¹³⁄₁₆ in.

When true exactitude is required, the woodworker puts measuring tools aside in favor of marking tools. In laying out half-blind dovetails, for example, we make the shoulders of the tails and the depth of the pins correspond precisely by marking them with a cutting gauge.

Think of marking as working to reality and measuring as working abstractly. This chapter presents the tools used by furniture makers for both purposes. Some, like calipers, dividers, center punches, and trammel points, are not necessities in many shops. Others, such as squares, measuring tapes, and the various marking gauges, are indispensable.

AWLS

Awls are common to many trades besides woodworking, such as leather working and sail making. They differ primarily according to the fineness of their points and the sturdiness of their shanks. There is no single tool called a "woodworker's awl," but there are two basic configurations that come in handy.

Awls with sturdy shanks and broadly ground points are particularly useful for marking hole centers preparatory to drilling, much like a machinist's center punch. Tapped with the palm or a mallet, such an awl leaves a dimple in the wood that provides an exact starting point for a drill bit. The firmness of the tap should suit the type of bit you are using. A gentle tap leaves a small dimple, which works well in conjunction with a brad-point bit. A firmer tap leaves a deeper, broader dimple more suitable to the wide nose of a twist drill.

The other end of the spectrum is the thin-shanked, sharp-pointed awl. This tool has a wide variety of uses in the woodshop, from marking lines to packing cane in seat holes. Many of its uses are improvisational, such as prying cracked wood apart to work in glue and cleaning gunk off bolt threads.

A totally different type of awl, which is next to impossible to find these days but easy to make, is a brad awl. The tip of a brad awl is sharpened to a chisel point, beveled from both sides like a screwdriver. Its purpose is to make pilot holes for screws and nails to keep them from splitting the wood. The technique is to place the cutting edge at 90° to the grain, then push and twist to sever fibers and push them aside.

Maintenance

It is simple enough to restore the point of an awl or change its configuration. For quick shaping, hold the point at the desired angle to a bench grinder or stationary sander and twirl with light pressure. You can also work the point against a coarse- to medium-grit honing stone.

TYPICAL AWL
CONFIGURATIONS

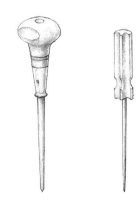

BRAD AWL

Buying awls

Awls can be found at any hardware store and through most wood-working catalogs and retail outlets. More expensive awls, such as those with rosewood handles, are priced on the basis of their aesthetic appeal. Inexpensive ones work just as well.

CALIPERS

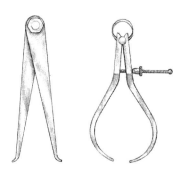

Firm-joint inside caliper   Spring-divided outside caliper

CALIPERS

Calipers measure and/or accurately transfer inside and outside dimensions. Their most common use in furniture making is to establish diameters when turning spindles on a lathe. Otherwise, they mostly sit on the shelf.

Inside and outside calipers

The simplest calipers, which are called firm-joint calipers, consist of two arms pinned together at the apex. Unfortunately, they are easily knocked out of position, much to the craftsman's chagrin. A more sophisticated version is the spring-divided caliper. By containing the expansion of spring-mounted legs with a threaded nut, the caliper succeeds in being more precisely adjustable and secure.

Vernier, dial, and digital calipers

The traditional machinist's tool for measuring inside and outside dimensions in thousandths of an inch is the vernier caliper. In recent years the vernier caliper has been supplanted, first by the dial caliper and, currently, by the new generation of digital calipers, both of which are much easier to read.

Rarely do woodworkers need to measure in thousandths of an inch, and many have led long, successful careers without vernier, dial, or digital calipers. The more engineer-minded among us enjoy them, though, particularly for the occasional metalwork that crops up.

How to use vernier calipers

Vernier calipers take some practice to master. They work by matching two scales against each other, the increments of which differ by one-thousandth of an inch. For example, if the main scale on the rule is divided into fortieths of an inch, the vernier plate takes the length of

VERNIER AND DIAL CALIPERS

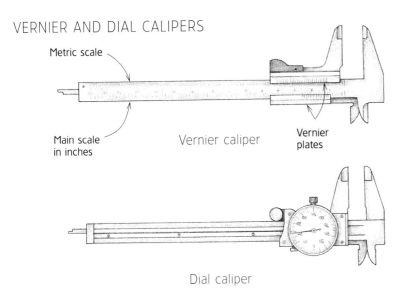

Metric scale

Main scale
in inches

Vernier caliper

Vernier
plates

Dial caliper

24 consecutive divisions on the main scale and divides it by 25. The difference between one division on the main scale and one division on the vernier plate is then one-thousandth of an inch.

The math looks like this:

$$\frac{1}{40} \text{ in.} = 0.025 \text{ in.}$$
$$24 \times 0.025 \text{ in.} = 0.600 \text{ in.}$$
$$0.600 \text{ in.} \div 25 = 0.024 \text{ in.}$$
$$0.025 \text{ in.} - 0.024 \text{ in.} = 0.001 \text{ in.}$$

To read vernier calipers, you note the location of the zero mark on the vernier plate. If it coincides exactly with a graduation on the main scale, that graduation is the correct measurement. Otherwise, you find the place where a graduation on the vernier plate lines up exactly with a graduation on the main scale. The correct reading is then the distance to the zero mark, plus one-thousandth of an inch for every increment on the vernier plate up to the point of coincidence.

As you might imagine, dial calipers are far easier to use. You simply read the number of thousandths right off the dial. Digital calipers are better still, because they remove the analog element entirely (as long as the battery isn't dead).

Buying calipers

All types of caliper can be purchased through industrial-supply outlets and catalogs. Firm-joint, spring-divided, and (sometimes) dial calipers are also available through woodworking catalogs and specialty stores.

CENTER PUNCHES

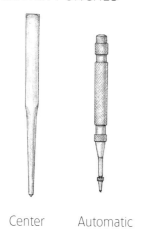

Center
punch

Automatic
center punch

DIVIDERS

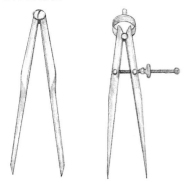

Firm-joint
divider

Spring-divided
divider

CENTER PUNCHES

The center punch is a machinist's tool that the woodworker occasionally finds useful for marking hole locations in metal and wood. The simplest model is a hardened steel punch, much like a pointed nail set, which is tapped with a hammer to create a dimple preparatory to drilling.

An automatic center punch has an internal trip spring that is released by pushing down the top of the punch. To regulate the force of the blow you turn the cap to adjust the spring pressure.

Center punches are available at your local hardware store and through industrial supply catalogs.

DIVIDERS

Dividers are built like firm-joint and spring-divided calipers, except that they have straight legs and sharp points. Dividers can be used as compasses for laying out circles and arcs. With one point sharpened to cut like a knife, they can cut discs of sandpaper and other thin materials. Perhaps most important, they can be walked end for end to divide a line into equal spacings without the risk of engaging in higher mathematics, as is sometimes done in laying out dovetails.

DOVETAIL GAUGES

Dovetails can be cut to an infinite number of angles, generally ranging between what is called "one-in-six" (about 80½°) to "one-in-eight" (about 83°). The correct angle is almost always that which the craftsman finds most pleasing aesthetically. Dovetail gauges are single-angle devices for marking pins and tails. They vary from rough-and-ready shopmade jigs to

DOVETAIL
GAUGES

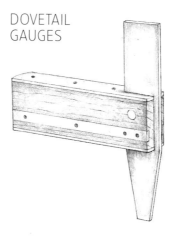

beautifully machined brass and rosewood heirlooms. Several types of dovetail gauge are available through specialty woodworking retail outlets and catalogs.

For the woodworker who uses the same angle on every project, a dovetail gauge is convenient. However, an inexpensive sliding T-bevel will perform the same task just as well and is infinitely more versatile because it can be set to any angle.

GAUGES (COMBINATION, CUTTING, MARKING, MORTISE)

The cutting gauge, marking gauge, and mortise gauge are invaluable tools for marking out joinery. The combination gauge unites the functions of the marking and mortise gauges. All share the same basic configuration: A beam slides through a fence that locks in position; projecting from one end of the beam is a metal knife, a pin, or a pair of pins.

In general, knives are better for marking across the grain, pins for marking with the grain and on end grain. Where a knife cut can be difficult to see along the grain or on end grain, a pin leaves an obvious trail. Where a pin scratched across the grain tears wood fibers in an unsightly manner, a knife leaves a clean cut.

Combination gauges

The combination gauge is constructed exactly like a mortise gauge (see p. 86), except that a fixed pin has been added to the back of the beam, which lets the tool double as a marking gauge. The sole advantage of the combination gauge is financial, in that one tool performs the work of two. Its disadvantages are twofold. First, only rarely can you use the marking and mortising functions at the same time, since they generally require different fence settings. Second, there is the omnipresent danger of pricking your thumb on the idle, upturned pin(s). There is only one compelling reason to buy a combination gauge: At present, you can't find a new stand-alone mortise gauge for sale in the United States.

For tune-up and use of the combination gauge, refer to the sections on marking and mortise gauges.

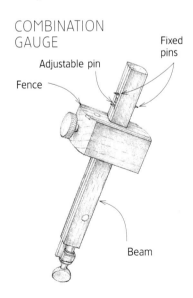

COMBINATION GAUGE

Fixed pins

Adjustable pin

Fence

Beam

CUTTING GAUGE

CUTTING-GAUGE
ACTION

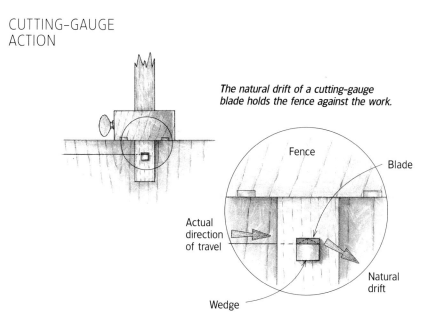

The natural drift of a cutting-gauge blade holds the fence against the work.

Fence

Blade

Actual
direction
of travel

Natural
drift

Wedge

CUTTING-GAUGE
WEDGE FIT

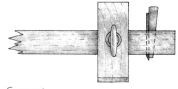

Correct
Wedge fits mortise snugly.

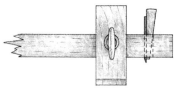

Incorrect
Wedge has play at thin end.

Cutting gauges

The cutting gauge, or knife gauge, gives a clean, sharp cut across the grain and is particularly useful for laying out the shoulders of dovetails and tenons. A small wedge holds the blade in a through mortise at one end of a wooden beam, with the beveled side of the blade facing the fence. As the blade cuts, the bevel's natural drift pulls the fence against the work.

Tuning a cutting gauge

The first step in tuning a cutting gauge is to be sure the wedge fits properly within the mortise. If the mortise in a new gauge is straight sided, the side farthest from the fence should be chiseled to the same taper as the wedge (see the drawing at left). If necessary, the angle of the wedge can be refiled slightly to match the mortise. However you achieve it, the wedge should fit snugly between the blade and mortise wall if it is to prevent the blade from changing position in use.

The second step is to shape and sharpen the blade. There are three possible configurations for a cutting-gauge blade (see the top drawing on the facing page). The choice depends on whether you are right- or left-handed and whether you work on the pull stroke (as I do), the push stroke, or both. In our school we use the V-configuration so the tool suits everyone.

You can reshape a new blade to your preference on a grinder. There is hardly any steel to remove, and the tiny blade can overheat quickly. You won't be able to use the grinder's tool rest, except to steady your hand. There is no prescribed angle for the blade shape. Try whatever looks right to you. The bevel itself should be angled much like a knife blade's. Too thin a cutting edge will bend over or chip in use; too thick an edge won't get sharp enough in the first place.

Generally, even if a new blade is the right shape, you'll need to regrind the bevel until it meets the back in a razorlike line. For some reason, manufacturers don't seem to grind new cutting-gauge blades all the way through.

Once the blade is ground, hone it to sharpness. You may want to refer to the appendix on pp. 185-195 for a full explanation of the sharpening process. Briefly, the steps for sharpening are as follows:

1. Flatten the back of the blade on a medium-grit honing stone.

2. Hone the bevel lightly on the same stone until you begin to feel a wire edge along the back or can see that the cutting edge is affected all the way across. Keep the bevel flat on the stone to maintain its angle during honing.

3. Pull the back flat on a fine stone (such as a 6000-grit waterstone or Hard Arkansas oilstone), removing any wire edge created by the previous step.

4. Hone the bevel on the fine stone, then pull the back flat again. The blade should now be quite sharp.

For subsequent sharpenings, begin at step 2, since you have to flatten the back of a blade only once in its lifetime.

Marking gauges

This simplest of gauges consists of a beam, fence, and fixed pin. It is particularly good for marking lines parallel to an edge on end grain and with the grain. In a pinch, a marking gauge can be altered to do cross-grain work by filing the pin to cut like a knife, but it is never the equal of a cutting gauge.

Out of the box a new marking gauge will work adequately, but its performance can be improved by filing a thinner profile on the pin. A further refinement (if you work consistently on the pull stroke) is to angle the inner face of the pin slightly so that its natural drift helps hold the fence against the work (see the top drawing on p. 86).

A most effective tool for reshaping pins is a portable grinder, such as a Dremel, outfitted with a small abrasive wheel. It cuts fast, so secure the beam of the gauge in a vise and work cautiously. Generally, I reshape just the inside of the pin as described above. However, if you want a knife-like cut for cross-grain work, grind the outside of the pin to meet the inside in a thin cutting edge.

CUTTING-GAUGE BLADE CONFIGURATIONS

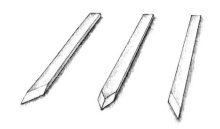

MARKING GAUGE

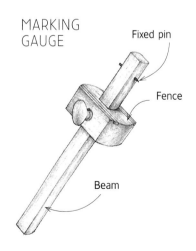

Fixed pin

Fence

Beam

TUNING A MARKING GAUGE

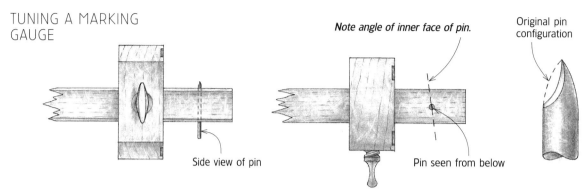

Note angle of inner face of pin.

Original pin configuration

Side view of pin

Pin seen from below

The performance of a marking gauge can be improved by grinding an angled face on the inside of the pin.

WHEEL MARKING GAUGE

Other tools for reshaping the pin are a diamond-coated slipstone, sandpaper wrapped around a stiff backing, or, if the pins don't have too hard a temper, a small file.

A second type of marking gauge has an all-metal fence and beam, with a sharp wheel mounted at one end instead of a pin. These "wheel marking gauges" work well for marking with the grain and on end grain. They also leave a clean mark cross-grain, but they don't cut aggressively enough to take the place of cutting gauges. Wheel marking gauges rarely require any sort of tuning or alteration.

Mortise gauges

The mortise gauge marks two lines parallel to an edge and is particularly suited to laying out the cheeks of mortises and tenons. One pin is fixed and the other slides in a track along the beam. Better-quality mortise gauges provide thumbscrew adjustment of the traveling pin. Cheaper gauges employ a manual slide, which can be difficult to position precisely. The pins of a new mortise gauge can be reshaped to improve their performance, just like the pin on a marking gauge.

MORTISE GAUGE

To set a mortise gauge, first adjust the distance between the two pins to the desired mortise width. Then move the fence to the same distance from the near pin that the mortise will be from the edge of the board. Tightening the mechanism (screw, thumbscrew, or lever) that holds the fence in place also locks the adjustable pin in position.

There is a another design for mortising gauges in which two beams slide independently through the fence, side by side. This style is more awkward to set and can't reach as closely into a corner as a single-beam gauge can.

FLATTENING THE FACE OF
A GAUGE FENCE

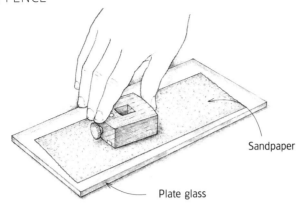

Sandpaper

Plate glass

General gauge maintenance

New gauges can require preparation beyond filing pins and sharpening
blades. You may also find it necessary to flatten the face of the fence or to
ease the beam to let it slide freely.

Test the fence for flatness by placing a straightedge across its working
face. The wood may not be flat or a brass inlay may protrude. If so,
remove the fence from the beam and abrade it against a piece of 220-grit
sandpaper adhered to a flat surface such as plate glass or a machine table
(see the drawing above). Hold the fence by its north-south axis to avoid
the sort of rocking motion that could make it convex across the face. A
newly flattened fence may no longer be perfectly lacquered, but it will be
reliable. If the beam of a gauge binds as it slides through the fence,
remove it and scrape or sand the sides just enough to let it move freely.

How to use a gauge

Gauges are most often used on the pull stroke. In principal there is no
compelling reason not to push, but pulling seems to be the more natural,
controllable motion.

When you are learning to use a gauge, concentrate on keeping the
fence flat against the work as you pull the gauge toward you. Also, keep
the beam parallel to the surface of the work, with the pins angled slightly
away from you so that they drag rather than jab.

Buying gauges

There are not that many makers of gauges to choose among, and the quality of manufacture seems to be declining. Until this situation reverses itself, my advice is to buy the best quality available. On a good gauge, the screw that holds the fence in place tightens against a piece of metal inlaid in the beam, not on naked wood. For superior wear, the face of the fence should be inlaid with brass. On the other hand, best doesn't always mean most expensive. Rosewood and brass are not necessities. My own knife gauge is of plain beech.

MARKING KNIVES

For cross-grain marking, such as laying out tenon shoulders, nothing beats a knife. Many woodworkers also prefer knives for scribing, as when tracing pins from tails. The best knives are thin edged, stiff, and razor sharp. The selection available includes single- and double-beveled knives, permanent- and disposable-bladed knives, and fixed, folding, and retractable knives. My own choice is a matter of happenstance as much as practicality. Twenty-five years ago, when I was a carpenter on Nantucket, a utility knife was an indispensable part of my kit, so it naturally came to hand when I began making furniture. Is it the best knife for marking joinery? Maybe not, but it does the job well.

For extreme accuracy, the best choice is a flat-backed blade that can be placed exactly against the work when tracing one part onto another. The action of its single bevel pushes the blade against the guiding surface and reduces the chance of wandering, much as the bevel on a cutting gauge does. Often, such a blade has a V-tip so it can cut in both directions. The included angle of the V should be less than 90° for the tip to reach interior corners. It is easy enough to make such a knife from a hacksaw blade or thin scraper, depending on the blade thickness you want.

What follows is an overview of knives sold specifically as woodworkers' marking tools. Keep in mind that a common penknife, properly sharpened, is perfectly adequate in most circumstances.

JAPANESE
MARKING
KNIFE

Japanese knives

Forge-welded much like Japanese chisels, Japanese knives will take a sharper edge than any jackknife. The cutting edge is a layer of high-carbon steel hardened to between 62 and 64 on the Rockwell hardness scale (Rc62 to Rc64). It is welded to a backing layer of more malleable, low-carbon steel or wrought iron, which compensates for its brittleness.

Japanese knives have flat backs and are available in right-bevel, left-bevel, and double-bevel versions. Like Japanese chisels (see p. 58), most single-beveled Japanese knives have hollow-ground backs to facilitate sharpening. The hollow grind makes it easier to flatten the back of the knife, because there is less material to remove. Japanese knives are sold without handles.

Sloyd knives

The sloyd knife is a traditional Swedish design intended for general craft work. It is double-beveled, has an oval-shaped wooden handle, and comes in a variety of blade shapes. Sloyd knives are made much like Japanese knives, with a layer of high-carbon tool steel laminated between two layers of milder steel. This allows the cutting edge to be hardened to a Rockwell hardness of 62, which will take a keen edge, without its attendant brittleness becoming a problem.

SLOYD KNIFE

Utility knives

The common utility knife has a replaceable blade and comes in numerous styles, with fixed, retractable, quick-release, and/or snap-off blades. Retractable-bladed knives are best, since they are safer to carry around or leave on a benchtop. Quick-release mechanisms may speed up blade changing by a few seconds, but they also shorten the life of a knife, because they are the first part to wear out. Snap-off blades are too flimsy for the task of marking.

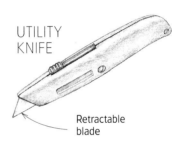
UTILITY KNIFE
Retractable blade

X-Acto knives

X-Acto knives feature an assortment of replaceable, throwaway blades and come in a range of sizes. They are great for small hobby work and for modelmaking in materials like foamcore and cardboard. However, the blades are too thin and flexible to make good marking tools.

X-ACTO KNIFE
#11 blade

Sharpening knives

The truly important part of a marking knife, however beautiful or utilitarian its handle and shape, is the last ⅛ in., the tip of the blade. This is where the work happens, and it should take and hold a razor edge.

There is more than one way to put a keen edge on a knife. Common methods usually involve some combination among grinding wheels, honing stones, buffing wheels, sandpaper, and leather strops. I find it convenient to hone on Japanese waterstones, although occasionally a nicked blade must first be reshaped on a coarse oilstone or grinder. To hone a Western-style knife, I hold the blade practically parallel with a 1000-grit waterstone (for an included angle of about 25°) and push it toward the bevel on alternating sides until the cutting edge is visibly affected. Then I repeat the process on the 6000-grit stone with just a few strokes, at which point the edge should be quite sharp. The process of honing a Japanese knife is the same, except that the back should be kept perfectly flat throughout.

Buying knives

Although you should consider blade shape, steel quality, and comfort when buying a marking knife, don't agonize over the decision. There is no one right choice, and an expensive knife doesn't so noticeably outperform an ordinary one as to matter. Perhaps the most important aspect to consider is comfort, as your knife is going to spend a lot of time in your hand. Before buying a knife, heft it. Get the feel of its shape and weight. Then make up your mind. Some craftsmen prefer to buy plain blades and fashion their own handles.

MEASURING TAPES AND RULES

The steel tape measure is a relatively recent invention. The "slide lock" that allows the tape to stand out, lock in place, and retract was patented by Stanley in 1963. Prior to development of the steel tape, woodworkers relied upon folding rules and straight rules for all but long-distance measurements, for which they used floppy steel tapes much like those still employed by surveyors. I learned this when I was a hungry young furniture maker in New York City in the mid-1970s and took part-time work framing a small addition at the Brooklyn Navy Yard. The other two carpenters on the crew were considerably older. If you have ever framed, you can imagine my surprise at seeing them lay out 40-ft. walls with 8-ft. folding rules. They had entered the trade before the steel tape was widely used and had never adopted the more efficient tool.

Steel tape measures are available in lengths from 8 ft. to 25 ft. The tape has an end hook that conveniently catches on board edges for taking outside measurements. For inside measurements, where the end of the tape must butt up against the starting point, the end hook slides over just enough to make up for its own thickness. On lower-quality tapes this movement can cause the rivets that fasten the hook to wear larger openings for themselves, thus altering the accuracy of the tool.

STEEL TAPE MEASURE

While it is possible to accomplish all the work in a furniture workshop with a tape measure, a folding rule (originally called a "spring-joint rule" or a "zigzag rule") is superior in many instances. Where a tape might flop or flex, a folding rule stays put and is easy to manipulate with one hand. The 6-ft. zigzag rule that lives in my back pocket is in constant use for measuring board thickness and width, laying out joinery, setting up machinery, and performing a thousand other daily tasks. The extension slide in the first joint is particularly handy when checking interior dimensions and diagonals. I reserve my steel tape for rough layout, measuring large-scale or curved work, and shop carpentry.

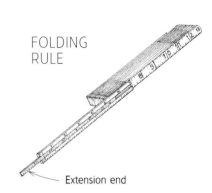

FOLDING RULE

Extension end

Folding rules come with plain, hook, or extension ends, in 6-ft. or 8-ft. lengths. Both sides can be numbered from the same end or in opposite directions. Eight-foot rules are cumbersome to handle. My preference is a 6-ft. rule with an extension slide at one end and both sides numbered in the same direction. The extension allows me to take accurate interior measurements and determine the depths of holes. Having both sides numbered in tandem makes the rule easier to work with, because I can flip it in an awkward spot without having to switch it end for end.

Another measuring device that has found favor with woodworkers is a 6-in. steel pocket rule with each edge graduated in a different scale: eighths, sixteenths, thirty-seconds, and sixty-fourths of an inch. The pocket rule is a convenient size to whip out when you need to check lumber thickness or set up a machine accurately.

Buying tapes and rules

Steel tapes are readily available at your local hardware store. Most name brands are reliable. A 16-ft. tape is a good length, given that furniture makers are unlikely to encounter anything longer in the way of lumber or work.

Purchase of a folding rule requires more attention. Those at the local hardware store are likely to be the less expensive sort, in which case they are prone to breakage and inaccuracy. Imagine the opportunity for error in manufacturing and assembling all those flexible joints. The standard-setter for reliable folding rules is the "Red-End" line made by Lufkin. The laths, made from select hard maple, are thicker and heavier than those found in less expensive rules. The brass-plated steel spring-joints lock in place with stiffness and accuracy; they should be lightly oiled on occasion.

Quality folding rules are available from some woodworking catalogs and retail outlets and can occasionally be found at local hardware stores.

SCHOOL
PENCIL

PENCILS

Two types of pencil come in handy for marking. For highly visible reference marks, a sturdy No. 2 school-type pencil is just the ticket. This is the pencil a woodworker parks behind his ear all day, at the ready for indicating which side of a board has been jointed, locating waste areas, orienting matching parts, and so forth.

A school pencil is worthless, however, when it comes to precise drafting and accurate marking of joinery. Its cylindrical, tapered point is all wrong for tracing outlines and working close up against a straight-edge, and the broadly tapered lead doesn't hold a fine point. The best tool for drafting and marking is an inexpensive architect's leadholder, made of plastic or metal (see p. 74).

The beauty of a leadholder is that the leads are thick enough to project some distance from the mouth of the holder without breaking (unlike the lead of a mechanical pencil), yet thin enough to mark accurately, much like a fine-pointed awl. Available leads span the full range of hardness, from 6B (softest) to 6H (hardest). Softer leads make darker lines, lose their points quickly, and break easily. The hardest leads are as likely to indent wood as they are to leave a trace of lead behind. The best leads for general marking and drafting are H and 2H—whichever suits the weight of your hand. Colored leads are also available: White is particularly useful for marking joinery on dark woods such as walnut, where an ordinary pencil line is difficult to distinguish.

Pointers for sharpening leadholders come in a variety of designs and a range of costs. Inexpensive portable pointers are perfect for the shop, as they travel with you from bench to drafting table. (See p. 75 for more information.) You can buy leadholders, leads, and pointers at art and architectural supply stores.

LEADHOLDER AND
LEADPOINTER

SLIDING T-BEVELS

The sliding T-bevel is almost as necessary to daily shop work as a square and a rule. Whenever an angle must be transferred, as in marking out joinery or setting up a special cut on the table saw, the T-bevel is likely to be the tool for the job. And whereas a competing tool such as a dovetail gauge is limited to a specific angle, the T-bevel has the virtue of infinite variability.

T-bevels come in a variety of materials and designs. The blade is usually made of steel, but the fence may be plastic, aluminum, steel, wood, or brass-inlaid wood. From a practical point of view, metal is the fence material most likely to be (and remain) straight.

Blade lengths vary, but 8 in. is sufficient for general shop work. The blade-locking mechanism may be a thumbscrew or cam lever at the pivot point or a knob protruding from the base of the fence. The latter is preferable. Although the thumbscrew is extremely common, it has the fault of occasionally projecting beyond the fence, thereby holding the fence off the work.

Buying T-bevels

When buying a T-bevel, look for a flat fence, a straight blade, and a well-designed lock that holds the blade tight. The best model I've found on the current market is Japanese made; it has an aluminum fence and tightens from the base. Sliding T-bevels are available through hardware stores and woodworking specialty stores and mail-order catalogs.

SLIDING T-BEVEL

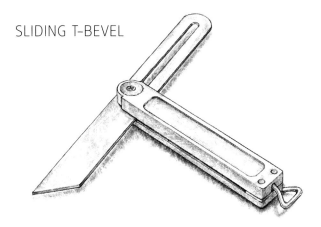

SQUARES

How square does a square need to be for woodworking? James Krenov, the respected furniture maker, considers expensive precision squares to be an indulgence. He suggests that what looks square to the eye is square enough. While I agree with Jim's emphasis on trusting one's perception, it is also true that most of us weren't born with his laser eye.

The accuracy of a square should be appropriate to the task for which it is intended. The 24-in. framing square with which I lay out rough lumber and square up large cases doesn't need to be as precise as the 9-in. engineer's square I use to true up machinery and mark tenon shoulders. I expect the latter to be true within the thickness of a hair over its full length, while in the former I can forgive $\frac{1}{64}$ in. or so.

The squares customarily employed in furniture shops include combination, try, framing, engineer's, and double squares. There is no reason to have them all. The only square I use besides the two mentioned above is a 4-in. double square, of which I am quite fond. However, if I could have only one square it would be a first-class 12-in. combination square—a tool that could practically replace the three I currently use.

Combination squares

The head of a combination square has two working fences, one at 90° to the blade, the other at 45°. It also contains a glass level tube mounted parallel to the 90° fence. The blade slides through the head, can be locked in place at any length, and is marked in increments like a rule. These features make the combination square capable of doing the work of a try square, miter square, depth gauge, height gauge, and level rolled into one. The 12-in. size is the most popular, but combination squares are also available with 6-in., 18-in., and 24-in. blades.

COMBINATION
SQUARE

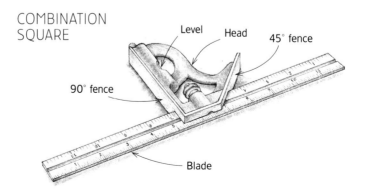

Level   Head   45° fence

90° fence

Blade

Combination squares run the full range from excellent to awful. Those at your local hardware store are as likely to belong in the trash barrel as in your tool cabinet. Often you will find the blades are not straight or square, the heads are inaccurately machined, and/or the locking mechanisms are sloppy. On the other hand, high-end combination squares made specifically for machinists are remarkable.

Double squares

The double square has a sliding head and lock mechanism much like a combination square, except that both faces of the head are at 90° to the blade and it doesn't contain a level tube. Double-square blades range in length from 2 in. to 6 in. and are graduated for measuring. Because they are made as machinists' tools, their quality is likely to be excellent.

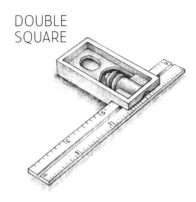

DOUBLE SQUARE

Engineer's squares

The engineer's square is similar to a woodworker's try square (see p. 96), the structural difference being that its fence is made of steel instead of wood, plastic, and/or brass. The other difference is the degree of accuracy the manufacturer feels compelled to live up to. Engineer's squares are expected to be square within a tolerance of perhaps 0.0005 in. per inch of length. Recently, however, some companies have begun to market inexpensive engineer-type squares specifically for the woodworking market. As you might expect, low prices are indicative of inconsistent accuracy.

Engineer's squares are available with blades from 2 in. to 12 in. long. They are handy for marking out joinery, setting up machinery, squaring stock, and so forth.

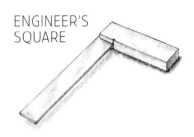

ENGINEER'S SQUARE

Framing squares

The framing square is really a carpenter's tool for laying out walls, floors, roofs, stairs, and just about everything else. It is constructed of steel or aluminum, with two arms about ⅛ in. thick set at right angles to each other. The standard size has one arm 2 in. wide by 24 in. long, which is called the blade, and one arm 1½ in. wide by 16 in. long, called the tongue. Often numerical tables are imprinted on the face of the square for laying out rafters and other carpentry esoterica.

In the hands of a skilled carpenter, the framing square can be a complex calculating machine. In a furniture workshop, it is simply a larger square, used for marking out rough lumber to approximate size, squaring up case pieces during assembly, and all sorts of odd jobs. Rarely is it expected to serve as a dead-accurate layout tool.

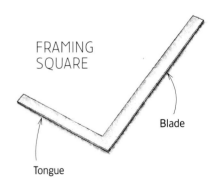

FRAMING SQUARE

Blade

Tongue

MITER
SQUARE

TRY
SQUARE

Miter squares

A miter square is made specifically for marking 45° angles. It is, perhaps, an overspecialized tool, since a good combination square will perform the same function and many others besides.

Try squares

The try square is the traditional furniture maker's square. Its fence may be wood, plastic, wood and brass, or steel. The blade is generally steel. Some of the more expensive try squares have brass blades, but these are less desirable for two reasons. First, brass is softer than steel and more likely to dent, nick, or be shaved by the blade of a marking knife. Second, brass blades, being made of weaker metal, are thicker, which makes them more difficult to mark against accurately.

A try square should be square inside and out, because it is used both ways. Often the fences are faced with metal on the inside only. Two metal-clad faces are preferable. Wooden faces are less reliably straight and more likely to deteriorate.

The best reasons for purchasing a try square are sentiment for tradition and an aesthetic preference for wood and brass. While the accuracy of try squares varies from manufacturer to manufacturer and from square to square, they are generally not up to the standard set by engineer's squares, which perform the exact same functions.

Buying squares

Purchasing a square can be a challenge, unless you are ready to pay the high price of machinists' tools that can be trusted right out of the box. Starrett is the brand of choice for combination squares and double squares. Chesterman Rabone is another reputable manufacturer. These tools are available through some woodworking catalogs and specialty stores, as well as through industrial-supply catalogs. In general, look for blades that are straight on both sides and fences that are either all-metal or faced with metal on both sides.

If you are buying a try square, framing square, or less expensive engineer's or combination square, there are a couple of ways to test for squareness. The simplest method is to match your potential purchase against another square that you know to be accurate. In a woodworking store you might borrow a Starrett off the shelf against which to test less costly squares.

TESTING A SQUARE FOR ACCURACY

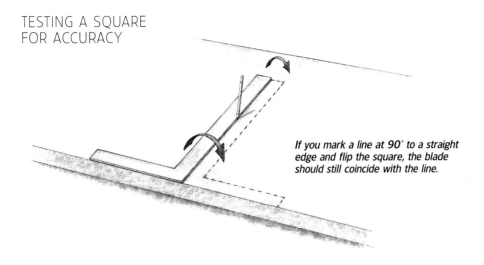

If you mark a line at 90° to a straight edge and flip the square, the blade should still coincide with the line.

A standard field test for squareness is to first mark a line at right angles to a straight edge, preferably with a knife or extremely fine pencil point. Then flip the square 180° (as shown in the drawing above). If the blade still coincides with the line, the square is fairly accurate.

How to use a square

Using a square is not a difficult task, although it does require practice at first. The most common problem among beginners is a tendency to hold the tool by the blade instead of the fence. For accuracy, the fence must be held firmly against the work at all times. The proper way to check a board for squareness is to introduce the fence to the work, then gradually slide the blade down till it meets the surface.

Maintenance

Many squares lead hard lives. Eventually someone drops them on a floor, and often that floor is concrete. The result may be as minor as a dented corner or as catastrophic as a loss of trueness. Dented corners are salvageable: File protruding burrs smooth so they can't hold the square off the work.

An out-of-true square is best discarded, unless it happens to be a framing square. To retrue a framing square, hammer the metal at the diagonal joint between the blades. As the metal spreads, the blades move. Hammering in the vicinity of the outside corner makes the square more acute. Hammering the inside corner leads to obtuseness.

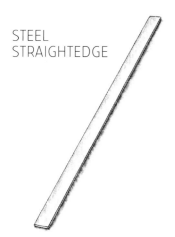

STEEL
STRAIGHTEDGE

STRAIGHTEDGES

A straightedge is most broadly defined as a piece of material of any length that has a straight edge. Thus, when I need to draw a long line on rough lumber for ripping on the bandsaw, my straightedge may be an 8-ft. plywood cutoff from the scrap pile.

More particularly, a straightedge is a flat steel bar that may or may not be scaled for measuring. Those in my workshop run the full range, from a little 6-in. pocket rule to a heavyweight 6-ft. machinist's straightedge. The latter is actually an anomaly—it is more accurate and expensive than necessary for the needs of a normal woodshop. I acquired it by accident as part of a larger purchase and use it primarily for leveling jointer tables once a year.

Straightedges play a part in drafting, layout, milling, marking out joinery, assembly, and machine setup. The most useful lengths are between 2 ft. and 4 ft. For smaller work, the blade of a square will usually do.

For most woodworking needs, there is no need to buy expensive machinist's straightedges. Wood, being an organic material, simply will not conform to the standards possible in metalwork. The degree of trueness should be appropriate to the type of work you do. Acceptable-quality straightedges are available through woodworking suppliers and artist's/architect's supply stores.

When selecting a straightedge, consider thickness and flexibility. For marking, a straightedge should either be thin or have one edge beveled thin. This reduces shadow and brings the pencil point closer to the paper. Thick, stiff straightedges are better for testing the flatness of surfaces, because they will stand on edge with minimal deflection. Suppleness becomes desirable when a straightedge is used to generate curves. The arc of a flexed straightedge constantly changes radius as it travels along. By comparison, the static arc of a circle is dead to the eye and hand.

Buying straightedges

Straightedges are available from hardware stores, woodworking specialty stores and mail-order catalogs, art/architecture supply outlets, and industrial-supply catalogs. One test for straightness is to trace an edge on a piece of paper, then flip the straightedge so the same edge is against the line from the other side. If it looks true, the straightedge is fairly good.

TRAMMEL POINTS

Trammel points are pairs of steel pins that clamp to a beam for marking out arcs of circles. They are particularly useful when the radius exceeds the capacity of a normal drafting compass. Sometimes one tip is replaced with a pencil for drawing instead of scribing.

Some trammel points are manufactured with a specially fitted beam. Others are fitted with clamps to latch on to a strip of wood or metal, a folding rule, a steel rule, or whatever else works.

Trammel points are not essential to furniture making. The need to draw large-diameter circles doesn't arise that often, and there are other means to do so. The simplest alternative is to drill two holes in a stick, separated by the desired radius. A nail through one hole fixes the center, while a pencil point through the other marks the circumference.

TRAMMEL POINTS

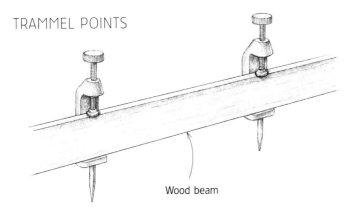

Wood beam

PLANING

The essential element of a plane is a chisel-like blade that cuts in relation to a sole. There was a time when carriage makers, coopers, coffin makers, chairmakers, cabinetmakers, and every other trade that fashioned wood had its own specialized planes. Since the heyday of the late 19th century the production of planes has narrowed extremely—a common form of cultural extinction arising from technological and economic change.

Fortunately, furniture making has not entirely gone the way of carriage making. We still have a wide variety of useful planes available from manufacturers (as well as the ability to make our own). The largest change of the past century has been the replacement of molding planes by the router and shaper.

The earliest known planes date from the Roman era. Their bodies had wooden cores sheathed in iron plate, and their blades were held in position with wooden wedges. It can only be assumed that these were preceded by all-wood bodies that haven't survived. Subsequent "improvements" included the development of all-metal bodies, the chipbreaker, mechanisms for raising and lowering the blade, and mechanisms for controlling the side-to-side angle of the blade. Many older plane designs are still in use, alongside those sporting the most recent innovations. Choosing among them is more often a matter of personal preference than of proven superiority.

Planes are categorized primarily by their function and design, not by the material of which they are made. A bench plane, for example, may have a wood, metal, or combination body. It might or might not have built-in mechanisms for blade adjustment. What defines it are the position of the blade in relation to the body, the presence of a chipbreaker, a flat sole, and its primary function of surfacing wood.

Although planes take many shapes, the principles upon which they work are constant. In order to avoid redundancy, I have corralled most of the theoretical and technical information into the sections on bench planes and block planes. I suggest you read these sections before moving on to descriptions of other planes.

Few planes come out of the box ready to use, and many require extensive alteration in order to perform their best. Tuning procedures specific to individual planes are explained in the sections on those planes. General sharpening information may be found in the appendix on pp. 185-195.

BENCH PLANES

Bench planes are the most important planes in the woodshop. Their function is to make wood flat and smooth, whether turning a roughsawn board into four-square stock, cleaning up an already flat surface for finishing, or shooting a perfect edge joint.

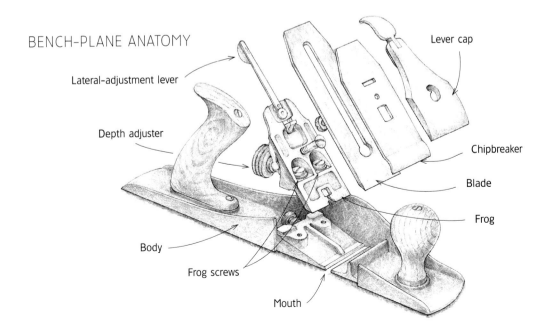

BENCH-PLANE ANATOMY

Lateral-adjustment lever

Depth adjuster

Lever cap

Chipbreaker

Blade

Frog

Body

Frog screws

Mouth

The essence of a bench plane is a blade and chipbreaker assembly mounted bevel down through a flat sole at an angle of 45° ("common pitch") to 50° ("York pitch"). The great majority of bench planes in use today also incorporate more sophisticated features in the forms developed by Leonard Bailey, of Boston, beginning in 1858, and by Stanley after they bought Bailey's patents and company in 1869. These features are a screw-adjusted frog that controls the size of the throat opening (patented 1895), a lateral-adjustment lever that controls the side-to-side angle of the blade, a yoke-shaped mechanism for adjusting depth of cut, and a cam-operated lever cap.

Bailey-style bench planes

Bailey-style bench planes are all-metal and were originally made in a range of sizes from the tiny No. 1 to the behemoth No. 8. Imagine an aircraft carrier calmly bridging the ocean swell as a nearby dinghy disappears in a trough, then mounts the onrushing wave, and you'll see why different-length planes are suited for different tasks. Long planes are best when a truly flat surface is desired, such as when making edge joints. Shorter planes are preferable for smoothing preparatory to finishing, since they can reach localized areas of a larger surface.

Although length is a guideline, there are no hard-and-fast rules regarding what one size plane may or may not do. One craftsman might like to flatten boards with a jack plane, whereas another prefers the heft of a jointer plane. In my own work, I tend to use a No. 7 jointer plane for edge jointing, a No. 5 jack plane for surfacing to make boards flat, and a No. 4 smoothing plane for cleaning up the surface in preparation for finishing.

As you will note in the chart on the facing page, smoothing and jack planes are available in more than one width. Whether wider planes are preferable is yet another matter of personal taste. One might argue that a wider blade would remove wood more quickly and leave a flatter surface. On the other hand, it also encounters proportionally more resistance.

The two largest makers of Bailey-style bench planes are the British manufacturers, Stanley and Record. Both companies designate their planes according to the original numbers assigned by the American Stanley company. The only difference is that Record puts an 0 in front of the number. Neither Stanley nor Record makes planes Nos. 1, 2, and 8 any more.

Bailey-Style Bench Planes			
Plane number	Length	Blade width	Name (if any)
1	5½ in.	1¼ in.	
2	7 in.	1⅝ in.	
3	9 in.	1¾ in.	smoothing plane
4	9¾ in.	2 in.	smoothing plane
4½	10¼ in.	2⅜ in.	smoothing plane
5	14 in.	2 in.	jack plane
5½	14¾ in.	2⅜ in.	jack plane
6	18 in.	2⅜ in.	fore plane
7	22 in.	2⅜ in.	try or jointer plane
8	24 in.	2⅝ in.	jointer plane

Anatomy and tuning of Bailey-style bench planes

There is no point in putting a bench plane to wood until it has been tuned up. This requires flattening the sole and the back of the blade, sharpening the blade, fitting the chipbreaker, making sure the frog seats well and the blade sits cleanly upon it, setting the throat size, and adjusting the tension of the lever cap. The parts of a Bailey-style bench plane are explained in the pages that follow, along with methods for improving their performance.

Sole   The sole is the bottom surface of the plane. For best results, it must be flat (within limits) and smooth. The critical points at which the sole needs to touch the work are the front of the mouth, the toe, and the heel. If some of the areas in between are hollow, it's okay, but if the toe and heel don't touch, the effective length of the plane is reduced.

The front of the mouth is the most important spot on the entire sole. Where it presses on the work, it keeps wood fibers from lifting ahead of the blade, inhibiting tearout. If the front of the mouth isn't in contact with the work, the effective throat is enlarged and the blade cuts poorly.

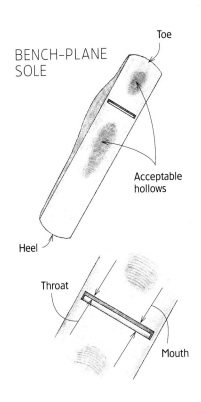

BENCH-PLANE SOLE

Toe

Acceptable hollows

Heel

Throat

Mouth

Bench planes are available with smooth or corrugated soles. In theory, soles relieved by lengthwise grooves are intended for use on resinous woods, where less contact should reduce friction. When you're working with furniture hardwoods, however, the resistance encountered by smooth and corrugated soles isn't distinguishable enough to matter. A most effective way to reduce friction on any sole is to rub on a small amount of paraffin or paste wax.

A good method for flattening the sole of a plane is to adhere strips of sandpaper to the longest flat surface in the shop, which is often the jointer table. Pressure-sensitive-adhesive sandpaper in rolls about 4 in. wide is most convenient. If you use this method, begin with 100-grit or 120-grit aluminum oxide, hold the plane down flat, and rub it back and forth with considerable pressure. Remove metal particles and loose grit from the paper with an air hose or brush from time to time. It is customary to keep the blade in the plane under normal tension but raised up out of harm's way, in case the pressure of the lever cap distorts the body in any way.

When the toe, heel, front of the mouth, and most of the rest of the sole are uniformly abraded, repeat the process with 220-grit paper until all the 120-grit scratches are gone. Going this far is sufficient, but continuing on to 320-grit paper and even beyond makes a sole impressively smooth. Afterwards, you might file or sand a tiny chamfer on the arrises of the sole, since they are quite sharp and prone to nicking otherwise.

Blade   The blade of a bench plane is often referred to as the iron, especially by collectors of older planes. It is forged and hardened in essentially the same way as a chisel blade, with the business end tempered and the upper section softer.

Blade thickness is a controversial topic in the woodworking world these days. Historically, plane irons were fairly thick, in the range of $\frac{1}{8}$ in. to $\frac{3}{16}$ in. (High-carbon steel was relatively valuable until the Bessemer process was developed in the mid-1800s, so blades were often made by welding a piece of high-carbon steel into a thicker piece of mild steel, much as they still are in Japan.) Then, about the time of the American Civil War, the thin blades (just over $\frac{1}{32}$ in.) that now dominate the market were introduced by Leonard Bailey. The current revival of interest in woodworking hand skills, however, has led to a fascination with thicker blades. They are now available to retrofit existing planes, and a few small manufacturers include them in new planes.

The advantage of thick blades is their mass, which, in some instances, reduces chatter and yields a cleaner cut. On the other hand, the added thickness makes them more time-consuming to grind and sharpen, so there is a trade-off. My own theory is that the craftsmen of yore were just as excited about the introduction of thin blades as those of today are about thick ones. They saw thin blades as a technological blessing that reduced sharpening time dramatically. Remember, this was in the days of human-powered, slow-speed, sandstone grinding wheels.

The shape of a bench-plane blade's cutting edge is often altered to suit its specific purpose. In theory, a straight, square edge is best for final smoothing and edge jointing, while a mildly convex edge is most efficient for rapid, rougher work such as planing boards to initial flatness. Some woodworkers grind the corners off a straight edge to prevent them from digging in when finish planing. My current preference is to use one shape for all bench-plane work. I grind the edge perfectly straight and then create the slightest of convexities by pressing down on the corners more than on the center as I hone. The resulting curvature is just a couple of thousandths of an inch, enough that a thin, full-width shaving feathers out to nothing at the edges.

The first thing to do with a new plane blade is to flatten the back (see the appendix on pp. 185-195), though not for the exact same reasons you flatten a chisel. On a chisel, the back guides the cutting action. On a plane blade, the flatness of the back is an aid to efficient sharpening and affects the angle at which the blade meets the wood (the cutting angle).

Like a chisel, a plane blade is sharpest when the included angle between the back and the bevel is the smallest that will hold an edge. On the other hand, that type of sharpness is not particularly important to the way a plane works. Instead of entering the wood in its entirety the way a chisel does, the blade of a plane has only one face in contact with wood. From the wood's point of view, it is meeting a sharp edge and sliding up a ramp of a certain angle. It has no way of knowing what the included angle of the bevel is.

Whether the cutting edge of a plane iron is honed to 25° or 35°, the initial sharpness of the edge is the same as far as the wood is concerned. However, the 25° angle stays sharp longer because it thickens more slowly as the edge wears away. This may seem to tip the scales in favor of a thinner edge, but it is balanced by the superior resistance a thicker bevel offers to crumbling as it encounters knots and other inconsistencies in wood grain.

The limit to bevel thickness is the need to maintain a clearance angle of at least 6° or 7° behind the cutting edge in hardwoods, more in softwoods. When the cutting edge severs wood, a tiny amount of compression and bending takes place in the fibers. As the cutting edge passes over, they spring back. Although the amount of springback is minuscule, it would be enough to lift the blade if there were no clearance angle whatsoever.

BLADE PROFILES

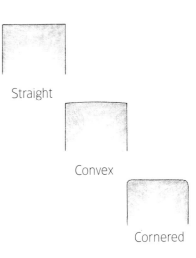

Straight

Convex

Cornered

BLADE-ANGLE TERMINOLOGY

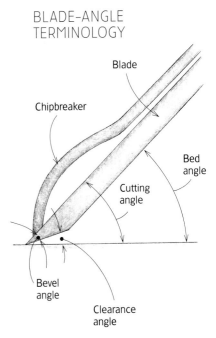

Blade

Chipbreaker

Bed angle

Cutting angle

Bevel angle

Clearance angle

Weighing all the previous factors, you can see there is a certain latitude in determining the "correct" bevel angle for a bench plane. For finish work in clear wood, particularly in softwood, 25° might be ideal. When taking thicker shavings from hardwood or planing knotty wood, the most effective balance of sharpness and longevity might be a bevel angle closer to 35°. That said, the truth is that most woodworkers get in the habit of grinding and honing their plane irons to some specific angle that they use in virtually all circumstances. Usually, I hollow-grind the bevel at anywhere from 25° to 28° and then hone the cutting edge a degree or two higher. If the edge of your blade begins to crumple in use, then make it a few degrees steeper, until you find the balance point between sharpness and edge retention.

CHIPBREAKER ACTION

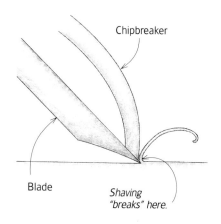

Chipbreaker

Blade

Shaving "breaks" here.

Chipbreaker   The chipbreaker (also called the cap iron) has three functions: to stiffen the blade; to direct shavings up and out of the throat; and, most important, to "break" shavings before they have a chance to cause tearout.

As a plane blade moves forward, it severs wood at the cutting edge and raises a shaving. The continuity of the shaving's fibers extends ahead of the blade, lifting them from the surface. Where wood grain travels downward, this can cause tearout. The strength of wood fibers is far stronger than the bond between them, so they are more likely to separate from their neighbors and leave craters than to break cleanly across at the surface. However, a close-set chipbreaker throws the shaving upward and forward, bending it severely where it passes the cutting edge. Theoretically, this bend sufficiently weakens the wood fibers so they suddenly find breaking easier than separating from adjacent fibers. Thus, instead of lifting out ahead of the blade, the fibers snap. This is similar to the action that makes scrapers so impervious to tearout (see pp. 163-164).

For taking fine shavings, the chipbreaker should be set immediately behind the cutting edge (about $1/64$ in. for hardwoods). For coarser shavings or work in softwoods, the chipbreaker should be between $1/32$ in. and $1/16$ in. behind the cutting edge.

The forward edge of a chipbreaker should make clean contact across the full width of the blade. Otherwise, shavings will jam underneath it and disturb the plane's cutting action. If you can see light between the back of the iron and the leading edge of the chipbreaker, there is too much of a gap. The way to fix the problem is to form the edge of the chipbreaker with a small mill file and/or honing stones (as shown in the drawing on the facing page). Usually this is necessary on new planes.

The leading face of a chipbreaker should be polished smooth with fine sandpaper so shavings slide easily against it.

TWO WAYS TO TUNE A CHIPBREAKER

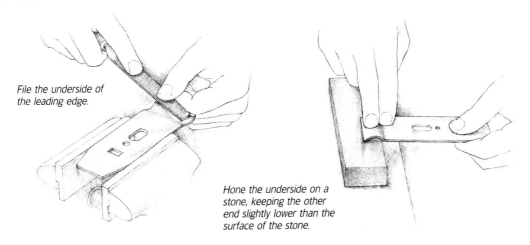

File the underside of
the leading edge.

Hone the underside on a
stone, keeping the other
end slightly lower than the
surface of the stone.

Frog   The frog is a roughly triangular block of metal that supports the blade at an angle of 45° on a standard bench plane. On all but the worst planes, the frog adjusts forward and back, effectively controlling the size of the throat. The frogs of cheaper planes move manually. Better planes utilize an external adjustment screw at the base of the frog.

In order to adjust the frog, you must first loosen the two screws that attach it to the body. Bailey-style planes require removal of the blade in order to gain access to these frog screws. An historic Stanley design known as the "Bedrock," now a collector's item, has externally accessible frog screws so it can be adjusted without removing the blade. Bedrock planes were developed by a Stanley employee, Justus Traut, and manufactured by Stanley from about 1900 up until World War II. Recently, they have been reintroduced by Lie-Nielsen Toolworks of Warren, Maine.

One distinguishing feature of a well-made plane is the milling of parts you don't normally see. This becomes evident when you remove the frog and look at the areas where it makes contact with the body of the plane. Beneath a cheap frog the contact points are rough-cast and painted over. Lift out a good frog, and you'll find the seats cleanly milled on both the frog and the body. To see the best, look at the extensively milled underside of a Bedrock frog (see the drawing on p. 108). The more firmly the frog seats in the body, the less likely the blade is to chatter. This is not to intimate that you must rush out and buy a Bedrock plane, since they are hard to find and expensive. The difference in performance between a Bedrock and a standard Bailey plane is only incremental, not compelling, and you can do excellent work with either.

TWO FROGS COMPARED

Bailey style

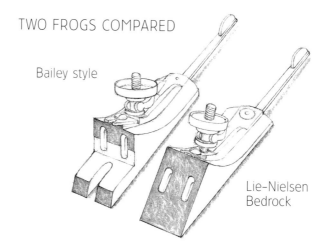

Lie-Nielsen
Bedrock

The more extensive the milled contact surface between the bed and the underside of the frog (shown shaded), the more stable the frog.

When tuning up a new plane, always remove and inspect the frog. The contact areas between the frog and the bed should be smooth, the frog should sit flat on the bed, and the frog should slide forward and back easily. The milled contact surfaces in the body can be difficult to reach with a file. The best way to work on them is to dab them with lapping compound and rub the frog backwards and forwards. Lapping compound is a paste of abrasive material available in tins from auto-supply stores. You should also examine the upper face of the frog and file off any roughness that might impede the up-and-down adjustment of the blade.

Throat   The throat is the clearance between the blade and the front of the mouth. A correctly set throat may be just as effective as a chip-breaker in minimizing tearout. Where the sole of the plane rests on the work in front of the mouth, it prevents wood fibers from lifting. Thus the smaller the throat, the less distance there is in front of the blade where tearout can occur. The limit to throat thinness is the width needed for shavings to pass through. This can be quite small for fine, finish planing on hardwoods.

Lever cap   The lever cap holds the blade/chipbreaker assembly in position against the frog. The amount of pressure it exerts is controlled by the height of the lever-cap screw. There should be enough pressure to keep the blade from shifting in use, but not enough to prevent its smooth adjustment up and down and side to side by means of the depth adjuster and the lateral-adjustment lever. You can easily find the right amount of pressure through trial and error, but err on the light side at first.

The leading edge of a lever cap should contact the chipbreaker cleanly across to apply even pressure. If the edge is rough or crooked, it should be filed.

Body   I've already mentioned two aspects of the body of the plane—the sole and the machined surfaces upon which the frog seats. Another consideration is whether the sides of a bench plane should be perfectly square to the sole.

The answer is not necessarily. The most you need expect of the sides is that they be within a degree or two of square and flat enough not to rock when the plane is on edge. The primary situation in which the sides affect a bench plane's performance is edge jointing with a shooting board (see the drawing below). A shooting board consists of two long, flat boards fastened together. The wider lower board forms a ledge upon which a plane can ride on edge. This keeps the plane at a constant angle to the work, which overhangs the upper board. The two halves of a joint are planed with opposite faces against the shooting board. The beauty of the system is that, even if the plane is not cutting perfectly square, the joined edges are at supplementary angles, ensuring a perfect match.

SHOOTING AN EDGE JOINT

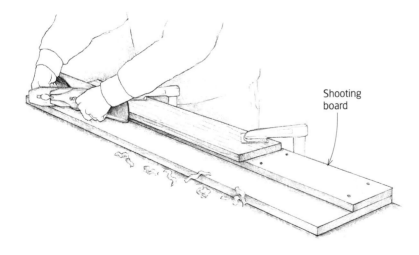

Shooting board

If there were a circumstance that required an absolutely square edge from the shooting board and the side of the plane wasn't square to the sole, you would simply set the blade to a compensatory angle with the lateral-adjustment lever.

Wooden and transitional bench planes

Not all bench planes are Bailey-style. The other types you are likely to encounter are wooden bench planes and transitional planes.

Wooden bench planes

Although the wood-bodied bench plane is probably the most ancient style of plane, there are excellent craftsmen who still think it the best. Students of James Krenov, in particular, learn early to make their own wooden planes and tend to stick with them throughout their careers. They find that the extra effort invested in making and adjusting their planes is rewarded with increased sensitivity, understanding, and control of the tool.

Not all wooden bench planes share the same design characteristics. The wedge and iron assemblies may be housed in grooves cut in the sides of the plane (as shown in the drawing below) or captured between the bed and a horizontal pin through the gullet. The bodies themselves may be carved out of a single block of wood or made by assembling the sides to the central elements. The sole may be a separate piece of denser wood, or simply the bottom of the body. This is not the place for a

WOODEN-PLANE ANATOMY

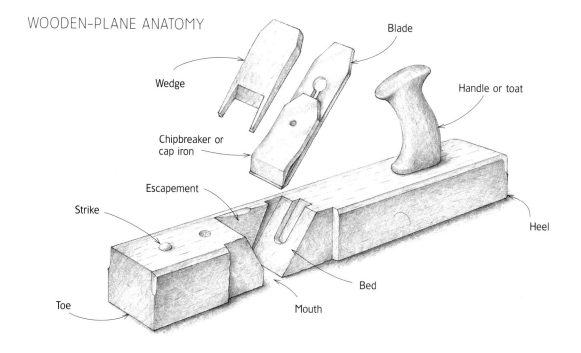

Blade

Wedge

Handle or toat

Chipbreaker or cap iron

Escapement

Strike

Heel

Toe

Bed

Mouth

treatise on plane making, but plenty of information is available in magazine articles and books. A few wooden planes are also sold commercially.

How do you adjust the cutting action of a wooden plane? To deepen the cut, you tap the back edge of the blade with a small hammer. To raise the blade, you tap the body from the rear. In order to remove the blade entirely, you smack the body hard enough to jar the iron loose, either on the stern or on the top of the body in front of the blade. Commercially made planes often have a metal strike button at one of these two points.

Wood has a tendency to warp, so the sole of a wood plane may need truing from time to time. In doing so, it is advisable to remove as little wood as possible. The mouths of wooden planes are narrowest at the bottom. Removing wood from the sole widens the throat, which can adversely affect the plane's performance. Too wide a throat should be remedied by inlaying a wood insert in the sole. Methods of flattening a sole include handplaning, scraping, lapping on sandpaper (my favorite), and machine-jointing (with the blade assembly removed for safety).

Transitional planes

Transitional planes combine wood bodies with sophisticated metal blade-adjustment mechanisms. The term "transitional plane" is usually applied to planes manufactured by Stanley in the second half of the 19th century. However, planes of this general description are still made by European manufacturers, so they should not be thought of as historic relics.

The theoretical advantage of the transitional plane is that it combines the best of both worlds: a lightweight, low-friction wooden body with precision blade setting. My own experience with the European planes is that when they work well, they're a dream. Unfortunately, the irons of all three European planes I own have a nasty tendency to shift their lateral angle spontaneously. I keep the planes around primarily for their decorative quality.

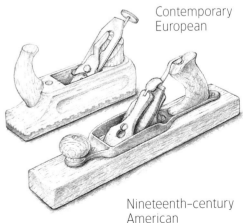

TRANSITIONAL PLANES

Contemporary European

Nineteenth–century American

PLANING WITH THE GRAIN

When the direction of the grain leads back up toward the surface ahead of the blade, tearout is avoided.

The physics of planing

In an ideal world, all planing would be done with the grain. Unfortunately, it's rare to find a board of such perfection. Trees are a lot like people: Environment and inheritance twist their growth, and there is often a core of early developmental knots at the center. So some amount of planing against the grain is inevitable. When it comes to working with contrary woods like bubinga and roey mahogany, planing can prove impossible. Fortunately, most of the time on most woods, some amount of planing against the grain is possible without incurring disaster. Just how much depends on the character of the wood and the set of the plane.

Holding a plane at an angle to its line of travel reduces the cutting angle and decreases resistance. It also produces a shearing cut that helps the plane enter easily at the start of a stroke. A shearing cut is effective in reducing tearout on end grain, but not on long grain. The time-honored way to reduce long-grain tearout is to raise the blade's cutting angle, not lower it. As the angle increases, the blade breaks shavings more aggressively, acting more like a scraper. Nowadays, bench planes are manufactured with their blades pitched to a 45° angle. But, traditionally, at least in Britain, a bench plane with a 45° pitch was meant for work in softwoods. Planes made for hardwoods had blades mounted at 50° and higher. A high cutting angle increases the amount of resistance the craftsman experiences but decreases the amount of tearout in hard and contrary woods.

One way to raise the cutting angle of a modern bench plane is to hone a back-bevel on the blade. This trick is commonly applied to the knives of thickness planers for coping with figured wood. If you explore this route, you may prefer to back-bevel a spare blade rather than deform your regular iron.

If wood is too squirrelly to plane successfully with the grain, you can plane diagonally or across the grain, and then finish up with a scraper. Planing across the grain virtually eliminates tearout but also leaves a rougher texture and increases the difficulty of making a board consistently flat along its length.

Setting the blade

When you are first learning to plane, it can be difficult to adjust the depth of cut correctly. Try setting the blade visually to start with. Sight down the length of the sole and raise or lower the blade until it just barely protrudes from the mouth and looks parallel across the width of the sole. Then take a test cut on a piece of wood, raising or lowering the blade until it yields a gossamer shaving. Watch to see which corner of the blade bites first or more heavily, and then correct the blade angle until the shaving is even across. Proper shaving thickness depends on the type of work and the character of the wood. When flattening hardwood, the shavings might start out as thick as construction paper and end up as thin as tissue paper; in finish planing they can be thin enough to read through. Softwood planes more easily and shavings tend to be thicker.

BENCH RABBET PLANES

Bench rabbet planes are similar in size and construction to smooth and jack planes, but their blades extend the full width of their soles. This enables them to plane up to interior corners. They can be useful for tasks such as fitting the cheeks of large tenons and trimming rabbets. However, they are not the best plane to make a rabbet from scratch, since they have neither the fence nor the depth stop of a true rabbet plane. (To make a new rabbet with a bench rabbet plane, you would ordinarily run it against a clamped-on fence.) Because they are engineered like bench planes, bench rabbet planes are better at cutting long grain than end grain.

The two sizes of bench rabbet plane currently in production have a 2⅛-in. by 8-in. sole and a 2⅛-in. by 13-in. sole. As is true of a few other planes described in this chapter, the bench rabbet plane is a specialty item not found in most furniture workshops. In scale and intent it was originally more of a carpenter's and framer's tool.

To tune up a bench rabbet plane, follow the procedure for bench planes. Because of the blade's T-shape, some craftsmen find it easier to install the blade from below the mouth and slip it under the chipbreaker; others put it in like a normal bench plane.

BENCH RABBET PLANE

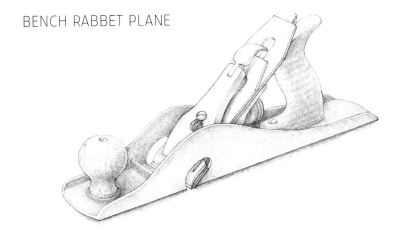

BLOCK-PLANE
ANATOMY

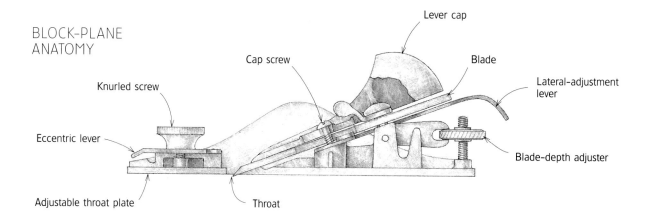

Lever cap

Cap screw

Blade

Lateral-adjustment
lever

Knurled screw

Blade-depth adjuster

Eccentric lever

Adjustable throat plate

Throat

STANDARD BLOCK
PLANE

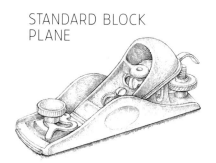

BLOCK PLANES

Like bench planes, block planes are considered essential in the
woodshop. Their small size and blade configuration make them handy
for all sorts of work on long grain and end grain, including smoothing
end-grain surfaces, chamfering edges, planing proud joints flush, and
making convex curves fair and smooth.

Block planes are small enough for one-handed use, generally from
5 in. to 6½ in. long. The blade beds directly in the body, bevel up, without
frog or chipbreaker. The bedding angle is 20° on a standard block plane
and about 12° on a low-angle block plane. Better block planes have
adjustable plates in their soles to vary throat size. Most block planes have
blade-depth adjusters, while standard planes often have lateral-adjustment
levers, too.

Most likely, the name "block plane" derives from the time when
butchers cut meat on massive, end-grain tabletops. (End grain survives
assault with a cleaver better than long grain.) The block plane, being less
prone to chatter and tearout in end grain, would have been the tool of
choice for dressing these original "butcher blocks."

Planing end grain

End-grain surfaces offer considerably more resistance to a plane blade
than long grain does. The blade must cut directly across the wood fibers,
which is the direction in which they are toughest and most compact. The
effect can be to make the blade flex and skip, leaving a series of irregular
cuts known as chatter.

A block plane is less likely to chatter than a bench plane for two reasons. One is that its blade is more closely aligned with the direction of thrust, making it less prone to deflection. The other is the bevel-up orientation of the blade, which allows the bed to support it right up to the cutting edge.

In planing end grain, the amount of resistance a blade encounters is a variable of two factors: the cutting angle and the thickness of the shaving. The steeper the angle, the more the blade pushes against the fibers ahead rather than just severing them. The thicker the shaving, the more reluctant the severed fibers are to part with their uncut neighbors. The worst result of resistance is when fibers ahead of the blade push over and break before they are severed, which is what causes tearout in end grain.

Surprisingly enough, the cutting angle of a standard block plane is identical to that of a standard bench plane, even though its blade is bedded at 20° instead of 45°. A glance at the drawing below shows why. A low-angle block plane blade meets wood at about 37°, making it preferable for end-grain work.

While the theoretical arguments for the superiority of block planes on end grain are clear, they should not be overemphasized. Good results on end grain may also be obtained with a sharp bench plane.

END-GRAIN RESISTANCE

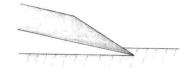

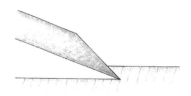

A low cutting angle and thin shaving (top) meet with less resistance than a high cutting angle and thick shaving (bottom).

COMPARATIVE CUTTING ANGLES

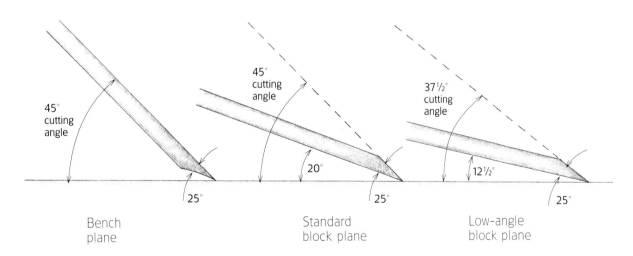

Tuning a block plane

The steps in tuning up a block plane for optimum performance are as follows:

1. Flatten the sole with the blade under tension but raised out of the way and the adjustable throat plate locked in place.

2. Check the bed for burrs and obstructions. Make sure the blade sits flat in the bed. File the bed where necessary.

3. If the edge of the adjustable throat plate is at all ragged at the throat, remove the plate and straighten the edge with a file to obtain uniform clearance at the throat.

4. Make sure the lever cap is straight and smooth along its front edge where it contacts the blade.

5. Flatten the back of the blade and then sharpen the edge (see the appendix on pp. 185-195). Be sure the cutting edge is reasonably square to the sides.

6. Many blades have a series of notches along the underside to engage one or two prongs on the depth-adjustment mechanism. As the blade shortens through repeated grinding and honing, higher notches come into play. When you install a blade, set the depth-adjustment wheel in the middle of its range and engage whichever notch puts the cutting edge closest to flush with the sole.

7. Adjust the cap screw so the pressure from the lever cap is heavy enough to keep the blade from moving in use yet light enough to permit easy adjustment.

Buying a block plane

The first question you face in buying a block plane is whether to get a standard model or a low-angle model. The difference isn't great enough to agonize about, so flip a coin if you must. That decided, weigh the following factors:

1. Adjustable throat. To get the most versatile performance from a block plane, an adjustable throat is a necessity. However, a plane that lacks this feature may still serve well for fine work in hardwoods if it has a small throat to begin with. In looking at planes with adjustable throats, be sure that the movable plate in the sole slides freely and tightens down flush. The plate is usually fastened with a knurled screw from above and adjusts forward and back by means of an eccentric lever.

2. Bed area. The more contact area there is where the blade seats in the bed of the plane, the less the blade is likely to chatter. Contact near the mouth is especially important. Compare block planes by removing their blades and looking at the extent of the flat-ground areas of the bed where the blade seats (see the drawing at left).

BLOCK-PLANE
BEDS

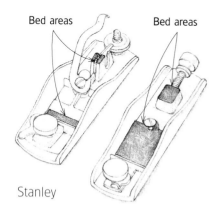

Bed areas   Bed areas

Stanley

Lie-Nielsen

3. Comfort in the hand. Because the block plane is so often used one-handed, it should fit your hand and present a comfortable, rounded surface to your palm. Be sure the lateral-adjustment lever tucks out of the way, if there is one.

4. Depth adjustment. A depth-adjustment mechanism greatly facilitates your ability to precisely control depth of cut.

5. Lateral adjustment. Although a lateral-adjustment lever is convenient, it is not indispensable. With a little practice, blade angle can be set by hand. Generally, standard block planes have lateral-adjustment levers and low-angle planes don't.

6. Cap design. The lever cap ought to be long enough to press the blade against the bed close to the mouth of the plane. Unfortunately, it is too short on many models. The most common tightening mechanism for the cap is a cam lever; a common alternative is a wheel-and-post mechanism. Both work.

CHISEL PLANES

The absence of a fore sole on a chisel plane exacerbates the blade's natural inclination to dive into wood. This makes it useless for ordinary surfacing. The chisel plane's major function is to extend a flat surface a short distance up to an obstruction, as when completing a rabbet in the corner of a frame. Other uses might include chipping glue off a flat surface and trimming plugs flush. All these jobs can be approached satisfactorily with other tools, making the chisel plane one of those specialized tools that you can readily do without but will find uses for if you have one.

Chisel-plane soles range in length from 6½ in. to 10 in. and in width from 1¾ in. to 2¼ in. The blade is bedded at a low angle (around 15°) with the bevel up. Tuning involves flattening the sole and the back of the blade, sharpening the blade, and making sure the bed is smooth. As noted on pgs. 124 and 126, some shoulder planes and bullnose planes convert into small chisel planes when their nose pieces are removed.

CIRCULAR PLANES

The circular plane, also known as a compass plane, has a flexible steel sole that adjusts to form convex and concave curves. While it is not commonly found in most woodshops, it is an effective tool for fairing curved surfaces.

Planing a curve of fixed radius is relatively easy, in that only one setting of the sole is required. To plane an irregular curve, the radius of the sole is adjusted in turn to match the flatter and more radical portions

CHISEL PLANE

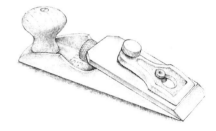

RECORD
CIRCULAR PLANE

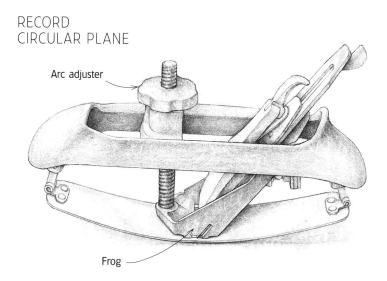

Arc adjuster

Frog

of the curve. All planing is done with the grain, which means that with concave curves you must often work from the ends to the center, while with convex curves you generally work from the center toward the ends. The circular plane is used in a straight line, not angled for a shearing cut the way a bench plane often is.

Tuning a circular plane

The blade of a circular plane is ground, sharpened, mounted, and adjusted like that of a bench plane. Since it has the same sort of chipbreaker, lever cap, depth adjustment, and lateral-adjustment lever, the principles of tuning are also the same, except there is no need to flatten the sole or worry about how the frog seats in the body. The arc of the sole is adjusted by means of a large, circular nut on top of the body, which must first be freed by turning a locking screw in the casting. The nut raises and lowers a threaded rod that connects to a platform on the front of the frog. The frog and sole are attached and move together.

Buying a circular plane

The first compass planes had wooden bodies of fixed arcs. As adjustable metal planes were developed, a few different mechanisms achieved popularity. You may find a variety of these on the used tool market. At this time, however, there is only one manufacturer of circular planes—Record, in England—so there's not a lot of comparison shopping involved in purchasing a new one.

COMBINATION PLANES

Once upon a time, separate wooden planes were required to make every shape and size of molding, groove, tongue, flute, and bead, so that an individual craftsman might have dozens and dozens of molding planes. In the late 19th century, metal planes were developed that combined many (sometimes all) of these functions in one tool. They had highly adjustable bodies and a multitude of interchangeable cutters. Their manufacturers christened them by various names, including Combination Plane, Multi-Plane, and Universal Plane.

Over the course of the 20th century, the router and shaper have rendered molding and combination planes virtually obsolete. Nonetheless, a few combination planes are still in production, while used ones have become collector's items. They are particularly useful in antique restoration since the marks a plane iron leaves on wood are more authentic than those of a router. Cutters can be custom-ground to match existing moldings. A typical combination plane is shown in the drawing at right.

Combination planes are most effective in soft and straight-grained woods. They have no throat or chipbreaker to prevent tearout, and the blade is insubstantially supported by the single skate that takes the place of an ordinary plane's bed and sole.

Combination planes are relatively complex instruments to set up and use. They come with instruction booklets detailed enough to make a strong mind go blank. A new combination plane may take anywhere from 18 to 40 separate cutters. Older ones, like the legendary Stanley 55, had as many as 96 different cutters and were incredibly versatile.

For detailed information about combination planes, see *Restoring, Tuning, & Using Classic Woodworking Tools* (Sterling, 1989), an excellent text by Michael Dunbar.

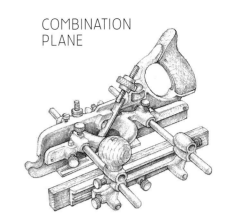

COMBINATION PLANE

EDGE-TRIMMING PLANES

These curious little planes have a vertically oriented blade set in a right-angled sole. Before the advent of chopsaws and table saws, edge-trimming planes may have fulfilled a real need in trimming the ends of boards square, shortening tongues, and so forth. Nowadays they are largely superfluous.

The blade of an edge-trimming plane is skewed to the sole and has a low bedding angle of about 12°, so it is particularly effective on end grain. But it also works well on long grain and plywood edges. At about 6 in. to 7 in. long, the sole is too short to accurately shoot any but the

EDGE-TRIMMING PLANE

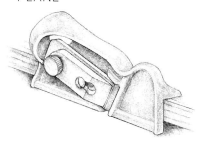

shortest edge joints. Edge-trimming planes come in left-handed and right-handed versions. Maximum width of cut is between ⅞ in. and 1 in. Blade depth and angle are set manually.

Tuning up a new edge-trimming plane is an uncomplicated procedure. Just flatten the back of the blade, sharpen it, and check the bed for obstructions. There is no need to flatten the sole, since it would be particularly difficult to keep the interior corner square while doing so. Instead, verify flatness and squareness at time of purchase, because that's as good as it's going to get.

When you plane across end grain, there is always the danger that the wood will split off at the far end. Tried-and-true methods for preventing splitting are to chamfer the far edge or to clamp a backing strip along the far edge, flush with the end of the board.

JAPANESE PLANES

Working with a Japanese plane might be compared to playing the violin. The effect can be sublime, but achieving it demands assured craftsmanship from two people: the one who makes the instrument and the one who keeps it fine-tuned and plays it. Japanese planes are not for the casual user.

The body of a Japanese plane (called the *dai)* is usually a block of air-dried Japanese white or red oak. The value of the plane is in part determined by the dai: the straightness and orientation of its grain, how long it has been drying, its likely stability. The dai has no handles, and the plane is used on the pull stroke.

The tapered blade is bimetal and hollowed, like the Japanese chisels described on pp. 58-60. The blade self-wedges in tapered grooves cut in the walls of the dai. Planes with chipbreakers have pins across their gullets to hold the chipbreaker against the blade. Traditionally, most Japanese craftsmen worked in softwoods, so standard bench-plane irons are at lower cutting angles than those of Western planes, about 37° to

JAPANESE PLANE

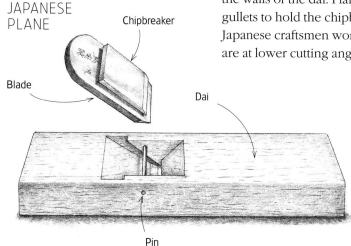

Chipbreaker

Blade

Dai

Pin

40°. If you work in hardwoods, be sure to ask the vendor for a plane meant for hardwoods. It will have a cutting angle somewhere between 43° and 45°.

Japanese planes are made in an immense array of styles, sizes, and shapes. There are functional equivalents for almost every Western plane, including bench, block, dovetail, molding, rabbet, and edge-trimming planes, as well as spokeshaves.

A new Japanese plane requires extensive preparation. The back of the blade must be flattened, the blade sharpened, the bed and grooves pared to accept the blade and to position it correctly, the sole flattened, the arrises of the sole beveled, the corners of the mouth pared out, and more. The plane's continued effectiveness demands renewed attention to these details throughout its life.

Japanese planes are sold through a few specialty importers. Don't hesitate to ask the vendors for advice as to which plane will best fit your needs and experience. Just as you wouldn't begin violin lessons on a Stradivarius, it would be disrespectful to start out with the finest of Japanese planes.

For a thorough account of the use and tuning of Japanese planes, see Toshio Odate's book *Japanese Woodworking Tools: Their Tradition, Spirit, and Use* (The Taunton Press, 1984) and Henry Lanz's book *Japanese Woodworking Tools* (Sterling, 1985).

LOW-ANGLE PLANES

The low-angle plane is a longer version of a low-angle block plane; it has a bevel-up blade bedded at about 12°, no chipbreaker or frog, and a throat that adjusts by means of a sliding plate in the sole. At present, the only manufacturer of low-angle planes is Lie-Nielsen Toolworks. They make one model the size of a jack plane. The sole is 14 in. long; the blade is 2 in. wide and ³⁄₁₆ in. thick.

The low-angle plane is highly effective for work on end grain but also a pleasure to use on long grain. The solidity with which the thick blade is bedded, as well as its low angle, virtually eliminates chatter. The throat adjusts to the narrowest of settings. Taken together, these qualities give the low-angle plane excellent working qualities, particularly for fine surfacing. A low-angle plane is tuned like a block plane.

LOW-ANGLE PLANE

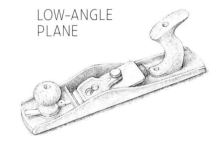

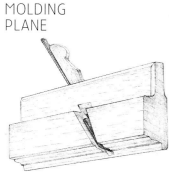

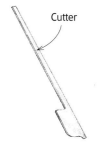

Cutter

MOLDING PLANES

Known in England as moulding planes, these are wooden planes, the soles and irons of which bear the inverse shape of some particular molding. The irons mount bevel down, and are held in place with wedges. Molding planes meant for hardwoods have their blades pitched particularly high, as much as 55° to 60°, while those for softwoods are lower.

Molding planes are about as central to contemporary furniture making as muzzle loaders are to hunting. They have been outmoded twice; the first time by the combination plane, the second by the router. While almost no molding planes are manufactured any more, they are still widely available in the second-hand and antique tool markets. Carpenters employ them for restoration work, and there are fine furniture makers who enjoy restoring and using them. If this interests you, you might read *Restoring, Tuning, & Using Classic Woodworking Tools* (Sterling, 1989) by Michael Dunbar.

RABBET, SHOULDER, AND BULLNOSE PLANES

As you look through tool catalogs and reference books, you'll find a certain amount of confusion in distinguishing among rabbet, shoulder, and bullnose planes. This is probably because their evolution was complex and prolific and their functions overlap. Today, relatively few of these planes remain in production. For purposes of description, these readily fall into three groups, to which I have assigned their historical names.

Rabbet planes

Rabbet planes cut rabbets, a task for which they are remarkably effective. If they are so scarce in the modern workshop, it is only because of the even greater convenience with which table saws and routers perform the same job.

The essential features of a rabbet plane are a narrow, high metal body with an integral cast handle; a bevel-down iron, the cutting edge of which extends the full width of the sole; a bedding angle of 45°; a fence; a depth stop; and a cutting spur. The purpose of the spur is to sever wood fibers ahead of the blade when working across the grain to prevent lifting and tearout along the edge. Often, rabbet planes have two iron locations, the forward of which is used for rabbeting into corners.

RABBET PLANE

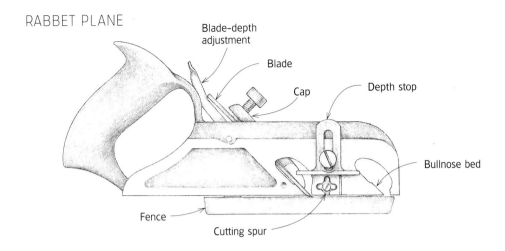

Blade-depth adjustment

Blade

Cap

Depth stop

Bullnose bed

Fence

Cutting spur

The standard rabbet planes made today have soles about 1½ in. wide and 8½ in. long. The sole and side of the plane should be square to each other. If they aren't, you have three choices. The best alternative is not to purchase the plane in the first place. Second best is to pay a machinist to mill the sole square. Last choice is to go ahead and use the plane anyway. It will work, but not as satisfactorily as it could.

Tuning a rabbet plane

The steps in tuning a rabbet plane are as follows (step 1 is optional):

1. Grind a slight taper up the right-hand side of the blade (the side against the work). This allows you to adjust the blade laterally without the side extending beyond the cutting edge, which could happen if the cutting edge hasn't been honed perfectly square across in the first place.

2. Flatten the back of the blade and sharpen it. Keep the cutting edge square to the left-hand side of the blade, which you haven't tapered.

3. Flatten the sole.

4. Check both beds to be sure they are cleanly milled and the blade sits flat upon them.

5. File the bottom edge of the cap, if necessary, so it presses cleanly and evenly upon the blade.

6. Lightly relieve the edges of the sole with sandpaper, because they will be quite sharp from flattening. Also sand off any burrs along the edges of the fence and depth stop, since they can scratch the work.

7. Sharpen one of the three spurs on the cutting wheel to a knife-like edge, using a file (or grinder) and honing stones. Usually the spur must be shortened to protrude only a little farther below the sole than the blade will. The outside of the spur is flattened like the back of a chisel. The bevel goes on the inside, toward the body of the plane.

How to use a rabbet plane

To use a rabbet plane, insert the sharpened iron so the right-hand corner of the cutting edge is flush with the side of the plane and the cutting edge itself is parallel with the sole. (In practice, the blade often protrudes a minuscule amount beyond the side of the plane, which is a lesser evil than having it shy of the edge.) Set the blade depth to take a fine, even shaving on a piece of scrap wood. Then set the plane's fence and depth stop to the dimensions of the desired rabbet. Finally, start planing with the fence flat against the work. If you plane deeper at the far end to start with and work your way back, it increases the likelihood that you'll be working with the grain. Plane almost to the full depth of the rabbet with a series of moderate shavings, and then finish with light passes to minimize tearout. Engage the cutting spur only when planing across the grain.

Shoulder planes

The bodies of shoulder planes are relatively tall and narrow; in place of handles, their tops curve to meet the hand. The T-shaped blade is the full width of the sole and beds like that of a block plane: bevel up at an angle of about 15°, so it is supported close to the cutting edge.

Shoulder planes are wonderful tools for fine trimming, particularly across end grain, as when truing up tenon shoulders. They also work well across long grain such as you encounter when fitting tenon cheeks, and they can be used to clean up rabbets. Some shoulder planes have fixed mouths, others are adjustable. In either case, the throat is properly set quite narrow for fine trim work, often to the thickness of a shaving.

Most shoulder planes made today are of all-metal construction with screw-adjusted depth controls and caps. Those with adjustable throats take several forms, as exemplified in the drawing at left. On the Record 73, the entire sole forward of the iron adjusts by means of a locking screw above the nose of the plane and an adjustment screw in the front of the plane. The Clifton 3110 has long and short detachable noses, so it can work as a shoulder plane or a bullnose plane. It can also be used as a chisel plane by leaving off both noses. Throat size is adjusted by inserting or removing shims between the body and the nose. The Stanley 93's nose detaches to leave a chisel plane behind. The throat is adjusted by sliding the nose casting over the rear part of the body.

The sizes of the shoulder planes currently on the market range in width from ½ to 1⅛ in. and in length from 5¼ in. to 8 in. As a general rule, a larger, heftier plane is preferable, even for small work. This may seem surprising, but greater weight and length minimize chatter and offer more precise control of the tool. The largest shoulder plane made by Stanley

SHOULDER PLANES

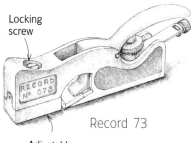

Locking screw

Record 73

Adjustable sole

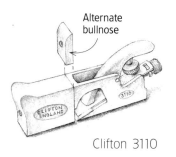

Alternate bullnose

Clifton 3110

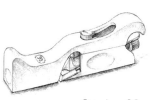

Stanley 93

and Record, the 73, was taken out of production a couple of years ago, but it is such a fine tool that we can only hope it will reappear before too many years pass.

It is important that the sole of a shoulder plane be square to the sides. Don't buy one that isn't. If you need to square the sole of an older shoulder plane, take it to a machinist, but ask him to mill off as little metal as possible to avoid unnecessarily enlarging the throat.

Tuning a shoulder plane

To tune a shoulder plane for optimum performance, do as follows:

1. The blade of a new plane may be too wide, in which case you should carefully grind it narrower, perhaps on a stationary disc sander. It should only barely protrude beyond the sides of the mouth when centered. One option is to grind a slight taper up both sides of the blade to give you a little leeway for lateral adjustment if the cutting edge isn't honed exactly square across. (Note that it is easier to determine the squareness of the cutting edge if you leave the sides of the blade straight.)

2. Flatten the back of the blade, and then sharpen the cutting edge, keeping it square to the length.

3. Flatten the sole with the plane assembled and the blade raised but under tension.

4. Check to see that the bed is cleanly milled and the blade sits flat upon it. File if necessary.

5. Lightly relieve the edges of the sole with sandpaper, since they will be quite sharp from flattening.

6. If your shoulder plane has an adjustable mouth, be sure you can get the throat as thin as a piece of paper. If not, try to make the necessary adjustments. This may be as simple as filing down a stop pin or as complex as having an intersecting face machined.

To adjust the blade depth of a shoulder plane, slack off pressure from the cap just enough to let the blade slide freely, then retighten.

Bullnose planes

The defining feature of a bullnose plane is the location of the blade, which has at most ½ in. of sole in front of it. A bullnose plane's primary purpose is to work close into corners. Its short nose is not optimal for normal surfacing of hardwoods. Bullnose planes are generally about 1 in. to 1⅛ in. wide and 4 in. long. Their small size makes them convenient tools for on-the-job trimming and fitting.

BULLNOSE
PLANE

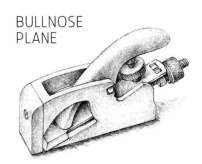

Most bullnose planes have bevel-up blades bedded at relatively low angles (about 20°), like standard block planes. But others have the blades installed bevel down, at the higher angles associated with bench planes. The cutting angles of the two are equivalent, but bevel-up blades are supported by the bed right up to the throat, which minimizes chatter. Some bullnose-plane bodies have removable front sections that transform them into chisel planes.

To tune up a bullnose plane, follow the procedures given for shoulder planes on p. 125.

Buying rabbet, shoulder, and bullnose planes

The most essential of these three planes in the modern woodshop is the shoulder plane, and I recommend buying the largest, heftiest you can find. With a good shoulder plane, you won't find much use for a bullnose plane. The rabbet plane is only for the craftsman particularly attracted to this peaceful method of making rabbets.

When purchasing any of these planes, don't rely on the name given to the tool by the vendor or manufacturer. You will find shoulder planes described as rabbet, shoulder rabbet, or trim planes, for example. Look at the design of the plane to understand what it is meant to do.

ROUTER PLANES

The primary function of the router plane is to lower a cross-grain groove or recess to uniform depth. It can also make a new cross-grain groove if the sides have first been established with a saw. Traditionally, the router plane was called "the old woman's tooth" in England.

ROUTER
PLANES

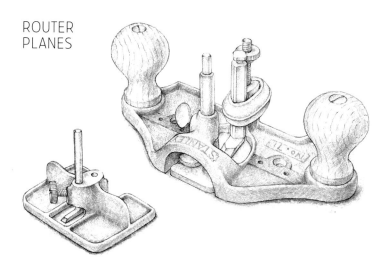

Router planes have L-shaped blades that extend through platformlike bodies. Although they come in many sizes and shapes, two are most commonly mass-produced. The sole of the smaller one measures 2 in. by 3 in. The blade is ¼ in. wide, square-edged, and manually adjusted. The larger-size router plane has a sole about 7 in. wide by 3½ in. long. Two of its three cutters are square-edged, measuring ¼ in. and ½ in. in width, respectively. The other cutter has a ½-in.-wide spear point; it approaches wood with a shearing cut for a smoother finish. Blade height is controlled with a screw-feed mechanism.

The blades of these router planes can be turned 180°. In one direction there is a toe in front of the blade. The other side is open for bullnose work. When clearing waste out of a cross-grain groove, it is best to remove the bulk with a chisel after the sides have been sawn and to reserve the router plane for smoothing out the bottom. For working in grooves that run with the grain, a shoulder plane would be preferable since it is far better engineered to avoid tearout. If you must use a router plane, try to work with the grain and take light passes.

Tuning up a router plane is pretty straightforward, although honing the blade can be awkward. First, flatten the sole, and then flatten the bottom of the blade. Finish by honing the blade to a sharp edge. The L-shape of the blade prevents access of the bevel to a grinding wheel, so shaping of the bevel, when necessary, must be done on a stationary sander or a coarse honing stone. The recommended bevel angle is 35°.

SCRATCH STOCKS AND BEADING TOOLS

Scratch stocks and beading tools are used to make beads, reeds, reveals, flutes, grooves, and other decorative edges. They are ideal for working with the grain in hard and curly lumber since their 90° cutting edges preclude tearout. They are less than satisfactory for cross-grain work in all but the densest woods, nor do they work well on softwoods.

Scratch stocks and beading tools are often perceived as hybrids of scrapers and planes. On the one hand, they have cutters and soles like planes. On the other, their cutting edges are ground at 90° like those of

DECORATIVE EDGES

Bead

Reeds

Flute

hand scrapers. A further source of confusion is that scratch-stock blades are often made from scraper stock. Nonetheless, it is most accurate to think of scratch stocks and beading tools as molding planes with 90° cutting edges.

Beading tools are manufactured with wood or metal bodies and interchangeable cutters capable of creating a wide variety of shapes. Scratch stocks are shopmade with wooden bodies and can hold an infinite variety of blade sizes and shapes. Both tools have limited application in a time when the router is the single most popular woodworking tool. They are slow cutting, less precise, and don't work well across the grain or on softwoods. They have two great advantages, though. One is the ease with which they allow you to create custom moldings and edges. The other is their ability to work on surfaces that curve in three dimensions, where a router base would have no purchase. An example would be a bead that sweeps up a French Provincial leg and around to the apron.

There are only a few beading tools in production (available through woodworking specialty stores and catalogs). One of the more popular is Lie-Nielsen's version of the classic Stanley No. 66, shown in the drawing at left. It has a bronze body shaped much like that of a spokeshave and two fences, one straight, the other curved to track on concave edges. The sole is 1¼ in. front to back and 4¼ in. side to side. The cutters, which are ⅝ in. wide and about 1/16 in. thick, come shaped for beading, reeding, fluting, and routing ⅛-in. and ¼-in. grooves. Blank cutters are included for making custom shapes. The blade inclines forward at 70° above horizontal, and the tool may be pushed or turned around and pulled.

There is no tune-up required for the Lie-Nielsen beading tool, other than sharpening the cutters as explained on the facing page. To install a cutter you slide it in place and tighten a knurled bolt, which pulls the holder tight. Then you set the fence and you're ready to work. However, the beading tool takes getting used to. It cuts slowly and is somewhat capricious, because the fence tends to slip sideways under moderate pressure. The normal process is to take incremental passes with only moderate downward pressure and little side pressure against the fence. Smaller cutters can be set to final depth from the beginning, but it's a good idea to set larger cutters for a partial cut and then lower them as you progress.

Scratch stocks offer more versatility in blade shape and size than manufactured tools. Commonly, their blades are made from old sawblades, scrapers, and such. Thickness is generally an advantage, because it averts bending and provides a heat sink to keep the tip of the cutter from overheating. The blade is ground or filed to the negative of the desired shape.

BEADING
TOOL

A typical scratch stock is made from a single piece of wood with a saw kerf in which the blade is inserted, a couple of bolts to pinch it tight, a sole that is convex across its width, and a fixed fence. The scratch stock shown in the drawing at right, designed by furniture maker Stephen Proctor, is made for beading. The distance from the cutter to the fence is adjusted by moving the cutter, but you can also make scratch stocks with adjustable fences. The convex sole allows you to control depth of cut with a rocking action. You begin with the scratch stock angled over so only the tip of the blade makes contact (see the drawing below) and end with the stock vertical and the blade at full depth.

SCRATCH
STOCK

This scratch stock is made for beading, but other cutter profiles can be introduced with equal success.

Sharpening scratch stocks and beading tools

Scratch-stock and beading-tool blades are most often filed and honed straight across, with no bevel angle, no burnishing, and no hook. This allows them to cut on both sides, so that beading-tool blades are reversible and scratch stocks can be worked in either direction as suits the grain.

New beading-tool blades can often be used right out of the box, but it's better to sharpen them properly from the start. This means flattening the two sides, beginning with coarse abrasives and ending with fine polishing stones. The edge is honed only when extreme wear makes it absolutely necessary; otherwise, the edge should be left alone since it can be difficult to maintain an exact profile.

USING A SCRATCH
STOCK

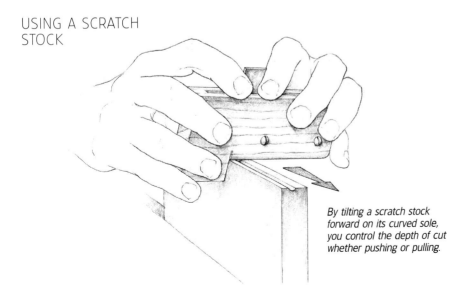

By tilting a scratch stock forward on its curved sole, you control the depth of cut whether pushing or pulling.

To make a scratch-stock blade, file or grind the negative of the shape you want with a 90° edge. Then polish the edge with slipstones or with fine abrasive paper wrapped around appropriately shaped pieces of wood. Finally, flatten the sides of the blade on successively finer sharpening stones. Even though the cutting edge is at 90°, it should be just as crisply polished as that of a plane iron. When the blade gets dull, rehone the sides on medium and fine honing stones until the cutting edge is restored. Leave the profile alone if you can.

SCRUB PLANES

The scrub plane is designed for rapid cross-grain removal of wood in the preliminary process of flattening a board by hand. In the modern shop, this usually occurs only when a board is too wide for the jointer, and only if the craftsman prefers handplaning to ripping the board into narrower sections, milling them, and then gluing them back together.

The sole of a scrub plane is narrow, measuring just under 2 in. wide by 9 in. or 10 in. long. Lightness is important, since the plane is used in a long series of short, repetitive strokes. The plane's mouth is wide, for rapid clearance of large chips. Scrub planes may have wood or metal bodies. Both work well, but at the moment only metal ones are commercially available in the United States.

The blade is bedded high (45°), bevel down, without a chipbreaker and, most important of all, has a convex cutting edge. A convex blade meets with less resistance than a straight-edged blade in removing a given volume of wood. Also, a convex blade planing across the grain efficiently severs the fibers it encounters, where a straight blade lifts and tears (see the drawing below).

CROSS-GRAIN
PLANING

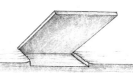

Convex cutting edge slices across wood fibers cleanly.

Straight cutting edge pries under fibers and lifts, leaving ragged, torn edges.

A scrub plane is not meant to be a precision instrument. It is for hogging off material. Nevertheless, the sole and blade back should be flattened, and the blade should be razor-sharp. It takes only a little practice to get the hang of sharpening a convex edge once you've learned how to sharpen a square-edged blade. The difference in grinding is that the iron is pivoted on the tool rest somewhat like a finger wagging back and forth. In honing, the cutting edge is rotated through its full arc in the course of every forward stroke. On waterstones, this must be done with unusually light pressure since they gouge so easily.

How to use a scrub plane

With its wide open throat and aggressive blade, the scrub plane is at its best working across the grain. Planing with the grain risks devastating tearout wherever the grain changes direction or a knot is encountered. A good technique for scrub planing is as follows:

1. Clamp the work lightly between bench dogs, convex side upward if it is cupped. (If the work isn't cupped, you can probably skip the scrub plane altogether.) The concave side sits flatter on the bench, and the convex side is easier to plane. Too much clamp pressure can distort a board's natural repose.

2. Set the blade about $1/16$ in. below the sole. Too little depth makes the job take too long; too heavy a set gouges the surface of the work unnecessarily. With practice, you'll be able to determine when to take more or less.

3. Start at one end of the board, planing straight across the grain. If the board is convex, remember there is no point in taking wood off the edges. They are already the lowest points, so why make them lower? Instead, start the stroke with the blade just inside the near edge and lift the plane off just before the blade reaches the far edge. Take contiguous strokes, one right next to the other, until you have worked your way to the far end of the board. Lift the plane on the return strokes to extend the life of the cutting edge.

4. Work your way back along the length of the board, again with contiguous strokes. But this time make them at a slight diagonal to prevent them from coinciding with the first series.

5. Keep working back and forth in this manner, using a slightly different stroke direction than that of the preceding row, until the convexity is gone. If some areas become flat before others, just plane the places that still need it. When the convexity is gone, the rest of the flattening process is usually done with bench planes.

It is possible to do the work of a scrub plane with a smooth or jack plane by opening up the throat, grinding the blade convex, and setting the chipbreaker away from the cutting edge. However, the scrub plane is better designed to the job.

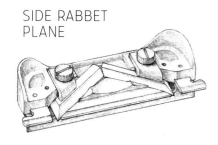

SIDE RABBET
PLANE

SIDE RABBET PLANES

In the woodshop, this specialized plane is meant for trimming the walls of rabbets, dadoes, and grooves that need widening. It is also useful in carpentry for tasks such as trimming rabbets on door jambs.

The sole of a side rabbet plane is vertical rather than horizontal, and thin enough to slip into a ⅛-in. groove. Two skew blades enable the plane to cut either way. The blades are set at extremely low angles, so they are effective on end grain as well as on edge grain. An adjustable stop regulates depth of cut to a maximum of ½ in. Removable skates enable the plane to work into corners where there is no obstruction above the height of the fence.

Tuning a side rabbet plane

To be more than a rough carpentry tool when it comes out of the box, a side rabbet plane often requires extensive tuning. The procedure is as follows:

1. Remove the fence, blades, blade holders, and skates from the body of the plane.

2. File the milled grooves in the body where the skates seat to remove any roughness. Flatten the rough edges and undersides of the skates themselves on sandpaper mounted on glass or on a coarse-to-medium diamond stone or oilstone. The skates should fit snugly into the body yet be easily removable. They should align closely with the plane of the sole.

3. Remount the skates and flatten the entire sole of the plane, which includes the skates. Attaching a wooden block on top of the sole with double-faced tape makes it easier to apply pressure where it's needed.

4. File the blade beds lightly to remove any roughness. On my new Stanley plane, just about every surface that should have been milled clean was gunked up with a heavy surface chroming.

5. Flatten the backs of the blades, grind their bevels, and sharpen them. It is important to retain the blades' original skew angle, so work carefully.

6. Round the edges of the fence with sandpaper to prevent it from marring the work.

7. Remount the blades and fence.

8. Set both blades to take thin shavings. If the lower edge of the sole extends down farther than the tips of the blades, it must be ground back. Otherwise, it acts as a fence to limit their penetration. A stationary disc sander is a good tool for shortening the sole, but you can use a file if necessary.

In actual use, it's best to set just one blade to cut at a time. The other should be raised out of range, or it will hold the sole off the work.

SPOKESHAVES

As its name implies, the spokeshave is particularly adept at making spindles and rounding edges. It is also indispensable for fairing and cleaning up surfaces that curve along their lengths.

The structure of the spokeshave is unique among planes. Two handles extend horizontally from the sides of a sole that is wider across than it is front to back. A typical metal spokeshave has a 2⅛-in.-wide blade set in a sole 2½ in. to 3 in. wide, while the distance from toe to heel is only ⅞ in. Spokeshaves can be used on the push stroke or the pull stroke.

Spokeshaves commonly come with four different sole configurations: flat, rounded front to back, and concave or convex along the cutting edge. The flat-soled spokeshave is by far the most popular and is the only spokeshave many woodworkers ever use. It is great for rounding edges and fairing surfaces that are moderately concave along their length. It can smooth convex curves, too, but so can a block plane to equal or better effect. In working a concave surface, a flat-bottomed spokeshave rides on

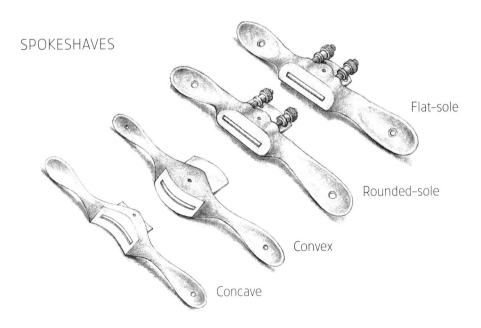

SPOKESHAVES

Flat-sole

Rounded-sole

Convex

Concave

the toe and heel of the sole. The limit to the tool's effectiveness is that, as the blade extends further from the sole to reach into more severe curves, it is more likely to chatter.

The rounded-sole spokeshave is for concave surfaces that are too extreme for a flat sole to handle. The curve of the wood should have a tighter radius than the sole, or the spokeshave will ride uncontrollably on the blade.

Convex-soled spokeshaves don't seem to be good for much of anything. Their rumored application is for scooping chair seats, but there are more effective tools. Concave spokeshaves, on the other hand, are particularly good for spindle making. They remove wood more efficiently and leave a softer edge than a flat-soled spokeshave can. Unfortunately, they are also considerably more trouble to sharpen, so the choice becomes a trade-off.

There are important structural differences between the original wooden spokeshaves and the all-metal ones that dominate the market today. Wooden soles extend to the front of the blade only, whereas metal soles enclose the blade completely. Also, the cutting angle of a wooden spokeshave is extremely low. With the blade set almost parallel to the sole, bevel up, the cutting angle can be anywhere in the range of 15° to 30°, depending on the bevel angle. A metal spokeshave has a cutting angle of 40° with the blade installed bevel down. These differences make for distinctly different cutting actions. The wooden spokeshave is great for finishing end-grain surfaces and for roughing out greenwood spindles. The more extensive sole of a metal spokeshave offers better control for fairing curves, while the cutting angle and the chipbreaking action of the cap make it theoretically better for smoothing hardwoods.

Spokeshaves with mechanical blade-depth adjusters are often preferable to those without. It is easy to set their blades precisely, and the adjusting nuts resist blade movement once set. On the other hand, there are serious spokeshave users who prefer manually adjusted blades because they fit more comfortably in the palm for one-handed work.

On the standard metal spokeshaves made by Record and Stanley, the depth adjusters are knurled nuts that engage slots on both sides of the blade. Since they work independently, the adjusters also control the blade's lateral angle. The cap must be loosened slightly to raise or lower the blade and then be retightened. The depth-adjusting nuts should be screwed down to take up any slack in the slots. This prevents the blade from retreating in use.

Some metal spokeshaves are made with adjustable mouths. These are of dubious value, especially as changing the throat size also seems to change the elevation of the toe. However, it is also true that the fixed mouths of most metal spokeshaves are excessively wide where a finish

WOODEN
SPOKESHAVE

surface is desired. This problem can be addressed in several ways. One is to install a thicker aftermarket blade. Another solution, courtesy of chairmaker Brian Boggs, is to wax the blade heavily, and then lay a bead of epoxy along the bed of the spokeshave right above the mouth and press the blade in just enough to establish the desired throat width. When the epoxy sets, the wax allows the blade to be removed and you have a flat bed with a small throat.

Tuning a spokeshave

Ninety-nine percent of the spokeshaves sold today are the metal-bodied type. Tuning them well will reduce chatter, improve their overall effectiveness, and make working with them more enjoyable. The steps in a full tune-up are given below. Few woodworkers take the time to implement them all, but the more you do, the better your spokeshave will work. An ordinary spokeshave with a firmly seated blade, small throat, and close-set chipbreaker works like a whole different tool.

1. Level the sole of a flat-bottomed spokeshave as you would that of any plane (see p. 104).

2. Install a thicker, aftermarket blade to reduce chatter and give the tool a smaller throat. These are available through a number of sources. If the throat becomes too small, the forward edge of the mouth can be opened with a file.

3. Flatten the back of the blade. In order to avoid sanding your fingers, you might double-stick tape a small block of wood on top to serve as a handle.

4. Grind and hone the cutting edge, as you would any plane iron. Honing a slight convexity onto the cutting edge gives you the greatest control of the cut (see p. 105).

SPOKESHAVE

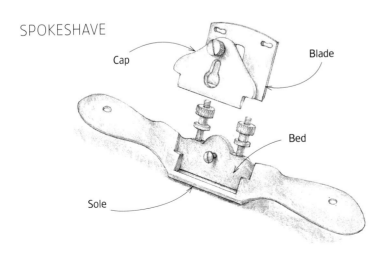

Cap

Blade

Bed

Sole

SPOKESHAVE
CAP

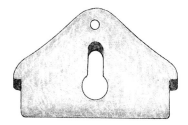

By filing away the indicated parts of a spokeshave's cap, you can lower it close to the cutting edge so it also serves as a chipbreaker.

5. Make sure the blade rests snugly against the bed, particularly at the mouth. If necessary, flatten the bed with a file. Work carefully—the soft iron of a spokeshave body files away quickly. You may also find it necessary to flatten the "top" of the blade, which is down against the bed of the spokeshave, for a good fit.

6. The lower edge of the cap should exert even pressure against the blade. Flatten the bottom of the cap, if necessary. Its front edge should meet the blade in a clean, sharp line all the way across.

7. On most spokeshaves, the cap is set too far back from the cutting edge. Sometimes you can lower the cap by lengthening the machined slot in its center with a round file and shortening the side projections with a mill file. If the cap drops to within $1/64$ in. or so of the cutting edge, it becomes a chipbreaker and reduces tearout significantly.

How to use a spokeshave

The spokeshave is often used to finish a spindle roughed out with a drawknife, but it can also make a spindle directly from square stock. Usually the work is held horizontal in a shaving horse or table-mounted vise. A good trick is to set the blade deeper to one side, shallower on the other. This allows you to go from rough removal to fine smoothing and back without constantly resetting the iron.

When smoothing a concave surface such as the inside of a curved leg, a shearing cut offers several advantages. With the blade at an angle to its line of travel the cutting angle is lower and the blade has more of a slicing action, so there is less resistance and less chatter. Also, the more you hold the spokeshave at an angle, the longer the effective sole becomes, which improves its function as a reference for making a fair curve. Elongating the sole also has the effect of lifting the blade farther off a concave surface. This trick can be used to advantage in controlling depth of cut as you move between gradual and steeper sections of an irregular curve.

BUYING PLANES

Some of the planes listed in this chapter are universally considered essential equipment in the workshop, others are rarities. The first planes I would suggest acquiring are a jack plane and a block plane. Additionally, I wouldn't want to be without a flat-soled spokeshave, a shoulder plane, and a jointer plane, but wait to acquire these until you have mastered the first two and are sure they fit your methods of work. In my shop, a scrub plane is also indispensable because I handplane wide boards.

At the other end of the scale are planes most woodworkers live without. These include combination planes, molding planes, edge-trimming planes, chisel planes, convex-soled spokeshaves, and rabbet planes. In acquiring new planes, a good policy is to buy a particular tool only when it meets a specific need that has arisen in your work.

At present, the minimum standard of acceptable quality in planes is set by the premium product lines of two British companies, Stanley and Record. But the best planes available today are being manufactured by a number of smaller companies, none of which yet offers a complete product line. The smaller companies' products tend to be more expensive, reflecting the attention they give to accurate machining of parts and top-quality materials. Their planes are also a joy to use. This is not to say you need to buy the most expensive tool every time. A standard $70 jack plane, properly tuned up, does good work. A $280 jack plane offers only marginal, not fourfold, improvement.

The other way to acquire a plane is to buy it used. A mystique has grown around American-made Stanley planes from before 1960, particularly those made before World War II. In the past few years I have bought and reconditioned several of these older planes, skeptically at first, but I have to admit there is something special about them. Point for point, they don't look much different from the planes still being made in England to the same patterns. Nonetheless, the accretion of detail in the quality of castings, machining, handle shaping, and finish is such that they are sweeter tools.

Better-quality new planes are available primarily through woodworking specialty stores and catalogs. Anytime you are buying a plane, inspect it with a reliable straightedge to make sure the sole and back of the blade are already reasonably flat. This will reduce your lapping time by hours. If you are acquiring a bench plane, remove the frog and examine the machining of the bed, as explained on p. 108. If you are buying a used plane, make sure that all of the parts are present and in good repair; otherwise, it's usually not worth the bother. Sometimes I find it worthwhile to pay a machinist to mill the sole of a used plane flat, when all the other parts are in good condition.

SAWING

Woodworker/philosopher David Pye perceived a dichotomy between the "workmanship of risk" and the "workmanship of certainty." Sawing by hand typifies the workmanship of risk, where the quality of result flows entirely from the skill of the craftsman and a moment's lapse can sometimes ruin hours or days of work. Sawing with machinery exemplifies the workmanship of certainty. Once the tooling is properly set up, the result can be guaranteed.

You might ask, "What is compelling about the workmanship of risk?" In many situations the answer may be "nothing." There are woodworking tasks, such as milling lumber and cutting production joinery, that machinery does quicker, better, and far less strenuously. On the other hand, there are times when handwork rules, especially when building one-of-a-kind pieces. Examples would be cutting compound-angle tenons and joining nonrectilinear pieces in general. In addition, the workmanship of risk is exciting, intimate, and gratifying compared to the rote of machine operation.

Unfortunately, many of us are so wedded to our table saws, chop-saws, jigsaws, circular saws, radial-arm saws, scrollsaws, and bandsaws that we never invest enough time to gain confidence with dovetail saws, panel saws, coping saws, and the other useful tools described in the pages that follow.

Structurally, hand-powered saws fall into three major divisions: handsaws, frame saws, and backsaws, all of which are commonly referred to as "handsaws." Japanese saws, which are listed under a separate heading, include both handsaws and backsaws.

Most Western saws cut on the push stroke, while Japanese saws cut on the pull stroke. The push stroke unleashes more power, but the pull stroke keeps the blade in tension so it can't buckle. Accordingly, Western sawblades tend to be thicker and more ductile—able to flex without cracking—while Japanese saws have thinner blades of harder temper.

Traditionally, saw teeth are patterned in two ways: for cutting across wood grain or for ripping with it. Crosscut teeth are set to alternate sides and sharpened to points that slice across wood fibers like a succession of fierce knives. They make two parallel cuts from between which the sawdust falls out to leave a kerf. Rip teeth also have an alternate set, but they are filed straight across to remove wood like a train of tiny chisels taking shavings. Rip teeth are hopeless for cutting cross-grain, but a crosscut saw will rip, albeit slowly.

The reason saw teeth are "set" (bent outward at the tips) is to create a kerf wider than the body of the blade to prevent it from binding. Better handsaws have their blades "taper-ground" to be thinner near the back and toe (see p. 151). Accordingly, their teeth require less set to prevent binding. Taper-ground saws leave a narrower kerf, so they move through wood with less effort.

Tooth size is described as "points per inch" (ppi) or "teeth per inch" (tpi). The number of points per inch always exceeds the number of teeth per inch by one. When there are fewer teeth per inch, they are generally

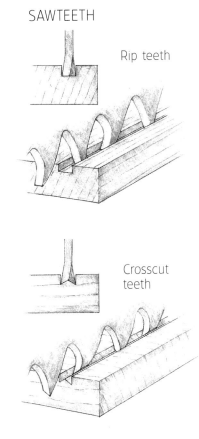

SAWTEETH

Rip teeth

Crosscut teeth

TOOTH SIZE

1 in.   1 in.

6 points per inch = 5 teeth per inch

For any given saw, the number of points per inch exceeds the number of teeth per inch by one.

larger, with stronger set and deeper gullets in between for efficient clearing of waste. Close-packed teeth are slower cutting but leave a finer, cleaner kerf.

As a general rule, handsaws and backsaws straight from the factory don't cut as well as they will from the hands of a skilled saw sharpener. This chapter ends with a section covering the general principles of saw sharpening.

BACKSAWS

A backsaw has a steel or brass spine folded along the back of its blade. The blade is parallel-sided, without taper. The stiffening action of the spine makes it possible to use thinner, harder steel than that found in handsaws. The result is a finer-cutting saw with more teeth per inch and less set, perfect for cutting joints such as tenons and dovetails.

Depending on the manufacturer, backsaw teeth may be sharpened for crosscutting, for ripping, or in a modified pattern meant both to crosscut and to rip. There are a variety of such patterns. Whereas a normal rip tooth has anywhere from 0° to 5° negative pitch, a modified pattern might have a 15° negative pitch.

Backsaws are categorized according to size. The smallest go by names such as "blitz" and "slotting," dovetail saws occupy the middle ground, and, for freehand use, tenon saws are the largest. The true behemoths of the backsaw world, though, are miter saws built for use in miter boxes.

BLITZ SAW

Blitz and slotting saws

Blitz saws were originally developed for use by jewelers on soft metals and plastics but have been adopted into some woodshops for extra fine work. Typically, their blades are only about 0.008 in. thick and 6½ in. long, with a 1-in. depth of cut. The tiny teeth (about 33 tpi) are too slow-cutting to be practical for most joinery. They come into their own when extremely precise work is called for on a miniature scale, such as cutting tiny dovetails into a jewelry-box drawer. Slotting saws are small backsaws about 6 in. long, with around 25 tpi and a 0.016 in. thick blade.

Saws with such tiny teeth are not considered sharpenable. They should be used just as they come from the factory and replaced when dull.

Dovetail saws

The dovetail saw is the most important backsaw in the furniture workshop. With a blade length normally in the range of 6 in. to 10 in. and a tooth count of 14 tpi to 22 tpi, it is just the right size for table, chair, and small carcase joinery.

Often, dovetail saws are manufactured with a crosscut tooth pattern. This works great for tenon shoulders but poorly for the equally important work of sawing tenon cheeks and dovetails, both of which are rip cuts. Saws manufactured or subsequently resharpened to a modified pattern that enables them to crosscut and rip are preferable, though they do neither task as well as they might. A third possibility, for the truly committed, is to have two dovetail saws, one sharpened as a rip saw, the other as a crosscut.

The exact length and tooth count of a dovetail saw aren't critical. What matters most for controlled, accurate work are a thin kerf and minimal set. A thin kerf allows you to saw closely along knife and fine pencil lines without obliterating them. The amount of set matters because when the kerf is substantially wider than the thickness of the blade, the blade tends to wobble around like a small boat in a heavy sea. It requires constant correction to stay on course. By way of contrast, a saw that fits into its kerf with little leeway wants to track without deviation. If you start the cut straight and true, the saw does the rest. In fact, having a saw with too restrictive a kerf can be a problem for beginners, because there isn't enough play in the cut to redress a crooked start.

Dovetail saws are available with three types of handles: closed, open, and turned. An open handle is sometimes called a "pistol-grip." A saw with a turned handle is known as a "gent's saw" and tends to have a narrower blade than the others. Every woodworker has his preference, but I find that all handle types work well. Don't be afraid to reshape a saw handle to make it more comfortable.

DOVETAIL SAW

DOVETAIL-SAW GRIPS

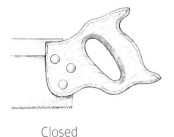
Closed

Open

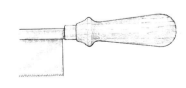
Gent's

OFFSET
DOVETAIL
SAW

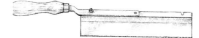

There is a version of the gent's saw that has an offset handle and blade, which allows you to saw close to a broad surface without interference from your hand or the spine of the saw, as might be desirable when trimming a through tenon flush to a surface. It is a special-purpose saw only, not suited for cutting most joinery. The offset handle puts your arm out of alignment with the blade and makes the saw difficult to control.

Buying a dovetail saw

When buying a new dovetail saw, look for one with a fairly thin blade, preferably no thicker than 0.030 in. (thirty thousandths of an inch). The general range of dovetail saws extends from 0.020 in. all the way up to 0.050 in. The number of teeth per inch can be anywhere from 14 to 22. But it's not the tooth count that matters so much as their being sharp and properly set. There's nothing wrong with starting with one of the inexpensive gent's saws that sell for as little as $15 if it meets these criteria.

Tuning a dovetail saw

Almost every new dovetail saw has its teeth set too aggressively for fine work in hardwoods. Not only is the kerf too wide, but also the teeth may catch and stutter. The first thing to do with a saw like this is to reduce the kerf. The steps are as follows:

1. Set a piece of scrap hardwood horizontal in a vise and make a test cut at least 1 in. deep across the grain (see the drawing below). To check for drift, hold the saw handle lightly so you won't impart any twist to the stroke. Usually a saw will cut straight, but if it pulls toward one side it means that the teeth on that side are sharper or more strongly set. Whether or not the cut is square to the edge doesn't matter, you just want to let the saw drift along in its own kerf.

CHECKING THE KERF

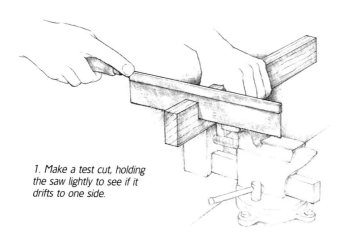

1. Make a test cut, holding the saw lightly to see if it drifts to one side.

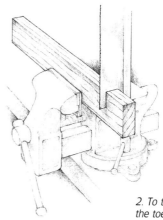

2. To test for wiggle, insert the toe of the blade into the kerf.

2. Stand the sawblade on end in the kerf to see how much wiggle room it has (see the bottom right drawing on the facing page). The ideal is not much more space than it takes to prevent the blade from binding.

3. If there is slop in the kerf, lay the blade on a clean piece of medium-density fiberboard (MDF) or other flat material with the spine hanging over the edge. This is easy to do with a gent's saw, but an enclosed or open handle must be removed in order to perform the next step properly. To do so, take out the bolts that go through the handle and slide it off.

4. Put some honing oil or kerosene on an India stone, hold it flat on the blade, and run it gently over the teeth (see the drawing at right). Apply consistent pressure from heel to toe. Flip the saw and do the same to the other side, treating both sides equally. Take no more than two strokes per side on this first round. If a saw is cutting crooked, take the second stroke only on the more aggressive side.

5. Make a new test cut (replacing the handle first, if you have removed it). The saw will run more smoothly, and its kerf will be detectably thinner than the original. Fit the nose of the blade into the new kerf and check for wiggle again.

6. Repeat step 4 as necessary, with only one stroke of the honing stone per side, until the kerf just exceeds the thickness of the blade. Don't overdo it or the saw will bind. Your test piece will have a progression of increasingly fine kerfs sawn along its edge as a running record of the process. The final result will be a blade that cuts easier and truer.

How to use a dovetail saw

A well-tuned dovetail saw will cleave to a straight line as if it had a mind of its own. All it needs are accurately marked lines to follow and a proper send-off. To start a cut, place your free thumb against the side of the blade near the point where it contacts the wood and begin with a backstroke or two to establish the location of the kerf. Then saw forward, and you're off and running.

The proper way to hold a backsaw is with a light grip, no harder than you would be willing to hold an egg. A white-knuckle grip is more likely to impart twist to the saw, since there is a natural tendency to rotate the wrist. The point is not to overpower the tool, but to "listen" with your hand.

Almost all the steerage way a saw has occurs as the teeth enter the wood. Where they exit, they are trapped within the walls of the kerf. This is the logic behind one traditional method of sawing shoulders to a line, which is as follows: Begin sawing at the far edge of the board with the saw pointed downward, just enough to establish a kerf (see the drawing on p. 144); then extend the kerf along the entire top shoulder by lowering the handle to the horizontal; finally, bring the saw down the near face of the board on an increasing diagonal as if it were hinged in the shallow kerf at the far corner where it started. To saw the next side, rotate the

REDUCING THE TOOTH SET

To reduce the amount of set, run an oilstone lightly over both sides of the blade.

SAWING A SHOULDER

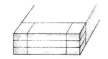

Mark out the location of the tenon.

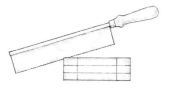

Begin sawing with a diagonal stroke at the far corner.

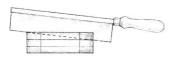

Lower the handle to horizontal and continue sawing down the near face until cutting any further would sever the tenon.

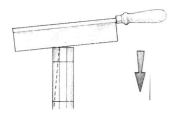

Rotate the board 90° and repeat the process.

wood away from you 90° and repeat. Now there is a horizontal kerf to guide the saw. Once there are kerfs on all fours sides, it is foolproof to complete the job by sawing in horizontally from each face.

Just for the record, I saw shoulders somewhat differently. I prefer to start on the near corner with an upward diagonal stroke and visually track the saw's progress along the vertical and horizontal faces simultaneously. Otherwise, I follow the same process of rotation.

Miter saws and miter boxes

Miter saws are manufactured for use in miter boxes. Their purpose is to make accurate, guided angle cuts. The length of miter-saw blades varies from 14 in. to 30 in., with widths up to 6 in. They are sharpened for crosscut work, with the larger saws having about 12 teeth per inch.

Before the advent of the power miter saw, miter boxes were a standard part of the carpenter's and cabinetmaker's toolkit, particularly for on-site trim work. Now they are disappearing fast, replaced by more accurate and efficient electric descendants. Even before the power miter saw, though, miter boxes were not that popular among fine furniture makers. They are clumsy to use and generally lack the requisite accuracy for precision joinery. If the saw isn't sharpened perfectly, it tends to drift. Also, the guide systems are subject to play.

Not all miter boxes are built for use with backsaws. Some on the current market utilize frame saws instead. These suffer an additional problem, which is the exaggerated tendency of a spineless blade to wander, as evidenced by the drift of bandsaw blades.

Maintenance

The sharpening of a miter saw must be excellent. A blade that cuts more aggressively to one side ruins any hope of accuracy. Other than that, the working parts of the guide system and table should be oiled to prevent rust and allow for easy movement without slop. The blade itself should be lightly oiled or waxed from time to time.

MITER SAW

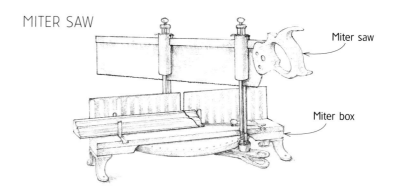

Miter saw

Miter box

Buying a miter box

Hardly anybody uses miter boxes any more, but if you want to acquire one, you might do best in terms of quality and price to look for an older one on the used tool market. The things to look for are a straight blade that is reasonably rust free, a guide system with absolutely no wobble or wiggle to it, a flat table and fence that are square to each other, and adjustable stops for locking the blade at precise angles. Adjustability is key, since factory-set positions are rarely perfect.

Tenon saws

Tenon saws normally have blades 10 in. to 16 in. long and 3 in. to 4 in. wide, with from 12 to 15 teeth per inch. Thickness can vary from about 0.024 in. up to a sturdy 0.050 in. Handles are closed-style. In furniture making, tenon saws are useful for cutting larger tenons such as you might find in doors and bed frames. They are also excellent for trim work in finish carpentry.

When selecting a tenon saw, consider that a thinner blade with more teeth per inch is likely to be more accurate, but also slower cutting. For fine work in hardwoods, the kerf size of a new tenon saw can be reduced by the same method given for dovetail saws (see pp. 142-143). However, a tenon saw that is to be used on softwoods needs a relatively aggressive set and widely spaced teeth. If you saw a lot of tenon cheeks, you'll probably want to refile the teeth of one tenon saw to a rip pattern and dedicate it to that purpose.

TENON SAW

FRAME SAWS

A frame saw consists of a thin blade, sometimes called a web, held in tension within a rigid structure of wood or metal. Contemporary frame saws vary quite a bit in scale, from a 5-in. fretsaw to a 2-ft. bowsaw. Historically, some frame saws had blades as much as 8 ft. long and 4 in. or 5 in. wide for resawing veneer.

Bowsaws

The bowsaw has a wooden frame consisting of two uprights (called cheeks) and a center bridge. The blade attaches across the bottom of the cheeks. At the top the cheeks are connected by a wire or cord, which tightens to put the blade in tension. Wire is shortened with a turnbuckle or eyebolt. Cord is wound with a toggle stick, which catches against the bridge to prevent unwinding.

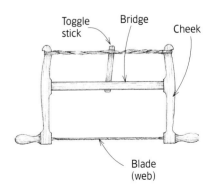

BOWSAW

Toggle stick   Bridge   Cheek

Blade (web)

In the British and American woodworking traditions, bowsaws were reserved for cutting curves—they were really just larger versions of the coping saw and fretsaw. In continental Europe, bowsaws were also outfitted with wide blades for cutting dovetails and other joinery. In today's workshop they are increasingly a rarity, displaced by the bandsaw and jigsaw for scroll work and by thinner-kerfed backsaws for hand-cut joinery.

Bowsaws may be used on the push stroke or the pull stroke. The blade can be turned to any angle by rotating the handles. Web lengths range from 12 in. to 27 in. Blades for scroll work can be as narrow as ⅜ in.; for straight sawing they go up to 1½ in. Scroll blades are sharpened to a crosscut pattern, while wider blades are available in both rip and crosscut patterns. Tooth size varies widely. At the low end is a long, wide blade with 4 tpi for coarse, straight sawing. At the fine end is a short, narrow blade with 16 tpi for curved work.

COPING SAW

INSTALLING A BLADE IN A COPING SAW

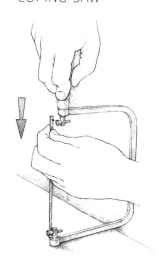

Coping saws

The coping saw has a springy metal frame that holds a narrow blade in tension. It is particularly useful for cutting small-radius curves, for removing the waste between dovetails, and for sawing wood from the interior of a form without passing through the circumference. This last task is done by inserting the blade though a drilled hole before securing it in the saw.

Coping saws work best with the blade oriented for the pull stroke, so it remains in tension. A normal coping saw takes a 6⅝-in. blade in a frame about 5 in. deep. Its versatility is enhanced by the blade's ability to turn to any angle within the frame. Coping-saw blades are disposable, with pins inserted through both ends for attachment. The number of teeth may vary from 10 to 28 tpi, but 14 or 15 tpi are good for general work in hardwoods. Because they are thin, the blades have a tendency to overheat, which can cause them to lose their edge or break. It is advisable to stop sawing once in a while to let the blade cool. You can also reduce friction by rubbing a little paraffin or paste wax on the blade.

To install a new blade in most coping saws, partially unscrew the handle to move the notched posts closer together. Then secure one end of the blade in either of the notches and force the ends of the frame together until you can slip the second pin into the other notch (see the drawing at left). Finally, turn the blade to the desired orientation and restore tension by screwing the handle on tight.

When buying a new coping saw, look for one that puts the blade in considerable tension. Some of those we see students bring to the school are so feeble that the blade practically sags.

FRETSAWS

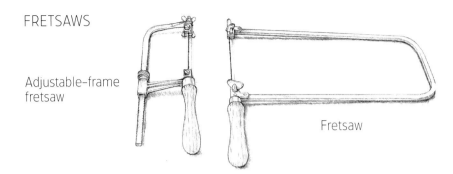

Adjustable-frame
fretsaw

Fretsaw

Fretsaws

A fretsaw is much like a coping saw with a deeper reach. One use is to
cut out shapes enclosed within the confines of a board, which is known
as "fretwork." Another is to cut veneer and other thin materials for
marquetry and inlay. Fretsaws currently on the market have frames up to
17 in. deep. Standard blades are 5 in. long. They have blank ends, which
are held in the saw by a clamp and thumbscrew or similar arrangement.
Unlike coping saws, the blades of fretsaws don't rotate within the frames.

A related saw, which woodworkers have borrowed from the jeweler's
trade, is called an "adjustable-frame fretsaw." It comes in a range of throat
depths, from 2¼ in. up to 8 in. Blades are held in clamp devices that can
be rotated to any angle within the frame. Tension is achieved by turning a
knurled nut to force the handle assembly farther down the frame. One
advantage of an adjustable-frame fretsaw is that when a blade snaps, as it
often does, the saw shortens to accept the remainder.

Fretsaw blades

For cutting solid wood, both types of fretsaw are fitted with blades much
like those of coping saws in thickness, width, and tooth count (14 to 32 tpi).
For cutting thinner wood, they take high-carbon-steel fretsaw blades
(Rc53 to Rc55), which are interchangeable with electric scrollsaw blades.

Woodcutting scrollsaw blades come in sizes from 2/0 (two-aught) to
12. (The progression, if all sizes were made, would be 2/0, 1/0, 0, 1, 2...,
12.) 2/0 is the smallest and most suitable for marquetry. It is 0.010 in. thick,
0.022 in. wide, and has 28 tpi. A 12 blade, by contrast, is 0.024 in. thick,
0.062 in. wide, with 9.5 tpi.

Scrollsaw blades come in five different tooth patterns. Skip tooth is
the most popular for electric scrollsaws and is also the best for fretsaws.
The other patterns are: reverse skip, where the teeth at the bottom are
reversed to cut upwards, so that both faces of the work saw cleanly;
double tooth, where there is a wide space between pairs of teeth;
precision ground, which have skip teeth that are ground instead of

FRETSAW-BLADE TEETH

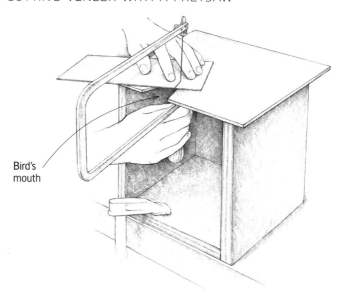

Regular teeth
(for metal cutting)

Skip teeth
(for wood cutting)

milled, making them sharper, cleaner cutting, longer lasting, and twice as expensive; and spiral, which cuts in all directions at once, so the work doesn't need to be rotated in order to saw curves. Spiral blades are relatively slow cutting and leave a rough finish. They are also the most difficult to control, since they cut even when you're backing up.

For fretsaw work in metal, ivory, and other thin, hard materials, jeweler's blades are preferable. Although they are made of the same high-carbon steel as scrollsaw blades, jeweler's blades are tempered harder (Rc60) and are more brittle as a result. They have a "regular" tooth pattern that is less effective on wood. Jeweler's blades come in lengths from 3 in. to 6½ in. They run considerably finer than scrollsaw blades, from 12 all the way down to 8/0, which has 96 tpi and is only 0.006 in. thick and 0.012 in. wide.

To choose the right blade, select one that will have at least two (and preferably, three) teeth in contact with the work at all times. For longevity, use the sturdiest blade that works. Obviously, a narrower blade will negotiate a tighter curve, but it will also be more fragile.

To cut veneer into irregular shapes for marquetry, the blade of a fretsaw is oriented for the pull stroke and used with a V-notched board called a bird's mouth. The procedure is to move the blade up and down near the point of the V, where the work is well supported. The blade remains stationary while you rotate the work. In the double-bevel system of marquetry, where the saw is held at a constant angle to the work (8° to 12°, depending on the thickness of the veneer), some craftsmen find it easier to keep the saw vertical and tilt the bird's mouth.

CUTTING VENEER WITH A FRETSAW

Bird's
mouth

A fretsaw has several disadvantages for cutting marquetry compared to an electric scrollsaw: The scrollsaw maintains a constant angle, leaves both hands free to maneuver the work, usually has a deeper throat, and supports the work better.

Hacksaws

Hacksaws cut metal—a need that arises surprisingly often in the woodshop. They are made in two frame styles: fixed and adjustable. Standard blade lengths are 10 in. and 12 in., with holes at both ends for attachment. Most hacksaws hold their blades with fixed pins or with square-sectioned pins that can rotate the blade to the four points of the compass. Blades are tensioned by turning a nut that draws back one of the pins. The greater the tension, the more control you have of the cut. Hacksaws are available at every local hardware store. They do not require any sort of tune-up.

There are four different types of hacksaw blade. The most common and inexpensive are carbon-steel blades, which meet most woodshop needs and can be purchased at any hardware or automotive supply store. They are tempered to Rc64 to Rc65 and will cut metals with hardnesses below Rc40. The biggest problem with carbon-steel blades is that they lose their hardness and dull quickly as they heat up from friction.

Far better are bimetal blades, with high-speed-steel cutting edges tempered to Rc64 to Rc67 and spring-steel backings tempered to Rc46 to Rc48. The high-speed steel holds up well to the heat of sawing, while the tougher backing keeps the blade flexible enough to resist breakage. Bimetal blades can be used on steel up to Rc58 or Rc59, which is handy if you want to cut down a scraper blade to make a scratch stock. They are available through industrial supply outlets and catalogs, cost about twice as much as carbon steel, and last up to 10 times as long.

The two other types of blade are solid high-speed steel, which can shatter if it twists since the whole width is hardened, and flex, which is high-speed steel with only the teeth hardened. Flex has similar cutting characteristics to bimetal but doesn't hold up quite as well.

ADJUSTABLE-FRAME HACKSAW

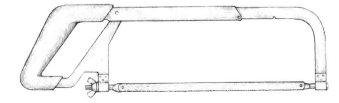

HACKSAW-BLADE TOOTH-SET PATTERNS

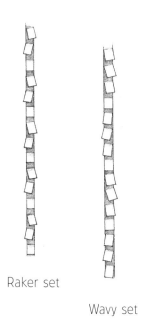

Raker set

Wavy set

Coarse hacksaw blades cut fastest, but finer blades are necessary when working thin material. This is because at least three teeth should be in contact with the work at all times or the saw will catch. Hacksaw blades come with 14, 18, 24, and 32 tpi. Coarser blades have a raker set that repeats a pattern of left, right, straight. Finer blades have a wavy set in which groups of teeth are set to the left and back to a straight tooth, then to the right and back to a straight tooth.

How to use a hacksaw

Hacksaws are meant to work on the push stroke. For maximum control and power, work with both hands on the saw, one on the handle, one at the front. Technically, downward pressure should not exceed 35 lb. To avoid vibration, locate the work in a vise so you are cutting just alongside of the jaws. If you are starting a cut on a corner, hold the saw almost parallel to one of the faces at first so that several teeth engage. Both the blade and the work have a tendency to heat up, so saw at a moderate pace of no more than 60 strokes per minute and take as long a stroke length as possible. You can also lubricate the blade with paraffin or light oil to reduce friction. Handle the hot ends of fresh-cut metal with caution.

HANDSAWS

Handsaws cut lumber to dimension, a task that most contemporary shops assign to power saws. Nonetheless, it is amazing how fast a sharp crosscut saw slices through a board and how accurate you become with practice. I particularly enjoy doing small framing and carpentry jobs with handsaws. In the absence of deafening sound the senses open up and work becomes a richer experience.

Handsaws are made to cut on the push stroke. They have wide blades, unsupported by any sort of spine or frame, thick and supple enough to flex without kinking or breaking. They say that in the old days you could test a saw's quality by bending the toe around to the handle. If it was good, the blade would return to perfect straightness. This may well be true, since the current standard for top-quality British saws is that they must spring back straight after bending around a cylinder 10 in. in diameter.

The manufacture of saws has changed greatly over the course of the last century. The old way was to cut the saw blank and teeth from soft, annealed steel, then taper-grind, harden, and temper it. The back was tempered a little softer than the teeth to keep the blade flexible. Because the hardening and tempering process tended to warp the blade, it was subsequently straightened with repeated hammer strokes. Finally, it was polished and sharpened. No one does this anymore. One disadvantage of the old way was that it was difficult to control the tempering process perfectly, so that hardness could vary from saw to saw or even along the teeth of the same saw. Even so, handsaw aficionados say that, overall, the old saws are far superior.

Today's version of the traditional handsaw is stamped out of pre-tempered cold-rolled steel, which may be high carbon or alloyed. Cheaper saws are made from steel in the range of Rc42 to Rc48, better saws run Rc50 to Rc54. A new category of saw has induction-hardened teeth in the range of Rc60+. These saws are made with either the traditional alternate-bevel tooth or one of several modified-set patterns that cut more aggressively and rougher. The advantage of induction hardening is that the saw stays sharp considerably longer, especially when cutting sheet goods such as particleboard and plywood. (Modern glues are hell on saw teeth.) The downside is that the teeth are too hard to be sharpened, so they are throwaway tools. The only way to keep them in use is to grind off the original teeth and cut new ones in the softer steel behind.

Better traditional handsaws are taper-ground, which makes them thickest along the teeth, thinnest along the back and toe. Taper-grinding reduces the amount of set required to prevent binding. Consequently, you get a thinner kerf, faster action, and a smoother, more controllable cut. Fifty years ago, handsaws were taper-ground as much as sixteen thousandths of an inch. Today they are ground only five to ten thousandths, because there is no modern machinery capable of doing better.

Another feature found in some saws is a skew back—a mild concavity that reminds me of a swaybacked horse. Folklore has it that skew-backed saws are lighter and better balanced. If so, it's a subtle effect. None of the saw experts I know think it matters.

TAPER-GROUND HANDSAW

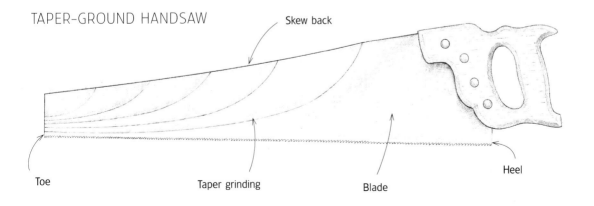

Skew back

Toe

Taper grinding

Blade

Heel

Today's crosscut saws can be 15 in. to 28 in. long, with anywhere from 6 to 12 ppi. Rip saws come in lengths from 24 in. to 28 in., with from 4.5 to 8 ppi. The term "panel saw" traditionally designated a crosscut saw with 10 to 12 points per inch and a length of 20 in. or 22 in.—a good saw for finish and cabinet work. Today it has been expropriated for all sorts of saws, including the toolbox-length, 15-in., induction-hardened saws that are the most popular selling saw in the United States.

Buying a handsaw

Handsaw aficionados don't buy new saws, they shop in antique barns, flea markets, and second-hand tool stores. The cream of the crop are said to be Disstons made in the first three decades of the 20th century, prior to the Depression. An older saw in good condition is easily restored, even if it has to go to a saw shop to have the old teeth filed off and new ones cut in. If you purchase an old saw, look for one that's still straight and has a minimum of rust. You can always make a new handle, but the steel is irreplaceable.

If you are working with solid wood and want a new saw that will last, look at the better British-made handsaws available through woodworking specialty stores and catalogs. Signs of quality are a taper grind and teeth that haven't been induction hardened. The teeth of the best saws are ground instead of punched, and hand-sharpened. The blades may be high carbon or spring steel, either of which is fine. The latter is harder and more durable but also more difficult to resharpen. Finally, be sure to get a saw with a wooden handle, and test the grip for comfort. The advantage of wood is that you can easily file contours and sand sharp edges to make it hand-friendly.

A good all-purpose, traditional crosscut saw for carpentry has 8 points and is 26 in. long. But if I had to choose just one handsaw for my workshop it would have 10 points and be 24 in. long—a saw with which I am comfortable cutting roughsawn planks to approximate size or trimming dressed lumber to final length. I use a rip saw much more rarely, but 5.5 ppi is a good all-purpose size.

The induction-hardened, disposable saws that dominate the market are a reflection of changing times and mores. They serve the cabinetmaker, carpenter, and "do-it-yourselfer" who is as likely to be cutting processed materials as solid wood. They eliminate the need to find a professional sharpener, now a rare species anyway. They are sold as a combination crosscut and rip saw, so there is no longer the need for two separate saws. And, of course, they please the manufacturer, who benefits from planned obsolescence.

Maintenance

A good handsaw will last forever with proper care and sharpening. Avoid rust by lightly oiling the saw once or twice a year and keep it in a dry environment. Existing rust spots can be sanded out with fine sandpaper. Store the saw so the teeth don't come in contact with other metallic objects.

How to use a handsaw

Most people know how to saw, but there are a few tips worth emphasizing.

- Position the saw against your thumb to start a cut, but be careful, because the saw can easily jump while the kerf is still shallow.
- Start a crosscut with a few backstrokes, until several teeth make contact at once and you can push forward without catching. Start a rip cut on the forward stroke, but hold the saw almost parallel to the face or edge of the work to engage several teeth.
- As a general rule, crosscut with the saw at about 45° to the work, rip with the saw higher, at about 60°.
- Both the forward and back strokes should be straight. If the saw whips in the kerf, you're pulling it crooked.
- Don't overpower the saw. Hold it gently. If you "listen" with your hand, the saw will follow easily in its own kerf.
- Make sure the waste side is free to drop off so the saw doesn't bind as you complete the cut.
- Put your weight into the forward stroke, not the return.
- Take long strokes, maintaining even pressure throughout.

JAPANESE SAWS

Japanese saws have become favorites with many Western woodworkers over the past two decades. Because they work on the pull stroke there is little danger of crimping the blade. Hence, they are made from thinner, harder steel than Western saws. This gives them several advantages. They stay sharp longer, leave a thinner kerf, and, in general, cut more quickly and precisely.

The tooth geometry of Japanese saws is more complex than that of traditional Western saws in that the teeth are longer and thinner, with more facets. There are at least five different tooth patterns, depending on whether they are for crosscut, rip, or angled cutting and whether in softwoods or hardwoods. However, wood being wood, the effective angles of the edges that do the actual cutting are quite similar between Japanese and Western saws. The number of teeth per inch is solely a

GEOMETRY OF JAPANESE
CROSSCUT TEETH

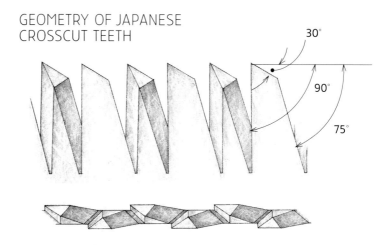

variable of blade length—longer saws have larger teeth with more set. Rip teeth are graduated in size, with the smallest teeth at the heel to start the kerf and the largest at the toe for rapid cutting.

Historically, most Japanese woodworking has been done with softwoods. Unfortunately, the same slender teeth that work so well in softwood have a tendency to snap off in hardwood, particularly those of less expensive saws. To ameliorate this problem, some saws imported for the American market specify that they have been modified for hardwoods, with shorter, blunter teeth.

The quality level of Japanese saws divides roughly into three tiers. The vast majority are factory-made, with induction-hardened teeth on replaceable, throwaway blades. A step up are factory-made saws that have been hand-adjusted at the end of the process, perhaps to straighten the blade and touch up the teeth with a file. At the pinnacle are saws made by individual craftsmen who work the steel at the forge, weld on the tang, cut the teeth, harden and temper the steel, scrape a hollow taper, and tension the blade with thousands of hammer strokes. This last step not only straightens the blade but is also supposed to impart memory to the steel so it will spring back straight when flexed.

For most Western woodworkers, amateur and professional, factory-made Japanese saws are more than satisfactory for accomplishing excellent work. Since they are not intended to be sharpened, the teeth are tempered harder and retain their sharpness longer than normal saw teeth. Handmade saws are appropriate for those few who develop the skill and passion to appreciate them. They are such particular objects that they are often sent back to their makers in Japan for resharpening.

Those saws most applicable to the needs of Western woodworkers are listed on the pages that follow.

AZEBIKI

Azebiki

The azebiki has no exact equivalent among Western saws, but it is like a cross between a veneer saw and an old-fashioned flooring saw. Its curved edges are used to start a cut on the interior face of a board, as you might in making a stopped cut or dado in carcase construction. The blade is flexible and can follow a straight or mildly curved line. Azebikis are two-sided, with crosscut teeth on one edge and rip teeth on the other. The smallest make good veneer saws, but they aren't readily available in the United States.

Dozuki

The dozuki is considered the Japanese equivalent of the Western dovetail saw. It has achieved the most acceptance among Western woodworkers of any Japanese saw. The usual blade length for furniture work is 8 in. to 11 in., with between 17 and 28 tpi. Blade width is only about 2 in., similar to that of a gent's saw.

Dozukis are relatively delicate instruments. Their blades are as thin as 0.012 in., and the teeth are fragile. For this reason, it is important that the dozuki you buy match its intended use. You will find them specialized to either ripping or crosscutting and for work in either hardwoods or softwoods. For a novice woodworker, the fineness of a dozuki's kerf is a problem, which practice can overcome. There is little room for correction if a cut starts off crooked.

DOZUKI

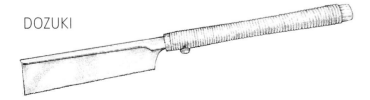

USING A KUGIHIKI
FLUSH-TRIM SAW

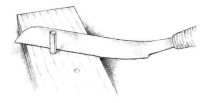

Kugihiki

Kugihiki saws flush-trim dowels, plugs, and proud joints. The blades are about 6 in. or 7 in. long and extremely flexible. The teeth are crosscut, with no set at all, so the blade can be used flat against work without leaving significant scratches. Kugihikis have from 19 to 26 tpi.

In use, the kugihiki is bent so that most of the blade lies flat on the work with the handle angled clear. It is an extremely useful saw, with no precise Western equivalent.

Ryoba

The ryoba is the functional counterpart of the Western handsaw. It has crosscut teeth on one edge, rip teeth on the other, with the blade taper-ground toward the middle. Although you can pass the full width of the blade through the kerf, the trailing set of teeth will roughen the cut surfaces and increase the likelihood of binding. For cleaner work it is preferable to mark all the way around the board and cut in from all four sides. The alternative is to use a single-edged version of the ryoba, called a kataba, which is taper-ground all the way to the back of the blade. There are rip katabas and crosscut katabas.

The ryoba and kataba come in a variety of lengths and are usually sized in millimeters. Thicker wood calls for a longer saw, since tooth size is a function of blade length. For general furniture work, where stock usually isn't over 2 in. thick, a 240mm (9½-in.) saw is appropriate. For finer joints, such as tenon cheeks, anywhere from 190mm to 200mm (7½ in. to 8 in.) is recommended. A 190mm blade has about 23 crosscut teeth and 11 rip teeth per inch. A 240mm blade has 16 crosscut teeth and 7 rip teeth per inch.

RYOBA AND KATABA

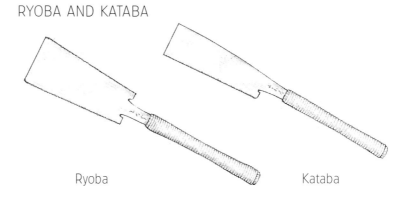

Ryoba

Kataba

Buying Japanese saws

Because of their thin, hard blades and unusual tooth geometry, Japanese saws have a certain fragility. When purchasing one, consider that the quality of the instrument should match your level of experience. For most of us, the imported, factory-made saws sold through woodworking specialty stores and catalogs are just right. Saws hand-forged by master smiths are available through a couple of Japanese tool dealers, but there is no point to buying one and then mangling it through lack of experience. Put another way, why throw money at a $200 bottle of wine when you're still working out the difference between a chardonnay and a chablis?

KEYHOLE SAWS

The keyhole saw has a long, narrow, unsupported blade for making small cutouts in large panels. It is of some use in areas too far inset to reach with a frame saw. Western keyhole saws cut on the push stroke, and it is unpleasantly easy to bend their blades. Japanese keyhole saws cut on the pull stroke, which is a slight improvement. But with their tendency to flex, keyhole saws aren't conducive to accurate work; they are a carpenter's tool that has been outmoded by the jigsaw.

Keyhole blades run about 5 in. to 8 in. long. Some Western-style keyhole saws have removable blades that slide through the handles, so they can extend as little as necessary in order to minimize flexing.

KEYHOLE SAWS

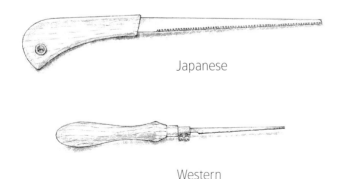

Japanese

Western

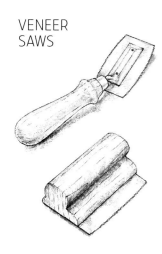

VENEER
SAWS

VENEER SAWS

The veneer saw is specialized for one purpose only, which is (you guessed it!) to crosscut and rip veneer. The essential elements of the saw are an offset handle and a convex cutting edge. In practice, you guide the blade against a straight-edged wooden fence.

The most commonly available design has a 3-in.-long, reversible blade with 13 teeth per inch. It works right-handed, on the pull stroke, which can be frustrating to left-handers. It also tends to split veneer at the end of a crosscut stroke, where little backup remains.

A second design has teeth that point from both sides toward the center, so it works for both left- and right-handers. It also solves the splitting problem, since you can work from both edges toward the middle. This saw comes in two sizes: one with a 4½-in., 14-tpi blade for fine work; the other with a 6-in., 12-tpi blade for not-so-fine work.

The veneer saw is most useful to craftsmen who work with veneer infrequently. Those who specialize in veneering are more likely to cut veneer to approximate size with a utility knife and then trim the edges straight and square with a router or table-saw fixture.

A veneer saw should be sharpened as if it were a single-bevel knife with teeth. The teeth should be flat on the back and beveled the full length of the front. This serves the double purpose of leaving a square edge on the veneer and encouraging the saw to press against the fence as it cuts, because of its natural drift.

Veneer saws may be purchased through woodworking stores and catalogs. New veneer saws are often useless until they are properly sharpened. To flatten the back of the teeth, remove the blade from the handle and hone the back on sharpening stones. To bevel the front of the teeth, use a grinding wheel, diamond stones, coarse honing stones, or even a mill file if the saw steel is soft enough.

SHARPENING SAWS

Like most craftsmen, I send my handsaws to a professional sharpener much of the time. I began to learn sharpening out of necessity, though, when I couldn't find a local sharpener with good enough eyesight to work on 20-point dovetail saws. Now I will sharpen a handsaw or backsaw a few times between professional ministrations.

Despite my own failing in this regard, there is no reason why the compleat craftsmen shouldn't do all his own sharpening, short of cutting new teeth (and even that is possible). When you sharpen a saw you have the power to alter the pitch, bevel, and set of the teeth. This gives you control of their aggressiveness and lets you determine the saw's suitability for crosscutting, ripping, or some compromise between the two.

The steps in sharpening are jointing, shaping, setting, and filing. Depending on a saw's condition, it is not always necessary to go through all four steps. If the saw has been properly sharpened and well cared for, it is possible to file several times between settings. Likewise, you can set the teeth a number of times before you need to joint and shape them again. I explain the essentials of sharpening below, but for a more thorough exposition refer to some of the sources listed in the bibliography on p. 196.

Saw-sharpening tools

Saw sharpening requires a few specialized tools. In addition to those listed below, some sharpeners find it helpful to use magnifying lenses that come with a headband or clip onto eyeglasses.

Mill file   An 8-in. or 10-in. second-cut or bastard works well for jointing. (See p. 7 for more information on mill files.)

Saw jointer   A manufactured holder that keeps a mill file square to the blade when jointing saw teeth. A shopmade, L-shaped, wooden block, notched to hold a file, serves the same purpose.

Saw set   A standard saw set has a squeeze grip that moves a beveled punch against a tooth (see the drawing on p. 161). On the other side, it backs the tooth with a wheel-shaped anvil that has a graduated bevel around the perimeter. Engraved numbers on the anvil's circumference often indicate the correct setting in teeth per inch. Saw sets cover different ranges of tooth size, usually from about 4 to 12 tpi. There are no sets fine enough for saws with 20 tpi.

Better saw sets also have built-in clamps that firmly grip the body of a saw every time you squeeze the handle.

SAW JOINTERS

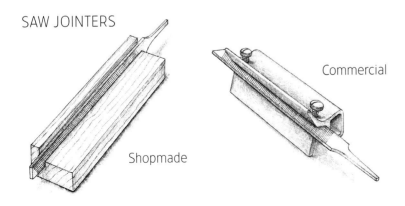

Commercial

Shopmade

SAW VISE

Saw vise   The first requirement of saw sharpening is a means to hold the saw straight and steady. Specialized metal vises are available new and secondhand, or you can make wooden jaws (called saw chops). There are many designs for holding saw chops together; one of the most straightforward is simply to clamp them in a shop vise. The jaws of a metal vise are 10 in. to 12 in. long, while saw chops can be as long as the saw itself. In section, the jaws of saw vises are narrow and rounded at the top to avoid interfering with the file. For jointing, shaping, and filing, the saw is held low in the vise to minimize flex and chatter, with the gullets just clearing the jaws. For setting, the blade is held higher to provide access for the saw set (see the drawing on the facing page). A saw longer than the vise is moved along section by section.

Taper saw file   Used to shape and sharpen the teeth. See pp. 7-8 for more information.

Buying saw-sharpening tools

With handsaw sharpening becoming a relatively obsolete skill, new saw jointers, sets, and vises can be difficult to find, even through woodworking stores and mail-order catalogs. Often the best bet is to look in second-hand and antique tool stores. Fortunately, it is easy enough to make your own saw jointer and vise.

Jointing

The teeth of a saw should be of even length, so that none bites in more than its neighbors. The overall shape of the line of teeth can be straight or convex but never concave. When either of these conditions no longer applies, a saw requires jointing. This is the process of running a mill file along the points of the teeth until you see at least a tiny gleam of light reflecting off each one when you sight down the blade.

It is advisable to hold the file so the teeth come out square across their tops. Usually this is done with a saw jointer, but you can also brave it with a steady hand and a keen eye.

Shaping

When you look at the teeth from the side, they should be consistent in size and spacing. If not, reshape them with a taper saw file. Mimic the pitch of the teeth, but don't worry about the bevel angle. Just file straight across as you would for rip teeth. You can file all the teeth from one side or do every other tooth and turn the saw around—it doesn't really matter at this stage. The flat spots made by jointing serve as a guide, in that you want them all to end up equally small. Since you are always filing the front of one tooth and the back of another at the same time, use side pressure to take more off the one that needs it most. If only mild shaping is called for, it can be done during the filing process.

Setting

The recommended amount of set for a handsaw varies, depending on its intended use and who you ask. Some authorities recommend that only the top half of a tooth be set to avoid snapping it off, others that the whole tooth be set. Some say the width of set should be one-third the tooth's length, others suggest one-half. The fact is that there is a certain amount of leeway in the geometry of saw sharpening. Until experience leads you to a different conclusion, a good starting place is to set the top half of each tooth.

The degree of set should be more for soft and green woods, less for hard and dry woods; more on a flat-sided saw, less on a taper-ground saw; more on a handsaw, less on a backsaw. Handsaws and tenon saws are set with a saw set. Dovetail saws with more than 16 tpi can be set by pushing the teeth with a screwdriver tip against a bevel filed along the edge of a metal plate. This is not easy, and if you try it on an induction-hardened saw, the teeth may snap off. Then there is the ever-practical Tage Frid's method of setting small teeth by inserting a screwdriver between them and twisting, but I can't claim to have tried it.

SETTING THE TEETH

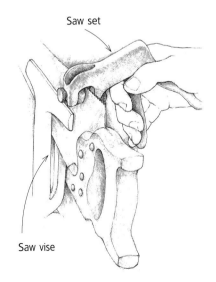

Saw set

Saw vise

Filing

If you think of saw teeth as a series of waves seen in profile, pitch is the angle of the leading edge as it crests. The typical pitch of a rip saw is 85° to 90°, while on a crosscut saw it relaxes back to 75° for hardwoods, 65° to 70° for softwoods.

If you look at saw teeth from above, the bevel (or fleam) is the angle at which the front facets are filed across. Normally the bevel is 90° on rip teeth, 65° for crosscutting hardwoods, and up to 45° for crosscutting softwoods.

When you file saw teeth, you hold a taper saw file at the desired angle and file the leading edges of those teeth that are set toward you. (Some sharpeners not only take into account the pitch and bevel, they also tilt the file upward to deepen the gullets on the near side, which improves chip clearance.) Then you turn the saw around and file the intervening teeth.

The file actually removes the front of one tooth and the back of the next at the same time. You control their relative sizes by exerting more pressure against one or the other. If the teeth are pretty even to begin with, you get into a rhythm, taking the same number of strokes with the same part of the file each time for consistency. There are adjustable saw-file holders made for this purpose, but experienced sharpeners find them ungainly and slow. Best to practice on your less important saws until you get the hang of it. You know that teeth are sharp when no light glints off their tips.

After sharpening a handsaw, run an oilstone down each side of the teeth to remove the burr left by the file. On a dovetail saw the burr is sometimes left to augment an insufficient amount of set.

SCRAPING

Scraping is the magic act of woodworking. With only a thin, flat piece of steel in your hands (and nothing up your sleeves) you can produce billows of gossamer shavings, leaving behind a smooth surface free of tearout even when working against the grain.

Scrapers have a multitude of uses in the woodshop, from removing scaly, old paint to skimming a final surface of lustrous perfection. They come in different forms appropriate to their disparate tasks, some with soles, some for freehand use. Scrapers are most effective on dense, close-grained hardwoods and are rarely used on softwoods.

The cutting edge of a scraper is a minuscule hook (or "burr") on the edge of a thin piece of high-carbon steel. The hook is sharp enough to sever wood fibers but unable to penetrate any farther than its own negligible length. Shavings raised by the hook immediately slam into the sheer wall of the scraper side. This bends them so severely that the fibers weaken and become more likely to break across their length than to split from adjoining fibers, which is why there is no tearout with a scraper

THE PHYSICS OF SCRAPING

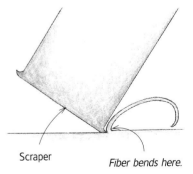

Scraper

Fiber bends here.

even when working against the grain. Shavings can't lift from beneath the surface because they are too weak to separate from their neighbors.

Although scraper planes and cabinet scrapers have soles similar to those of handplanes, the mechanics differ. The sole of a plane works to limit the penetration of the blade and to provide a reference for flatness. The sole of a scraper is only a reference for flatness; the blade limits its own penetration.

The names given to scrapers can be contradictory among both historical and contemporary sources. One person's cabinet scraper is another's card scraper. In this chapter I have chosen contemporary names that best distinguish one scraper from another: hand scraper, cabinet scraper, and scraper plane. The chapter also includes a section on burnishers, the specialized tools with which scrapers are sharpened.

BURNISHERS

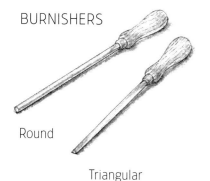

Round

Triangular

BURNISHERS

A burnisher is a polished length of steel used to form the hook of a scraper. The steel must be tempered substantially harder than the scraper itself. Good burnishers have a hardness in the range of Rc62 to Rc64. Common shapes are round, oval, triangular, and teardrop in section. Lengths range from approximately 6 in. to 11 in.

The crucial aspect of a burnisher, besides hardness, is a smooth polish. A scratched burnisher will leave a tooth on a scraper edge that lessens its effectiveness, just as a 1000-grit stone fails to get a chisel as sharp as a 6000-grit stone does. For this reason, burnishers should occasionally be polished bright with a buffing wheel and compound.

Manufactured burnishers are preferable for convenience and quality, but you can improvise your own. I once saw eminent furniture maker Tage Frid burnish a scraper with the back of a chisel. The sharp cutting edge makes a chisel potentially hazardous as a burnisher, but otherwise it fits the parameters of hardness and polish.

Which shape of burnisher is best? Good reasons may be adduced for each, and the truth is that you become adept with whichever you use on a regular basis. I started using a round burnisher because it was a gift and

SECTIONS OF BURNISHERS

Round   Oval   Triangular   Teardrop

have been happy with it since. Some claim that oval and teardrop burnishers are advantageous, since you can vary pressure by using sharper or gentler sections of their curves. Mostly, though, it is hand pressure that controls the aggressiveness of burnishing, whatever the shape. Triangular burnishers are the most difficult, though. They are generally worked on the narrow edges where the faces intersect, so pressure focuses in an extremely small area.

Many woodworkers lubricate their burnishers with a little "nose grease," paraffin, or oil. Nose grease is applied by twirling the burnisher in the seams alongside one's nostrils. My grandfather taught me this trick 40 years ago on the banks of the Schuykill River, where I would spin the ferrule of a fishing rod against my nose before assembling it. The purpose of lubricating a burnisher is to reduce abrasion so it doesn't tear the softer steel of the scraper.

Burnishers can be purchased from woodworking specialty stores and catalogs. They should be highly polished and hard enough to resist being scratched. A secure handle is desirable, but not necessary.

CABINET SCRAPERS

The cabinet scraper is capable of taking thicker shavings than a simple hand scraper and can make wood almost as smooth. Its primary advantages are a sole to keep surfaces relatively flat and handles that reduce fatigue and eliminate the risk of cooked thumbs. Common applications for cabinet scrapers include flattening and smoothing wild-grained wood that handplaning would tear out, removing dry, squeezed-out glue from panel surfaces, and cleaning veneered surfaces of glue and tape. In the sequence of surface preparation, a cabinet scraper is generally followed with a hand scraper for the final touch of perfection.

The cabinet scraper has a small, flat sole, about 2¾ in. front to back by 3¼ in. side to side, suspended between spokeshave-like handles. It is most often used on the push stroke. A steel pressure plate holds the bevel side of the blade against a 110° bed. A thumbscrew flexes the blade much as one's thumbs flex a hand scraper. To adjust or remove the blade you loosen the two bolts that secure the plate.

When you acquire a new cabinet scraper, flatten the sole as conscientiously as you would a plane's. Afterwards, gently break the arrises along the sole's edges and mouth with sandpaper just so they aren't sharp. Finally, clean any obvious lumps of paint or other material from the bed with a file. The bed of a cabinet scraper doesn't need to be anywhere near as perfect as that of a plane. When flexed by the thumbscrew, the blade doesn't rest flat against it anyway.

CABINET
SCRAPER

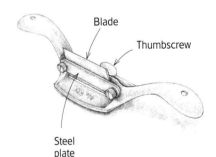

Blade

Thumbscrew

Steel
plate

CABINET-SCRAPER BEVEL ANGLES

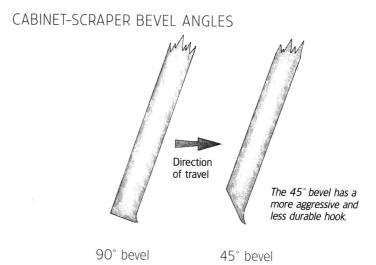

Direction
of travel

*The 45° bevel has a
more aggressive and
less durable hook.*

90° bevel   45° bevel

The bevel angle on a cabinet-scraper blade can be as low as 30° but commonly varies from 45° to 90°. The geometry is such that at 45° you can burnish a more aggressive hook than you can at 90°. But it is also a weaker hook, since it is more extended with less steel backing it up. As the bevel approaches 90°, the cabinet scraper works more like a hand scraper. It has a less aggressive bite but yields a potentially finer surface.

Sharpening a cabinet scraper

The back of a new scraper blade should be flattened and polished just like that of a plane or chisel. The flattened area must extend along both cutting edges, even if interior hollows remain. The best method I know is to work on pressure-sensitive-adhesive sandpaper mounted on a flat surface such as plate glass or a jointer table. Start with 100 grit if necessary, step up to 220 grit, and then go on to polish the back on medium and fine honing stones. The blade can be awkward to manipulate unless you attach a small block of wood on top with double-stick tape to serve as a handle.

Putting a cutting edge on a scraper involves polishing the bevel and back to form a crisp, sharp intersection that is burnished into a hook. Once the back has had its initial flattening, a suggested procedure is as follows:

1. Hold the blade in an upright vise so you have comfortable access to the cutting edge throughout the process.

FILING A FRESH BEVEL ON A CABINET-SCRAPER BLADE

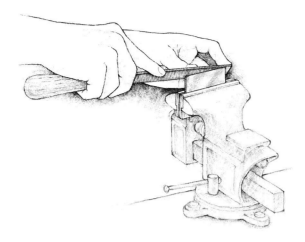

2. Put a fresh, straight bevel on with a file at any angle from 45° to 90° (see the drawing above). I prefer to use an 8-in. smooth or second-cut mill file, but you could also use a bastard mill file, which is coarser but more commonly available. It is also possible to create the bevel on a grinder or stationary sander.

3. Hone the bevel smooth with medium and fine stones to remove the file marks and leave the edge polished (see the drawing at right). I prefer to use oilstones when working at the vise, because the softness of waterstones makes them more likely to be grooved or wear unevenly. A medium India stone alone will create a good working edge, but polishing up to finer grits makes for a sharper edge and better performance.

4. Hone the wire edge off the back of the blade with the finest stone you've used on the bevel (see the drawing below). At this point, the scraper blade should have a crisp, sharp edge.

HONING THE BEVEL

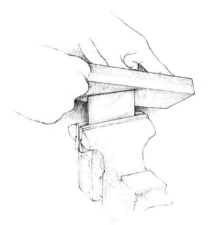

HONING OFF THE WIRE EDGE

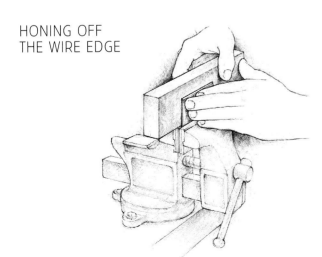

BURNISHING A CABINET-SCRAPER BLADE

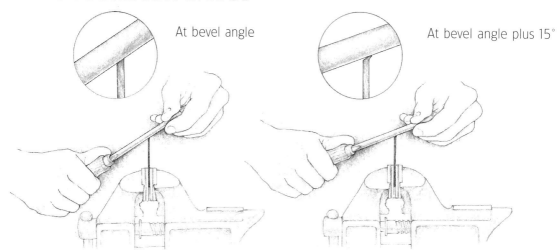

At bevel angle

At bevel angle plus 15°

5. The final step is to turn a hook with a burnisher. On a cabinet scraper, this seems to take more pressure than is required on a hand scraper. Run the burnisher along the bevel several times. Then angle the burnisher an additional 15° for a few more strokes, until you feel a definite hook across the back (see the drawing above).

DRAWING THE SPENT HOOK FLAT

When a scraper blade gets dull, you can reburnish it a few times before it needs refiling. To do so, place the blade on a table, back side up. Hold the burnisher flat on the back of the blade and draw it across and off with significant pressure (see the drawing at left). Take several strokes until you can no longer feel the hook. Then burnish as directed in step 5 above, this time with less pressure.

How to use a cabinet scraper

To set up the scraper for normal use, loosen the steel pressure plate and the thumbscrew. Insert the blade upward through the mouth to avoid damaging the hook, with the beveled face against the bed. Place the tool on a flat wooden surface and let the blade drop to it, so that the cutting edge is flush with the sole. Tighten the steel plate without lifting the blade off the wood. Make a test pass over the surface: nothing (or very little) should happen. The idea is to have the blade exactly even with the sole. Then, as you apply pressure from the thumbscrew, the blade will flex below the sole. The more you turn the thumbscrew, the more aggressive the cut. When using the cabinet scraper, it is best to overlap your strokes thoroughly to avoid corrugating the surface with the scalloped blade.

The sole of a cabinet scraper is relatively small as far as planes go, so it is not ideally suited to making a large surface perfectly flat. To coax the best possible performance, vary the direction of your strokes, working first with the grain, then on a diagonal, then on the opposite diagonal, and so forth, so you fair out as large an area as possible. In general, working directly across the grain leaves an unnecessarily rough surface, particularly on open-grained woods.

Buying cabinet scrapers

The cabinet scraper is a somewhat underappreciated tool and may not be easy to find, even though the original Stanley No. 80 is still in production in Britain and a few other manufacturers make their own versions. Look for cabinet scrapers in woodworking specialty stores and catalogs.

HAND SCRAPERS

HAND SCRAPER

The hand scraper is also called a card scraper in some quarters because of its shape. Mechanically, it is the simplest tool in the shop—just a small, flat rectangle of steel. Conversely, it may be the most challenging tool to master. But once you get the hang of it, the hand scraper is indispensable.

The hand scraper is a smoother-cutting, more delicate instrument than either the cabinet scraper or the scraper plane. Its primary application is smoothing flat and curved surfaces preparatory to finishing, after they have been milled, handplaned, filed, and/or prepared with a cabinet scraper or scraper plane. In capable hands, a hand scraper can take dense hardwood to a level of perfection where, if you felt the need to use sandpaper, you might begin as fine as 220 or 320 grit. Softer hardwoods, such as poplar, don't scrape as cleanly. They might require sanding beginning at about 150 grit. In any case, the scraper eliminates time spent sanding with coarser grits and yields a superior surface. Other uses include removal of dried glue and veneer tape.

The hardness of manufactured hand scrapers varies considerably. Softer scrapers may be in the range of Rc38 to Rc42, while harder ones are Rc48 to Rc52. A harder scraper must be burnished with more force, but it holds its edge longer. In fact, you can use any piece of tool steel as a scraper, as long as you have an even harder burnisher with which to turn a hook. Old handsaws make good scraper stock. Cecil Pierce, a legendary Maine woodworker who recently died at age 90, showed up at our school unannounced some years ago carrying a few favorite hand tools. One was a 1½-in. chisel that he used as a narrow scraper. In his firm opinion a chisel made the best scraper because its hard steel retained a hook "forevah."

GOOSENECK
SCRAPER

Manufactured scrapers (available through woodworking specialty stores and catalogs) come in a variety of thicknesses ranging from 0.4mm (0.015 in.) to at least 1mm (0.042 in.). A thinner scraper is easier to flex but also heats up and seems to lose its edge more quickly. Thin scrapers are great for work on gentle curves, to which they readily adapt. Thicker scrapers tire your thumbs more but burn them less. The dean of scrapers, made by Sandvik, measures 2½ in. by 6 in. and is 80mm (0.030 in.) thick. Anything thicker is too stiff to be flexed comfortably but may be used flat on the pull stroke.

Hand scrapers are also available with curved profiles for scraping rounded surfaces. The gooseneck scraper is a good example. Curved scrapers don't have to be store-bought. You can grind and file any scraper edge to the exact shape you want.

Sharpening a hand scraper

HAND-SCRAPER
EDGE ANGLES

90° edge   80° edge

A hand scraper with an 80° beveled edge takes a more aggressive hook than a 90° edge.

While it is standard good practice to file and hone hand-scraper edges at 90°, it is by no means an absolute rule. A mildly beveled edge allows for a more aggressive hook. The hook on a 90° edge can be turned only 5° or 10°. Otherwise, you must hold the scraper uncomfortably far over to engage the hook, by which time your knuckles are scraping as well (see the top drawing on the facing page). With a beveled edge, you can file a more angled hook and still hold the scraper in a comfortably upright position.

It is customary to burnish hooks on both sides of both long edges, for a total of four hooks. The advantage of having so many hooks is efficiency: more time between burnishings, plus, when the edge you are working with begins to heat up too much, you just flip to the other. In the days when scrapers were still something of a mystery to me, I figured that the real reason for putting on four hooks was to increase the odds that at least one would actually take shavings. In fact, now that I've finally acquired a feel for the tool, I burnish only one hook on each long side. I can't claim it's a better method, just that it helps me keep track of what I'm doing.

Sharpening a hand scraper is a two-part process. First, you create polished surfaces that meet in crisp arrises. Then you burnish them into minuscule hooks. There are many paths to this particular mountaintop. One is as follows, assuming a 90° edge:

1. Place the scraper in an upright vise, as shown in the bottom drawing on the facing page. File the two long edges straight and square. A smooth or second-cut 8-in. mill file works well. If you wanted to, you

HOOK ANGLES

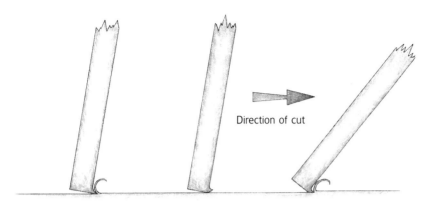

Direction of cut

90° edge burnished at 5° will cut with scraper held almost upright.

90° edge burnished at 30° will not cut in upright position.

Scraper burnished at 30° must be held at considerable angle for hook to engage.

could actually take shavings with the burr left by the file; I sometimes remove paint, finish, or glue in just this manner. But it's not yet a fine surfacing edge.

2. Remove the scraper from the vise and hone the edges on a medium-grit stone, such as a 1000-grit waterstone (see the top drawing on p. 172). Keep the scraper at 90° to the stone without rocking. Skew the scraper to its line of travel so it won't groove the stone. Hone until the file marks vanish from the edges. A magnifying lens will reveal the scraper edges clearly while you're learning.

FILING A NEW EDGE ON A HAND SCRAPER

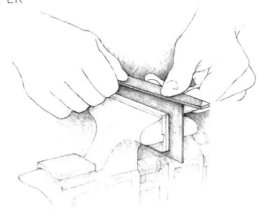

HONING THE SCRAPER EDGE

3. Hone the faces of the scraper on the same stone. Keep your fingers pressed along each edge in turn, since a scraper is so flexible. Hone until you can see that the faces have been affected all along the cutting edges.

4. Repeat steps 2 and 3 on a fine stone such as a 6000-grit waterstone. The sharpest scraper is one that has the smoothest intersecting surfaces at the cutting edges, just like a chisel or plane iron. A rounded arris is anathema.

5. This step is optional when you have followed the first four well but is the crucial starting point for reburnishing. Lay the scraper flat on a tabletop. Hold the burnisher flat upon it and draw the burnisher along and off the edge in one motion, several times, with pressure (see the bottom drawing on p. 168). Do this to every edge you plan to put a hook on, until you can't feel the old hook anymore.

6. Place the scraper upright in a vise or lay it down so the cutting edge overhangs a benchtop, whichever you find more convenient. With the burnisher square to the sides, run it along and off the edge (see the drawing below). Take two or three moderately hard strokes in this fashion. You should feel a faint burr, which is the beginning of the hook. Then tilt the burnisher approximately 5° and turn the edge with several more firm strokes. Not too firm, though. Harder strokes make larger hooks, but smaller hooks are equally effective and can be reburnished more times before they expire.

BURNISHING A HAND SCRAPER

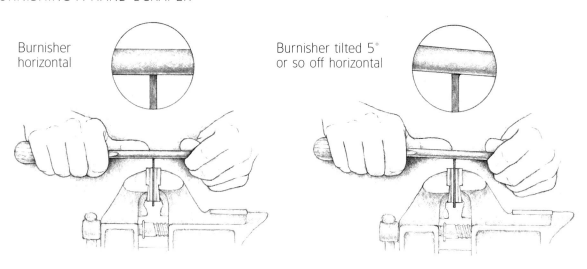

Burnisher horizontal

Burnisher tilted 5° or so off horizontal

The scraper is now ready to use. When it stops taking shavings and only makes dust, burnish again, beginning at step 5. When reburnishing is ineffective, start again at step 1.

Curved hand scrapers may be sharpened in essentially the same way, but often they are used to good effect with just the burr from the file or with the unburnished, sharp edge right from the stones.

How to use a hand scraper

A hand scraper is most often used on the push stroke, while flexed into a mild arc, but it may also be used flat on the pull stroke. To push, grasp the scraper with both hands, fingers to the side and thumbs in the middle near the cutting edge (see the drawing at right). Flex it slightly by thrusting your thumbs forward. Now place the scraper on the work, leaning away from you at about 5° off the vertical, and try to take a shaving. If the hook doesn't bite, lean the scraper a little farther forward until you find the most upright position where it takes fine, continuous shavings. An upright scraping position is more comfortable. It also yields a flatter surface, since less of the scraper's curvature translates to the wood.

For beginners, I liken the motion of a scraper stroke to touching an airplane down on a runway and lifting off again. Not that the scraper must be raised from the wood, but it works best if you exert pressure gradually at the beginning of the stroke and ease off at the end.

Scrapers give the fairest surface and chatter least if held at a slight angle to their line of travel for a shearing cut. When removing a defect from a particular location, take down a larger area around the spot, working on diagonals as well as straight ahead. Scraping too locally can leave an obvious depression.

Singed thumbs are a common scraping hazard for beginners, since friction heats thin steel quickly, particularly if the edge is dull. There are a number of solutions, one of which is to wrap your thumbs in tape. Perhaps the cleverest is to cut a piece of refrigerator magnet a little smaller than the scraper and apply it to the side that contacts your thumbs. Unlike commercially sold scraper holders, the thin magnet still allows you full sensitivity to the action of the edge.

HAND POSITION FOR SCRAPING

PAINT SCRAPERS

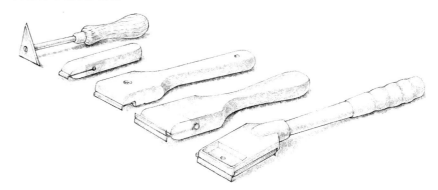

PAINT SCRAPERS

A paint scraper, also known as a glue scraper, basically consists of a handle and a replaceable, hooked blade. As the names suggest, paint and glue scrapers work well to remove dried glue, paint, and other finishes. They are not tools for surfacing wood in the manner of cabinet or hand scrapers. Paint scrapers are used on the pull stroke with either one or two hands, depending on their size.

To sharpen a paint scraper, simply file a fresh edge at the original angle. Push the file toward the head of the scraper, so no burr overhangs the cutting edge. A smooth or second-cut mill file works well.

Paint scrapers are sold mostly through hardware and paint supply stores, though you may find them in some woodworking specialty stores and catalogs.

SCRAPER PLANES

Scraper planes are used like cabinet scrapers to remove tool marks and tearout from machined and handplaned surfaces. On wood that is too wild to be planed, they are the tool of choice for flattening and surface preparation. They are also excellent for smoothing veneered panels. Generally, a scraper plane is followed with a smoother-cutting hand scraper.

Scraper planes have longer soles than cabinet scrapers, but there are important mechanical differences as well. First, the blades of scraper planes pivot forward from just under 90° to about 125°, while the blades of cabinet scrapers are fixed at 110°. Second, the blades of scraper planes stay flat across, whereas those of cabinet scrapers are flexed by thumbscrews.

The net effect of these features is that the two tools handle differently. Scraper planes are better at maintaining flatness, which can be particularly important when working with veneer, where it would be a disaster to scrape through the thin surface. They also have the potential to remove more wood more quickly, since the flat blade takes shavings across its entire width. On the other hand, cabinet scrapers are less prone to chatter, and their thumbscrews make it easier to control the setting for fine work.

In the first half of the 20th century, Stanley made many varieties of scraper plane. Three of these are still available, although from other manufacturers. The most well regarded among furniture makers is the No. 112, which is shaped somewhat like a smoothing plane. It has a 3⅜-in. by 9-in. sole, the longest of any scraper, which makes it the first choice where flatness is an important consideration.

The No. 212 is sized like a small block plane, with a 1⅜-in.-wide blade and a 5½-in. sole. It is too small for most surfacing needs and is useful primarily to craftsmen who work with small parts, such as instrument makers. The original Stanley No. 212 had a standard thin scraper blade, which was burnished with a hook to form a cutting edge. The only No. 212 currently in production, by Lie-Nielsen Toolworks, has a thick blade. The manufacturer suggests that it is sufficient for a beginner to use it with the blade simply sharpened to a keen edge, although it definitely works more aggressively with a burnished hook. The 212 also offers two optional toothing blades, with 18 and 25 teeth per inch, respectively. Toothing blades are used to roughen the ground prior to applying veneer with hide glue.

The No. 12 has a 3⅜-in. by 6⅜-in. sole and a crossbar handle. It was the first scraper plane Stanley put in production (in 1869) and was originally called a "veneer scraper."

Stanley took all of its scraper planes out of production in the 1940s. Recently, there has been only one manufacturer of the Nos. 12 and 112, the German firm of Kunz, and their quality is not up to that of the original Stanleys'. One can only hope another company will step in to fill the void with superior products.

One oft-cited problem with the Kunz scraper planes is that the frog tends to shift side to side and back and forth, causing the blade to chatter. This can be ameliorated by expanding the heads of the pins that anchor the frog, using a center punch and hammer.

STANLEY NO. 112 SCRAPER PLANE

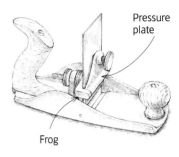

Pressure plate

Frog

LIE-NIELSEN NO. 212 SCRAPER PLANE

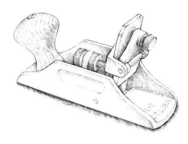

STANLEY NO. 12 SCRAPER PLANE

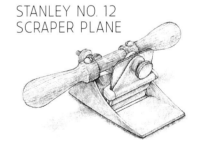

Tuning and using scraper planes

The most important aspect of tuning a scraper plane is flattening the sole. Afterwards, it's a good idea to break the arrises around the sole with sandpaper so they aren't sharp. The bed should be flat too, but access is restricted by the pressure plate that pivots against it. About the most you can do is slip in a very small file and remove any obvious lumps of paint.

The blade of a scraper plane is prone to chatter. Also, if the bed is at all concave, the corners of the blade are thrust forward and likely to dig into the work. However, there are two types of modification that address these problems. One is to sharpen the blade with a barely perceptible convexity across the width of the cutting edge. The other is to attach tiny shims to the center of the bed and the outside edges of the pressure plate to force the blade into a mild flex, much as the thumbscrew of a cabinet scraper does. While these modifications may not entirely eliminate chatter, they will certainly prevent the corners of the blade from scoring work.

Scraper-plane blades are sharpened like those of cabinet scrapers (see pp. 166-168). To install a newly sharpened blade, set the frog angle to about 5° forward of vertical and slide the blade up through the mouth to avoid damaging the hook. Then place the plane on a flat surface and tighten the pressure plate so the blade is flush with the sole. To take shavings, lower the blade angle just enough to pivot the cutting edge below the mouth (about 10° forward of vertical). As a blade dulls, you may be able to extend its utility by resetting it flush to the sole and then further lowering the pivot angle.

The suggestion of 95° as a starting angle is an approximation that can vary according to the geometry of the hook you turn. To get an idea of the minimum angle to which the frog can be set, first try scraping freehand to observe the most upright angle at which the hook is effective.

The process of working with a scraper plane is much like using a handplane, except that you can safely work against the grain. As with a handplane, you get less chatter if you skew the body to the line of the cut.

Buying scraper planes

Scraper planes are available through woodworking specialty stores and catalogs. Original Stanleys are hard to come by, since they have become collector's items, but you might look for them in antique stores or contact dealers who specialize in old Stanley tools.

STRIKING

The tools furniture makers use for striking fall into two categories: hammers and mallets. Hammer heads are made of metal, usually steel. Mallet heads generally offer striking surfaces of wood, plastic, or rubber. Their blows are less forceful, but they are also less destructive to the objects of their attention. Hammers and mallets are most often specified according to the weight of their heads.

HAMMERS

Throughout history, hammers have taken about as many shapes as human ingenuity could devise. A glance at 19th-century hammers turns up a butter firkin hammer, fruiterer's hammer, grocer's hammer, clogger's hammer (for shoe work), coach trimmer's hammer, cooper's hammer, glazier's hammer, and many others pertaining to specialized fields of labor now defunct or altered beyond recognition. Even as I write this,

CLAW-HAMMER ANATOMY

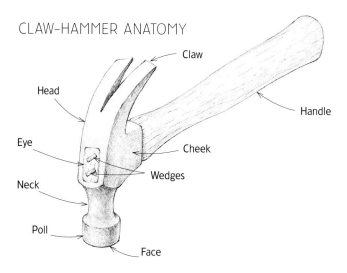

HAMMER PEENS

Ball peen   Cross peen   Straight peen

air-powered nailers are displacing the once-ubiquitous claw hammer on construction sites, and young carpenters are beginning to call nails "hand nails."

Hammers with claws are considered carpenter's hammers, while hammers with peens are sometimes categorized as metalworker's hammers. There are three types of peen: the ball peen, cross peen, and straight peen (see the drawing at left).

A good hammer is distinguished by the forging, tempering, and machining of the head, the strength and shock-absorbing quality of the handle, the permanence of the bond between handle and head, and the hammer's balance and heft.

A contemporary furniture maker is likely to have at least two hammers around the shop: a 16-oz. claw hammer for general construction and assembly and a lighter hammer, such as a 10-oz. Warrington, for driving brads and miscellaneous tapping. There is little danger that the hammer will become obsolete in the woodshop. If nothing else, it is the ultimate persuader when a glue-up goes awry and parts must be bashed together or knocked apart before the glue sets irreversibly.

Claw hammers

Carpenters were pounding and pulling nails with claw hammers in the heyday of the Roman Empire, 2,000 years ago. However, the particular design of the wood-handled hammer we use today was perfected by blacksmith David Maydole of Norwich, New York, in the 1840s. The ongoing problem that Maydole solved was how to keep the head on the hammer. He forged a long-necked head with a rectangular or oval elongated eye that tapered inward toward the neck. This shape, which was typical of adzes, allowed a more substantial section of the handle to be firmly wedged in place than did contemporary "plain-eye" hammers (see the drawing at right). The hammer Maydole developed is properly called a bell-faced, adze-eye, claw hammer. Similar hammers made today offer a choice of round or octagonal polls.

Claw hammers are commonly sized from 12 oz. to 28 oz., although I have seen them as small as 7 oz. A 16-oz. curved-claw hammer is standard for general carpentry, whereas straight-clawed hammers weighing in at 20 oz. or more are popular for framing. Curved claws are best for pulling nails. Straight claws are superior at ripping woodwork apart. Well-made claws have clean, sharp edges for gripping nail shanks, with crisp V-notches to grab small nails. Their ends are tapered, rather than blunt, for effective prying. If necessary, these characteristics can be improved with files.

Although older hammers offered a choice of flat or crowned (convex) faces, contemporary claw hammers are uniformly crowned. A flat face makes it easier to hit nails squarely; a convex face is better for sinking nails below the surface without leaving dents. Perhaps more to the point from the manufacturer's point of view, a convex face is less likely to spall (chip around the rim). Scuffing the face of a hammer with sandpaper or concrete will stop it from skidding on nail heads.

The handles of modern hammers may be wood, steel, or fiberglass. Wood and fiberglass are kindest to muscle and ligament because they absorb shock well, while steel is the most indestructible. Hickory is the wood of choice because of its strength, flexibility, and resistance to splitting. Handle lengths range from 14 in. to 17 in., with heavier hammers usually having longer handles. The grip of a hammer should be neither too slippery nor too sticky. A wood handle can be made less slick by removing the varnish and roughing up the grip area with a file—a trick sometimes applied to oars. Friction from a rubber handle is more likely to blister soft hands.

Good hammer heads are drop-forged tool steel. The face and claw are separately oil-tempered: the face in the range of Rc50 to Rc55, the claw Rc48 to Rc55. The body in between remains more malleable, somewhere between Rc18 and Rc35. "Rim-tempered" hammer faces are tempered about 5 points softer around the rim than at the center to prevent spalling.

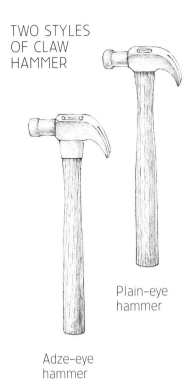

TWO STYLES
OF CLAW
HAMMER

Plain-eye
hammer

Adze-eye
hammer

HAMMER
CLAWS

Curved
claw

Straight
claw

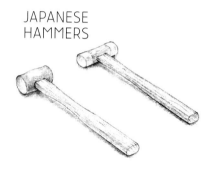

Japanese hammers

In Japan, chisels are driven with steel hammers instead of mallets. There are two basic styles of head used for this purpose. One is square-sectioned and relatively long; the other is cylindrical and compact (see the drawing at left). Both types have a flat face on one side and a convex face on the other. The flat side is less likely to glance off chisels, nails, and rounded surfaces, while the crowned face is better for setting nail heads, assembling wooden parts without leaving dents from the rim, and striking flat surfaces with minimum deflection.

Japanese hammer faces are tempered harder around the rim than at the center—the opposite of rim-tempered Western hammers. A softer center is considered desirable to absorb shock and give the head better purchase on nails and chisels. Brittleness around the rim is minimized by careful oil tempering.

In Japan, it is traditional for carpenters to buy the head of the hammer separately and make their own handles. This enables them to custom-fit the length of the handle and the shape of the grip. Japanese hammers imported into the United States have surprisingly slender handles, because they are sized to the relatively small hands of the Japanese.

In addition to the square- and round-faced hammers, other Japanese hammers include light, octagonal-headed hammers for adjusting plane irons (and driving chisels); boatbuilder's hammers with one face tapered to form a nail set; and saw-setting hammers.

Japanese hammers may be drop-forged like Western hammers or have harder steel faces laminated to softer steel or wrought-iron cores in the traditional hand-forged style. They come in a range of weights comparable to Western hammers. Japanese hammers are sold through woodworking specialty stores and catalogs. The best sources are those outlets that specialize in Japanese tools.

Tack
hammer

Split peen

Upholsterer's
hammer

Tack and upholsterer's hammers

In contemporary usage, tack hammer and upholsterer's hammer are generally synonymous terms. They are light hammers (4 oz. to 12 oz.) made specifically for driving upholstery tacks. The style most often called an upholsterer's hammer has an arched head and an inward-canted striking face. A tack hammer most often has a straight head and a squared-off face.

Tack and upholsterer's hammers usually have magnetized peens for picking up and setting tacks. The best hammers have bronze heads with a steel face welded on one end and a steel magnet welded into the other.

Less expensive hammers have all-steel heads and may have an old-style, magnetized split peen, one tine being the north pole, the other the south.

The customary way to set tacks is to take about a dozen in your mouth and present them one at a time, head first, through your lips. You pick up the tack on the magnetized face of the peen and set it. Then you roll the hammer over to drive the tack home with the striking face. One of the main disadvantages of a split peen, in comparison to a welded-on magnet, is that the space between the tines tends to collect a paste of steel, dirt, and saliva.

Tack and upholsterer's hammers are sold through suppliers to the upholstery trades. The best way to find one in your area is to call local upholsterers and ask where they buy their tools.

Veneer hammers

The veneer hammer is an anomaly. Its primary use is not striking but pressing out excess glue and air when laying veneer with hide glue in the traditional manner. The head may be metal or wood, but it ends in a hoe-shaped blade about ⅛ in. thick and 2½ in. to 3½ in. across. Better blades are made out of stainless steel or brass, since ordinary steel can leave oxidation stains on veneer. Hammers with steel heads often have a smaller face behind, which is square-sectioned and crowned for driving nails and pressing out small sections of veneer with high pressure.

The blade of a veneer hammer should have rounded arrises and be smooth so it won't leave scratches. Defects can be cured with a file, sandpaper, and/or honing stones. Veneer hammers are sold through woodworking specialty stores and catalogs.

Warrington hammers

The Warrington hammer has a cross peen for starting tiny nails without hitting your fingers and a round face for driving nails in. The cross peen is also appropriate for tapping the irons of wooden planes into lateral position.

Warrington hammers come in a lighter weight range than claw hammers: from 3½ oz. to 10 oz. The peen can be reshaped with a file or honing stones if it is uneven or too thin to strike a nail well. Warrington hammers are sold through woodworking specialty outlets and industrial-supply houses.

MALLETS

Mallets are used in place of hammers where steel would be too damaging to the contact surface or where their shape lends an advantage of efficiency or control. Mallet heads tend to be larger than hammer heads, so they make it easier to hit the target. The most common applications of mallets in the woodshop are driving chisels and gouges and assembling and disassembling joints and carcases. Their hardness varies from the ringing denseness of lignum vitae to the muffled softness of rubber.

CARPENTER'S
MALLETS

Carpenter's mallets

Wood is preferable to steel as a material for striking chisels: It does less damage to the handles and has less bounce. The best mallet woods are close grained, dense, and resist splitting. The traditional carpenter's mallet, also known as a jointer's mallet, has a wooden head assembled to wooden handle. The head is rectilinear, while the handle may be squared-off or rounded in section. The flat striking faces cant inward to follow the angle of a natural swing. Carpenter's mallets are preferable to carver's mallets for heavier work where the tool must be swung some distance, since their broad faces make it easy to hit the target.

Customarily, carpenter's mallets are made of solid beech. Traditionally, the heads were saturated in linseed oil, which increased their weight and diminished crushing (since liquid-filled fibers don't compress as easily). Nowadays, heads of laminated beech are also available; they are considerably harder, heavier, and more resistant to splitting. Contemporary mallets also are made from denser, heavier exotic species such as sapodilla and tonca. Common weights range from 11 oz. to 26 oz.

A closely related form of mallet has a cylindrical wooden head much like that of a croquet mallet. It is made of similar materials to the standard carpenter's mallet and is used in similar fashion. Sometimes the head is banded in iron to prevent splitting.

Carver's mallets

Carver's mallets are usually turned from a single piece of wood, although they are also made with urethane heads. The head has a tapered conical section, following the same ergonomic logic as a carpenter's mallet. Common wisdom says that a major advantage of the carver's mallet is that no matter how you pick it up, a striking face presents itself. However, anyone who has used a carpenter's mallet knows that you feel where the striking face is as soon as you heft it, without having to look. I prefer to drive chisels with a carver's mallet, but only because that's what I'm used to.

Carver's mallets can be made out of any dense, fine-grained hardwood that resists splitting. Beech is often used but is on the light side. Denser exotics such as sapodilla, lignum vitae, and tonca wood have more punch. Some subspecies of lignum vitae are threatened, and the wood has been off the market in recent years. You can also turn your own mallets out of whatever's available locally. Mallets made from exotic woods are often turned green and are prone to check as they dry. For this reason, they usually come coated in thick wax, and it's beneficial to keep them waxed, particularly on the end grain. The professional carvers I know stay away from the carver's mallets with urethane heads. Urethane absorbs shock more than wood, so the blow it delivers is less crisp.

Carver's mallets may be sized by weight or head diameter. As a rough guide, you might consider that a 2½-in.-diameter head of tonca wood, which is fairly dense compared to beech, weighs about 10.5 oz. A 3½-in. diameter weighs about 18.5 oz., and a 4-in. diameter weighs about 20.5 oz. The proper weight of a mallet is entirely dependent on your strength and the type of work at hand. Personally, I find 16 oz. to 20 oz. a good weight for general use, including joinery.

Deadblow mallets

The head of a deadblow mallet is metal or plastic filled with small steel balls, iron shot, or a similar material. The striking faces are plastic, usually urethane or nylon. Because of the shot's inertia, a deadblow mallet delivers a heavy, solid blow without the bounce associated with hammers

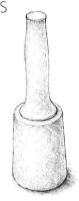

CARVER'S MALLET

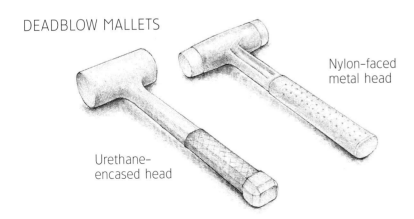

DEADBLOW MALLETS

Nylon-faced metal head

Urethane-encased head

and other types of mallets. The plastic heads are less damaging than steel and hardwood but can still leave dents if not plied carefully, particularly on softer woods. Urethane-encased heads are the most forgiving.

Deadblow mallets are made with head weights from 5 oz. to 50 oz. Those in the 12-oz. to 28-oz. range are extremely handy for assembly and disassembly of furniture.

RUBBER MALLET

Rubber mallets

Rubber mallets usually have black rubber heads on wooden handles. They will not dent hardwoods, no matter how hard you pound, so they are ideal for knocking joints and furniture parts together or apart. However, they don't deliver as much power as a deadblow mallet or a hammer does. A second disadvantage is that glancing blows can leave black streaks on raw wood, though these are readily sanded out. Rubber mallets usually come in weights from 12 oz. to 2 lb.

Buying mallets

It's good to have an assortment of mallets in the shop. My own preference is a medium-weight carver's mallet for driving chisels and a urethane-encased deadblow mallet for assembly.

Carpenter's, carver's, and deadblow mallets are available through woodworking retail outlets and catalogs. Rubber mallets might be more easily found at hardware stores, automobile-supply stores, and industrial-supply outlets.

APPENDIX : Sharpening Chisels & Planes

When we teach our Basic Woodworking course at the Center for Furniture Craftsmanship, the first thing students learn is how to impart a razor-sharp edge to their chisels and plane irons. This is not coincidental. Without sharp tools, it is impossible to master the fundamental hand skills that are the foundation of craftsmanship. This appendix presents an overview of sharpening equipment, followed by a step-by-step explanation of the sharpening process.

Sharpening Equipment

Sharpening is a process of abrading steel in a controlled manner. There is a wide variety of effective sharpening tools available, and it may not always be easy to know which is best for the task at hand. This section presents information on the equipment woodworkers most commonly employ for sharpening, including bench grinders, grinding wheels, dressing tools, and sharpening stones.

GRINDERS

In the 25 years I've been woodworking, I've seen quite a few grinders come and go. For hollow grinding (where the circumference of the wheel leaves a concave bevel on the tool) there have been a variety of slow-speed, water-cooled wheels, specially designed belt sanders, hand-cranked wheels, standard machinist's bench grinders, and hybrids thereof. For flat grinding there have been water-cooled Japanese grinders with horizontally mounted wheels and see-through abrasive discs where you grind from underneath, among others. Some of these have been good tools, some have been gimmicky, and many have included sophisticated tool-holding systems.

To put things in perspective, picture the grinding technique of Tage Frid, one of the outstanding woodworkers of the past 50 years. I've seen Tage grind chisels to a perfect hollow against the drum of a stationary belt sander in seconds, freehand. No fancy gizmos for Tage! Not that you need to copy his example, but I do encourage you to adopt a simple system and trust your eye and hand. Avoid expensive sharpening systems with NASA-engineered, computer-guided, laser-activated tool holders. In the long run they slow you down.

My own preference is a standard machinist's bench grinder, such as the one shown in the drawing below. Bench grinders are sized according to their speed, wheel diameter, and horsepower. Mine is a relatively slow-speed (1,800-rpm), 6-in., ¼-hp grinder made by Baldor. Most bench grinders run at speeds closer to 3,600 rpm, but a slower grinder reduces friction and the consequent risk of burning the blade. (When excessive heat turns steel blue or black, the carbon content burns off and the steel loses its temper—it becomes too soft to hold an edge. The arduous cure is to grind the end of the blade back to good steel without burning it all over again.)

Generally, new bench grinders come with gray aluminum-oxide wheels. On mine, I replace one of these with a 60- or 80-grit, white

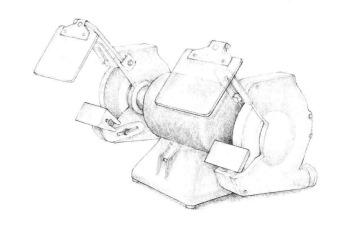

aluminum-oxide wheel. The binder that holds the abrasive together in a white wheel is softer than that of a gray one. It enables dull abrasive particles to slough off more readily, exposing fresh, sharp ones beneath, so that a white wheel cuts faster, with less friction. Even so, the surface of any grinding wheel will eventually collect enough metal debris to slow down its cutting action and generate excessive heat. When this happens the wheel should be dressed (see below).

Bench grinders are available with 6-in. wheels, 7-in. wheels, 8-in. wheels, and in even larger sizes. A standard 6-in. grinding wheel is ¾ in. wide, which is perfectly adequate for a wood-worker's needs. The 1-in.-wide wheels of a 7-in. grinder are easier to use, but a 7-in. machine also costs considerably more.

When you acquire a grinder, look for one with cast-iron tool rests. Pressed-steel rests commonly found on cheaper grinders tend to be small and flimsy.

Electric grinders that run at anything more than 100 rpm can be dangerous unless treated with respect. The crucial safety rules are as follows:

1. Every time you turn on a grinder, stand away from the wheel until it comes up to speed. If a wheel is faulty or has been damaged, it is most likely to shatter at this time. To test a new wheel for soundness, put your finger through the hole and rap the stone with a piece of wood. If it doesn't ring, there's a crack somewhere and you shouldn't use it.

2. Never grind against the side of a bench grinder's wheels. They are engineered for grinding on the circumference only.

3. Always wear eye protection and place the grinder's translucent face shield between your eyes and the work.

DRESSING TOOLS

Grinding wheels require dressing when they become clogged with metal particles, develop chatter, or lose their shape. The tools available include dressing sticks, diamond-point dressers, and wheel dressers. The first two will both resurface and reshape a wheel, while the latter is for resurfacing only. Whichever you use, always wear a particle mask. You will be sending up a small cloud of fine stone dust.

Dressing stick

A dressing stick is a round or square block of silicon-carbide or aluminum-oxide abrasive about 1 in. thick and 6 in. long. Often it is the same material as the grinding wheel, but coarser. To use a dressing stick you place it on the tool rest, turn on the grinder, and

work the end of the stick against the wheel as if you were grinding a chisel (see the drawing at left below). You can also work the stick lengthwise against the wheel, but be sure to use the full length evenly or you'll wear it concave.

When a wheel needs extensive restoration you can apply substantial pressure with the dressing stick. However, it is best to finish up with a gentle touch to remove any eccentricity and keep the wheel from chattering.

Diamond-point dresser

The standard diamond-point dresser consists of a small diamond mounted on the end of a steel rod. It is more aggressive than a dressing stick and highly effective when used with a holding guide.

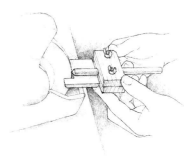

To dress a wheel flat, set the grinder's tool rest straight on to the wheel, as shown above. Adjust the holding guide so that the diamond point barely grazes the wheel when the guide is held against the back of the tool rest. Then turn the grinder on and run the dresser across the face of the wheel, back and forth, until it stops cutting. Instructions for making a holding guide are usually included in the packaging of diamond-point dressers.

The diamond-point dresser is also excellent for putting a special profile on a grinding wheel, such as a molding-plane iron might require.

Wheel dresser

The wheel dresser, also called a star dresser, consists of a handle with a hardened-steel star cutter mounted at one end. The cutter is a cylindrical wheel that resembles a gear more than anything else. It is set at enough of an angle so that as it spins against a rotating grinding wheel the "teeth" around its circumference clear away embedded metal particles and glazing with a shearing action. There is often a foot on the handle that can be mounted against the tool rest to steady the cutter and apply leverage.

A wheel dresser resurfaces but doesn't reshape or retrue a wheel. The fresh surface left behind is rough compared to those created by diamond-point dressers and dressing sticks. It is more appropriate to the needs of the metalworking industry than to sharpening woodworking tools.

SHARPENING STONES

When I started woodworking, it seemed as though oilstones were the only type of sharpening stones there were. Within 10 years, however, Japanese waterstones had become favorites among many woodworkers, and their popularity continues to rise. More recently, we have seen the introduction of diamond stones and dry ceramic stones.

A sharpening stone consists of an abrasive held in place by a binder. Their combined qualities give each type of stone its particular working characteristics. The ideal sharpening stone would abrade steel quickly and evenly without clogging or wearing away and stay sharp forever. None has yet achieved this ideal.

The sharpening stones discussed in the pages that follow are flat honing stones applicable to sharpening chisels and planes. Each type of stone is also available in other shapes, such as rods and slipstones, for sharpening carving tools, router and drill bits, and so forth.

Ceramic stones

Ceramic stones consist of an aluminum-oxide abrasive captured in a high-temperature glass matrix. The aluminum oxide is a powder fused under high pressure into a monolithic structure, so there are no individual particles of grit to be dislodged. The net result is a stone that is advertised to "last a lifetime."

Because of the hardness of their bond and the fused quality of the abrasive, ceramic stones are the slowest-cutting type of sharpening stone. They come in a range of grits referred to by names such as medium, fine, and ultrafine. Since they are not made from grit particles screened for size, equivalencies to other types of sharpening stones are difficult to specify precisely.

The working characteristics of ceramic stones are quite different from those of oilstones and waterstones. They are meant to be used dry, without a liquid wash. When their surfaces blacken and clog with metal debris, which is often, you clean them in the sink with water, household cleanser, and nonwoven nylon abrasive pads. The coarser ceramic stones are designed to wear away slowly in use and may need flattening against a diamond stone from time to time. The fine, white stones are supposed to resist erosion entirely and stay sharp forever. The fine and ultrafine are the same stone, but the surface of the latter has been lapped to remove the peaks. The ultrafine ceramic stone imparts a chrome-like polish to steel that approaches an 8000-grit waterstone's.

Because they are so slow cutting, the only situations in which ceramic stones are preferable to waterstones and oilstones are where cleanliness matters, as when working in your living room or traveling.

Diamond stones

Diamond stones consist of steel or plastic plates with fine industrial diamond particles adhered to their surfaces, usually in a nickel bond. Two distinct types of manufactured diamond particles are used. Monocrystalline diamonds are most resistant to wear, since each particle of grit is a single diamond crystal. Polycrystalline diamond grit is made up of smaller diamonds fused together, and it fractures into finer particles as you hone. Monocrystalline diamonds are better for sharpening stones, while polycrystalline are better for polishing applications.

As the hardest known material, diamond will hone any type of steel, including carbide. Grit for grit, it imprints a rougher surface than other types of sharpening stones. Depending on the manufacturer, diamond stones range from coarse (150 to 325 grit), through fine (600 grit),

to extra fine (1200 grit). These grit specifications are diamond-industry numbers, which are compared to other types of stones on the chart on pp. 194-195. As you will see, diamond stones don't reach the levels of fineness appropriate to final honing of a cutting edge. Their favored applications in the woodshop are preliminary flattening of tool backs and small plane soles, shaping cutting bevels, and lapping other types of sharpening stones.

Diamond stones are available in sizes as large as 2½ in. by 11⅜ in. They will not dish out in use, but if they aren't flat to start with, they can't be trued up. Check initial flatness carefully at time of purchase. Both the plastic- and metal-plated stones sold for woodworkers are manufactured to reasonably high standards, but not necessarily to what a machinist would expect. Also, plastic can warp from heat or pressure, metal from radical temperatures and impact, so take good care of them.

When woodworking catalogs first introduced diamond stones, the copy sometimes implied they were indestructible. Unfortunately, it turned out that diamonds aren't forever. I have found that one of my Basic Woodworking classes can wear out a large polycrystalline stone in less than two weeks, flattening chisels and plane irons. However, for the solo craftsman, a monocrystalline diamond stone should last for years.

Diamond stones can be used dry, but they cut more efficiently with the addition of water, liquid soap, or a combination of the two. If used dry, they should be washed with soap and water occasionally to remove metal grit. If used wet, they should be rinsed out thoroughly each time to remove metal filings that can flash-rust.

Japanese waterstones

The traditional sharpening stones of Japan are mined from various sedimentary rock formations, which, like sandstone, work best when lubricated with water. As top-quality natural stones began to become more scarce and costly, Japanese manufacturers successfully developed a full range of synthetic stones to mimic their properties. Natural Japanese stones in the finer grits are still the first choice of those craftsmen who knowledgeably use the finest Japanese tools, but man-made Japanese stones are excellent for the rest of us.

Of course, not all waterstones are Japanese. Belgian waterstones have been used in Europe for centuries. But the quality of the synthetic Japanese stones is such that they have come to dominate both the market and our consciousness. Also, not all "Japanese" waterstones are made in Japan anymore. At least one United States manufacturer has introduced its own version within the past few years.

One outstanding feature of Japanese waterstones is that their binders are significantly softer than those of oilstones. As a result, the abrasive particles in Japanese stones wear off as fast as they wear out. The good news is that fresh, sharp particles constantly come into play, so clogging is not a problem and steel is efficiently abraded. The bad news is that waterstones saddle quickly, gouge easily, and require flattening more often than other types of stones.

Synthetic Japanese stones are graded on a different scale from Western abrasives. For purposes of discussion, we can divide Japanese stones into three main groups:

80 to 220 grit Various abrasives are used in these stones, including silicon carbide. They are exceptionally coarse and might be used in place of a rough grinding wheel to re-form a badly nicked or chipped cutting edge. A grinding wheel is preferable, though, because the stones dish out so quickly.

800, 1000, 1200 grit These mid-range stones are made of aluminum-oxide abrasive in a clay matrix. The 800-grit stone might be appropriate to hone out a minor nick. Either the 1000- or 1200-grit stone is best for the first step in normal honing (see p. 193).

4000, 6000, 8000 grit Often called "finishing" or "polishing" stones, these generally have an aluminum-oxide abrasive in a resin or clay binder. They are usually sold attached to wooden bases because they are fragile. As you can see in the chart on pp. 194-195, these finishing stones are finer than any oilstone, even the Black Hard Arkansas. They also cut quicker. Japanese finishing stones are unsurpassed for polishing a cutting edge to razor sharpness.

Before sharpening, Japanese waterstones should be thoroughly saturated. Many woodworkers store them permanently in water, often in plastic food containers. Finishing stones with wooden bases store best upside down in shallow water, with the wood above the surface. Even so, the stone and base occasionally separate. To reattach them, let the stone dry out thoroughly, then glue it to the base with silicon caulk. Waterstones should never be allowed to freeze, because any trapped moisture can break them apart.

Sometimes, reading about the process of sharpening with Japanese stones, it can sound as complex and ritualistic as a tea ceremony. It doesn't have to be. The straightforward sharpening process described on pp. 190-193 uses only the 1000- and 6000-grit stones to get chisels and planes as sharp as fine craftsmanship demands. But, as with most tools, there are further levels of refinement to explore.

When you sharpen on a Japanese stone, a slurry of abrasive, binder, and metal particles builds up on the surface. Because the abrasive in the slurry breaks down into smaller units, it can take a tool to a finer finish than the raw surface of the stone could alone. The amount of water matters. Too much water on the stone washes the slurry off, while too little allows metal particles to embed themselves in its surface. A small dressing stone, often called a "nagura" stone, is sold for the purpose of working up an advance slurry on finishing stones. It is not a necessity.

When Japanese stones become dished or gouged they should be flattened right away, because they work so much better with clean, flat surfaces. The technique I prefer is to lay a 9-in. by 12-in. sheet of wet/dry silicon-carbide sandpaper on a piece of ⅜-in. glass, with water in between to keep the paper from sliding. Then I thoroughly wet the surface of the sandpaper and rub the stone back and forth on top with moderate pressure, as shown in the drawing below. Keeping the surface wet, I continue until the entire surface of

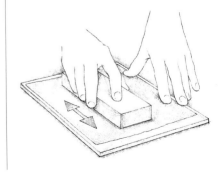

the stone is affected, which I can usually tell by its fresh color. A sheet of 220-grit paper is good for flattening mid-range stones, 400 grit for finishing stones. However, a sheet of 220 paper worn from flattening a mid-range stone is often just right for a finishing stone.

Oilstones

Oilstones are a family of natural and man-made sharpening stones. Their commonality is that they are meant to be lubricated with light oil to float away metal particles and prevent surface clogging. The wash can vary quite a bit in viscosity and content. Examples include pure kerosene, light mineral oil, and mixtures of kerosene and lubricating oil. It is also possible to use water or soapy water, but neither one is as effective as oil.

Natural oilstones are made from novaculite mined in Arkansas. From coarsest to finest they are called Washita, Soft Arkansas, Hard Arkansas, and Black Hard Arkansas. As deposits have been mined out, the availability of high-quality Black Hard Arkansas stones has declined, but they are still available and getting more valuable all the time. Washita and Soft Arkansas stones are more plentiful.

Man-made stones are at the coarser end of the oilstone continuum. Their abrasives are either aluminum oxide (India stones) or silicon carbide (brand names such as Crystolon and Carborundum) in vitrified ceramic bonds.

The abrasive particles of oilstones are tightly bonded, so they wear away slowly. This is an advantage in that the stones tend to stay flat a long time. It is also a weakness. Oilstones are relatively slow cutting because the surface particles wear down without sloughing off. Oilstones are also messy. Oil may start off on stones and tools, but it inevitably migrates to bench, wood, and clothing.

In our shop we use oilstones infrequently, mostly when their wear-resistance gives them an advantage over waterstones. This includes sharpening gouges and very narrow chisels, reducing the set of sawblades, and honing drawknives. In each case, a waterstone would be too likely to wear unevenly or have its surface scored.

There are a number of ways to flatten an oilstone when it finally needs it. They include use of a diamond stone, a lapping plate and compound, or wet/dry silicon-carbide sandpaper (silicon carbide being harder than aluminum oxide) on a flat surface lubricated with water. The abrasive shouldn't be too coarse relative to the stone being flattened, or it will reduce its effectiveness. Only the tops of the microscopic ridges left by the lapping agent make contact.

How to Sharpen

The first thing to do with any new chisel or plane iron is to flatten its back properly. With luck, you need to do this only once in the lifetime of the blade. After that, there are only two steps in sharpening. The first step is to give the bevel its correct shape and remove any gross imperfections such as nicks. This is generally done on a grinder. The second step is to hone the intersecting faces that form the cutting edge to extreme smoothness, which is generally done on sharpening stones. There are many combinations of sharpening tools and techniques that can achieve satisfactory results. The method we use at the Center For Furniture Craftsmanship is described below.

FLATTENING THE BACK

The back of a new blade should be flattened against increasingly fine abrasive surfaces until it is polished to the capability of your finest sharpening stone. It is not necessary that the entire back be perfectly polished. Hollows are permissible as long as they aren't contiguous to the cutting edge, which should make full contact whenever the back of the blade is on a flat surface such as a honing stone.

The flattening tools we use are:
- a piece of ⅜-in. plate glass measuring 5 in. by 12 in., with 120-grit aluminum-oxide sandpaper adhered to one side and 220-grit paper on the other; rolls of pressure-sensitive adhesive sandpaper about 4 in. wide are convenient, but you can also mount standard sheet sandpaper with spray adhesive;
- a 1000-grit waterstone; and
- a 6000-grit waterstone

The technique is to hold the blade down on the sandpaper or stone and move it back and forth along the length of the abrasive, as shown in the drawing below. It is crucial to keep the back of the blade flat on the abrasive at all times. Lifting the handle will put a small back-bevel on the cutting edge, which is ruinous. To correct it, either the back has to be flattened that much further or the bevel must be ground back extensively. When working on a sharpening stone, try to use the entire surface so it wears down evenly.

Often, it's worthwhile to begin flattening on the 1000-grit stone, just to see if you can get away with skipping the sandpaper. After a minute of honing, look at the newly abraded areas on the back, which are gray and dull compared to the bright polish the tool probably came with. If they are already closing in on the cutting edge, you might continue on the stone. If a substantial amount of steel will have to be removed before the edge is affected, go back to the 120 or 220 sandpaper. With a little experience you'll know which abrasive is needed.

When the entire area within ⅛ in. or more of the cutting edge has been uniformly abraded and no deeper scratches remain than those left by the abrasive, step up to the next grit (120 to 220 to 1000 to 6000) and repeat the process. Once the back has been polished with the 6000-grit stone, it should never touch a coarser abrasive again.

Flattening the hollow-ground back of a Japanese chisel is done in the same way. However, as repeated sharpenings shorten the blade, the cutting edge can retreat into the hollow in the back, as shown in the drawing below. When this happens, there are alternative solutions. The traditional method involves hammering the softer steel on the cutting bevel to reshape the back of the blade, then reflattening. The other technique is to abrade the back extensively, removing enough of the hollow to establish a new flat area behind the cutting edge. This second method requires less skill but may also thin the blade more than desirable.

After you have flattened the back of a chisel, the arrises along the sides can be sharp enough to slice your fingers. To avoid injury, sand them lightly with fine sandpaper (perhaps 320 or 400 grit), just enough to dull the sharpness. The amount of roundover should be almost imperceptible.

SHAPING THE EDGE

Most chisels and plane irons have their cutting edges ground straight across, at right angles to the sides. The exceptions are skew blades (which are ground straight, but not square) and curved blades (found in convex and concave spokeshaves, scrub planes, and sometimes, mildly, in bench planes).

Bevel angles vary according to the character of the steel, the hardness of the wood, and the way in which the tool is used. The correct bevel angle for a chisel or plane iron is the slimmest at which the steel will hold an edge in use. This can range anywhere from 20° to 35°. The following list of suggested bevel angles should be taken as an approximate guide only, subject to results:

Paring chisels 20° in clear softwoods and straight-grained, clear hardwoods; 25° in most hardwoods and across end grain

Firmer chisels 25° in softwoods and straight-grained, clear hardwoods; 30° in normal hardwoods and for cutting across end grain

Mortise chisels 30° in softwoods, 35° in hardwoods

Bench planes 25° for finish work in clear woods, particularly softwoods; 30° in most hardwoods; 35° in highly figured woods

Block planes 20° in clear softwoods, 25° in hardwoods

All other planes 25° to 30°

Japanese blades are traditionally ground with flat bevels, so that the brittle steel of the cutting edge gets maximum support from behind. Western chisels and planes don't need this extra support. In fact, the hollow bevel created by a grinding wheel is preferable on a Western tool because it makes sharpening quicker and more efficient. When a flat bevel is placed on a honing stone, steel must be abraded from the entire face in order to affect the edge. A hollow bevel in the same position needs to lose only a little steel off the cutting edge and heel to achieve the same result. Even if you lift the blade to establish a secondary bevel, some advantage retains to the hollow grind. A blade can be honed many times before enough of the hollow disappears to warrant regrinding.

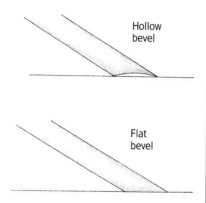

Hollow bevel

Flat bevel

To grind a hollow bevel with a bench grinder, you first adjust the tool rest. With the top of the blade flat on the rest, the cutting bevel should meet the grinding wheel at the desired angle (see the top drawing at right). Also, the tool rest should be reasonably close to the wheel so there isn't a wide gap in between.

To grind, you turn the machine on and advance the blade until it just kisses the wheel, then move it evenly from side to side. Do not, however, slide the blade too far beyond either edge of the wheel: Grinding only a corner of the blade can get it too hot. Pushing

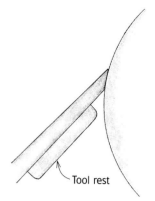

Tool rest

too hard will also make the blade heat up quickly and can force the blade to ride up the wheel, reducing the bevel angle.

From time to time, pull the blade from the wheel and touch the cutting edge to see how hot it's getting. With practice, you'll develop a light, sure hand and be able to grind a blade from start to finish without any need to cool it in a cup of water. In the meantime, quench the blade if it threatens to burn your fingertips. Grinding is complete when you have established a single, continuous hollow grind across the full cutting bevel of the tool.

HONING

When honing a blade, you have the choice of maintaining the grinding angle or putting a secondary bevel on the cutting edge. There are no major advantages either way, but with a secondary bevel there is less steel to remove, so sharpening is somewhat more efficient.

The process of honing begins on a 1000-grit waterstone, placed on a bench hook or other holder for convenience (see the drawing below). To establish the correct honing angle, find the "flat" spot where the toe and heel of the hollow grind touch the stone simultaneously. To create a secondary bevel, raise the handle a degree or two. Keeping your arms still, rock from your legs to move the blade forward and back. Put pressure against the stone on the forward stroke only. You can put moderate weight on a wide chisel, but anything more than light pressure can encourage a narrow chisel to slice into the stone. Work the full length and width of the stone in parallel strokes to wear the surface down as evenly as possible.

With a freshly ground blade, it takes only a few strokes on a 1000-grit stone to affect the entire cutting edge. As soon as you see a honed surface extending along the entire edge (as shown below), stop. In order to get as many honings as possible between regrindings, you want to remove the minimum of steel each time.

As a blade dulls, the steel at the cutting edge wears away to become rounded. This reveals itself visually as a silver thread of light across the cutting edge when you look from the back. Rehoning involves abrading away just enough steel from the bevel side to remove the rounded part. To know when you have reached this point, it is easier to rely on tactile rather than visual cues. When the cutting edge has been restored on a 1000-grit stone, you can feel a "wire edge" on the back. It needn't feel any larger than the finest hair would in the same position.

The remaining steps take place on the 6000-grit stone:

• Hone the back, effectively removing any wire edge. This takes just a few strokes. Remember that the back of the blade must be flat on the stone at all times or you'll create the dreaded back-bevel.

• Place the cutting bevel on the stone just as you did on the 1000-grit stone to establish the same honing angle. Again, hone with pressure on the forward stroke only. Ten to fifteen strokes should be enough, but this time there probably won't be a discernible wire edge.

• Hone the back again, anyway.

• Then take 10 more strokes on the bevel side, hone the back one last time, and you should have a cutting edge sharp enough to shave hair off your arm. Don't run a thumb along the edge to test it— your chisel may be sharper than a razor blade!

If you don't succeed, try again. Start at the step where you hone the cutting edge on the 1000-grit stone until you feel a wire edge. You don't need to regrind until much of the hollow has been honed away.

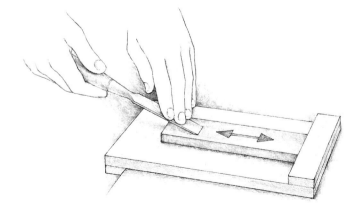

ABRASIVE COMPARISON CHART

Unfortunately, abrasive materials are not categorized according to a single, uniform scale. This makes it difficult to compare precisely the various abrasives used for sanding and sharpening in the woodshop. This chart aligns abrasive scales and materials according to particle size measured in microns. The chart gives only an approximation of performance, since cutting characteristics vary among the different types of abrasive particles and are additionally affected by their binders, backings, and methods of application.

Microns	ANSI (CAMI) U.S. Sandpaper	FEPA European (P-mesh) Sandpaper	JIS Japanese Waterstones	ANSI Bonded Abrasive Oilstones	Diamond Stones
1.2	-	-	8000	-	-
2.2	-	-	6000	-	-
3.0	-	-	4000	-	-
5.4	-	-	3000	-	-
6.0	-	-	-	Hard Arkansas	-
6.5	1200	-	-	Hard Arkansas	-
6.6	-	-	2500	-	-
8.2	-	-	2000	Soft Arkansas	-
9.2	1000	-	-	Soft Arkansas	extra fine
10.5	-	-	1500	Soft Arkansas	-
12.2	800	-	-	Soft Arkansas	-
12.5	-	-	1200	Soft Arkansas	-
15.0	-	-	1000	Soft Arkansas	-
15.3	-	1200	-	Soft Arkansas	-
16.0	600	-	-	Soft Arkansas	-
18.3	-	1000	-	Soft Arkansas	-
19.0	-	-	800	Soft Arkansas	-
19.7	500	-	-	Soft Arkansas	-
21.8	-	800	-	Soft Arkansas	-
23.6	400	-	-	-	-
25.8	-	600	-	-	fine
26.0	-	-	600	-	-
28.8	360	-	-	-	-
30.0	-	-	500	-	-
30.2	-	500	-	-	-
32.0	-	-	-	fine India	-
35.0	-	400	400	-	-
36.0	320	-	-	-	-
40.0	-	-	360	-	-
40.5	-	360	-	-	-
44.0	280	-	320	fine Crystolon	coarse
46.2	-	320	-	-	-
50.0	-	-	280	-	-
52.2	-	280	-	-	-
53.5	240	-	-	-	-
54.5	-	-	240	-	-
58.5	-	240	-	-	-
60.0	-	-	220	-	extra coarse
63.0	-	-	-	medium India stone	-
64.0	220	-	-	-	-
66.0	-	220	-	-	-
74.0	-	-	180	-	-
79.0	180	180	-	-	-

Microns	ANSI (CAMI) U.S. Sandpaper	FEPA European (P-mesh) Sandpaper	JIS Japanese Waterstones	ANSI Bonded Abrasive Oilstones	Diamond Stones
88.0	-	-	150	-	-
95.0	150	-	-	-	-
98.0	-	150	-	-	-
110.0	-	120	-	-	-
113.0	120	-	-	-	-
122.0	-	120	-	medium Crystolon stone	-
131.0	-	-	100	-	-
136.0	100	-	-	-	-
157.0	-	100	-	-	-
173.0	-	-	-	coarse Crystolon and India stones	-
189.0	80	-	80	-	-
196.0	-	80	-	-	-
262.0	-	60	-	-	-
266.0	60	-	-	-	-
274.0	-	-	60	-	-
324.0	-	-	50	-	-
328.0	-	50	-	-	-
341.0	50	-	-	-	-
385.0	-	-	40	-	-
412.0	-	40	-	-	-
457.0	40	-	-	-	-
523.0	-	36	-	-	-
536.0	36	-	-	-	-
540.0	-	-	36	-	-
626.0	-	30	-	-	-
643.0	-	-	30	-	-
646.0	30	-	-	-	-
731.0	24	-	-	-	-
743.0	-	24	-	-	-
768.0	-	-	24	-	-
886.0	20	-	-	-	-
973.0	-	20	-	-	-
984.0	-	-	20	-	-
1238.0	-	-	16	-	-
1292.0	-	16	-	-	-
1293.0	16	-	-	-	-

Notes

Most of this information is courtesy of the Norton Company.

ANSI is the American National Standards Institute, which publishes a standard grading scale for coated abrasives (sandpaper) and a separate scale for bonded abrasives (grinding wheels and sharpening stones).

CAMI is the Coated Abrasive Manufacturers Institute, which has adopted ANSI standards for grading sandpaper. However, U.S. manufacturers are also beginning to make sandpapers according to FEPA and JIS grading systems.

FEPA is the European standard-setting organization that established the P-scale by which European-made sandpapers are graded. Generally, the grit number is preceded by the letter P.

JIS is the Japanese grading system for abrasives, including waterstones.

Diamond stones are not manufactured according to a standardized grading system. The information in the chart uses the system developed by DMT, a major U.S. manufacturer of diamond sharpening stones.

Ceramic stones are not manufactured according to a standardized grading system. The technology is such that particle size cannot be equated with performance. The leading U.S. manufacturer, Spyderco, was unable to provide any objective method for comparing ceramic stones to other abrasives.

BIBLIOGRAPHY

Blackburn, Graham. *The Illustrated Encyclopedia of Woodworking Handtools, Instruments and Devices.* New York: Simon & Schuster, 1974.

Browne & Sharpe. *The Young Machinist's Handbook.* North Kingston, R.I.: Browne & Sharpe Manufacturing Co., 1974.

Bureau of Navy Personnel. *Tools and Their Uses.* New York: Dover Publications, 1973.

Chinn, Garry, and John Sainsbury. *The Garrett Wade Book of Woodworking Tools.* New York: Gallery Books, 1979.

Dunbar, Michael. *Restoring, Tuning, and Using Classic Woodworking Tools.* New York: Sterling, 1989.

Landis, Scott. *The Workbench Book.* Newtown, Conn.: The Taunton Press, 1987.

Lanz, Henry. *Japanese Woodworking Tools.* New York: Sterling, 1985.

Law, Tom. "Handsaws." *Fine Homebuilding* 20 (April, 1984).

Lee, Leonard. *The Complete Guide to Sharpening.* Newtown, Conn.: The Taunton Press, 1995.

Morgan, Alfred P. *Tools and How to Use Them.* New York: Gramercy Publishing, 1948.

Odate, Toshio. *Japanese Woodworking Tools: Their Tradition, Spirit, and Use.* Newtown, Conn.: The Taunton Press, 1984.

Payson, Harold H. *The Cutting Edge: Setting and Sharpening Hand and Power Saws.* Brooklin, Me.: WoodenBoat Publications, 1983.

Salaman, R. A. *Dictionary of Woodworking Tools.* Newtown, Conn.: The Taunton Press, 1990.

Sellens, Alvin. *The Stanley Plane: A History and Descriptive Inventory.* Albany, N.Y.: Early American Industries Association, 1975.

Watson, Aldren A. *Hand Tools: Their Ways and Workings.* New York: Lyons & Burford, 1982.

Weygers, Alexander G. *The Making of Tools.* New York: Van Nostrand Reinhold, 1973.

INDEX

BOOK PUBLISHER / Jim Childs

ACQUISITIONS EDITOR / Rick Peters

PUBLISHING COORDINATOR / Joanne Renna

EDITOR / Peter Chapman

DESIGNER / Henry Roth

ILLUSTRATOR / Kathy Bray

INDEXER / Harriet Hodges

TYPEFACE / Garamond

PAPER / 70-lb. Utopia Two Matte

PRINTER / Quebecor Printing/Hawkins, Church Hill, Tennessee